hearing from
GOD
each morning

365 DAILY DEVOTIONS

hearing from GOD

each morning

365 DAILY DEVOTIONS

JOYCE MEYER

Faith
Words

NEW YORK   BOSTON   NASHVILLE

Unless otherwise indicated, Scriptures are taken from the Amplified® Bible. Copyright © 1954, 1962, 1965, 1987 by the Lockman Foundation. Used by permission.

Scriptures noted KJV are taken from the King James Version of the Bible.

Scriptures noted The Message are taken from The Message. Copyright © 1993, 1994, 1995, 1996, 2000, 2001, 2002. Used by permission of NavPress Publishing Group.

Scriptures noted NIV are taken from the HOLY BIBLE: NEW INTERNATIONAL VERSION®. Copyright © 1973, 1978, 1984 by International Bible Society. Used by permission of Zondervan Publishing House. All rights reserved.

Scriptures noted NKJV are taken from the NEW KING JAMES VERSION. Copyright © 1979, 1980, 1982, Thomas Nelson, Inc., Publishers.

Scriptures noted NLT are taken from the Holy Bible, New Living Translation, copyright © 1996. Used by permission of Tynsdale House Publishers, Inc., Wheaton, Ill. 60189. All rights reserved.

FaithWords
Hachette Book Group
237 Park Avenue
New York, NY 10017

www.faithwords.com

Printed in China

10 9 8 7 6 5 4

First Edition: January 2010

FaithWords is a division of Hachette Book Group, Inc.

The FaithWords name and logo are trademarks of Hachette Book Group, Inc.

Library of Congress Cataloging-in-Publication Data

Meyer, Joyce
   Hearing from God each morning: 365 daily devotions / Joyce Meyer.—1st ed.
      p. cm.
   ISBN 978-0-446-55785-6
   1. Devotional calendars.   I. Title.
   BV4811.M446 2010
   242'.2—dc22

                                                            2009023967

hearing from
GOD
each morning

365 DAILY DEVOTIONS

God Will Tell You Everything You Need to Know

The woman said to Him, I know that Messiah is coming, He Who is called the Christ (the Anointed One); and when He arrives, He will tell us everything we need to know and make it clear to us.

(JOHN 4:25)

Learning to hear from God and be led by the Holy Spirit is an exciting adventure. God wants to speak to you and tell you what you need to know to enjoy your life, be blessed, be wise, and fulfill the good plans He has for you. He always has something good and helpful to say, but sometimes people miss knowing these things because they fail to recognize that God is speaking to them. They need to learn how to hear and obey His voice.

Earthly parents talk to their children all the time, so why wouldn't our heavenly Father speak to us? Human parents do not expect their children to know what to do if they don't tell them, and God feels the same way toward His children. He wants to tell us everything we need to know in life.

We often want to go our own way so we can do what we want to do, when we want to do it. But, when we live this way, we end up losing our way and wasting our lives. We need the Holy Spirit to guide us through each day of our time on Earth, and He is committed to doing so by speaking to us and telling us everything we need to know.

GOD'S WORD FOR YOU TODAY: You have a guide and a comforter in the Holy Spirit, who is with you 24-7.

A Vital Necessity

*One thing have I asked of the Lord, that will I seek, inquire for,
and [insistently] require: that I may dwell in the house of the Lord
[in His presence] all the days of my life, to behold and gaze upon
the beauty [the sweet attractiveness and the delightful loveliness]
of the Lord and to meditate, consider, and inquire in His temple.*

(PSALM 27:4)

If we desire to hear from God, then seeking Him must be a priority in our lives. David summarized life's one requirement in the verse for today. He required God's presence as a *vital necessity* in life.

David had enjoyed many opportunities to succeed and gain confidence. Empowered by the presence of God, he had killed an imposing giant with nothing more than a slingshot and five small stones. God chose this simple shepherd boy to become king of Israel even though he was the youngest brother of a family of men. His eventual fame and wealth offered everything most people might think would bring satisfaction.

David's pursuit of more of God, even after experiencing God's presence in many ways, should give us a realization that we must continue seeking God no matter how many victories we have enjoyed. After all, even David needed to know God more intimately.

Many people want guidance from God, but they don't want to lay aside other things in order to hear His voice. But David narrowed down everything he wanted to just one thing—more of God all the days of his life. I believe the only thing that truly satisfies the longing within us is to know God more intimately today than we did yesterday.

GOD'S WORD FOR YOU TODAY: Pursue "more of God" in your life—today and every day.

Come Close

Come close to God and He will come close to you. (JAMES 4:8)

Not everyone is willing to pay the price required to be close to God. Not everyone is willing to simply take the time required or make the investments needed for spiritual growth. God doesn't ask for all of our time. He certainly wants us to do things we don't consider "spiritual." He designed us with bodies, souls (minds, wills, and emotions), and spirits, and He expects us to take care of all these areas.

Exercising our bodies and caring for our souls takes time and effort. Our emotions need to be ministered to; we need to have fun and be entertained, and we need to enjoy being with other people. Our minds need to grow and be renewed daily. In addition, we have a spiritual nature that needs attention. To stay balanced and healthy, we must take time to take care of our entire being.

I believe the whole issue of intimacy with God is a matter of time. We say we don't have time to seek God, but the truth is that we take time to do the things that are most important to us. Even though we all have to fight distractions every day, if knowing God and hearing from Him is important to us then we will find time to do it. Don't try to work God into your schedule, but instead work your schedule around time with Him.

Getting to know God is a long-term investment, so don't get discouraged if you don't get instant results. Be determined to honor Him with your time and you will reap the benefits.

———————

GOD'S WORD FOR YOU TODAY: Just like physical exercise, spiritual exercise needs to be done regularly. You're sure to see the results.

Let Peace Be Your Umpire

Let the peace (soul harmony which comes) from Christ rule (act as umpire continually) in your hearts. (COLOSSIANS 3:15)

I try to run my life by finding peace. If I am shopping, I don't buy something if I don't have peace about it. If I am involved in a conversation and find myself losing my peace, I become quiet. When I make decisions, I look at the options before me and see where the peace is. When I am trying to discern between the voice of God and the other voices that compete for my attention, I listen to see which voice or message brings the peace of God into my heart.

I have learned that maintaining peace is important in order to maintain power in our lives. When we don't have peace, we may very well be making a serious mistake. I would go so far as to say we should never act without peace. We might say that peace is an "internal confirmation" that God approves of the decision we have made.

God leads us by peace. The verse for today says peace is like an umpire that decides what is "safe" or what is "out." If there's no peace, it's "out"! We are to let the inner harmony in our minds and souls rule and act as an umpire continually in our hearts, deciding and settling with finality all the questions that arise in our minds and the decisions we must make in our lives.

We must learn to obey our own sense of right and wrong and resist doing things our inner conscience is uncomfortable doing. God gives or takes peace from our conscience to let us know whether or not we are on track.

———————

GOD'S WORD FOR YOU TODAY: Let peace be your umpire today. Know that your decision is "in" when you have peace, and "out" when you don't.

God Is Not Hiding

The heavens declare the glory of God; and the firmament shows and proclaims His handiwork. (PSALM 19:1)

God does not hide from anyone. He reveals Himself to all humankind (see Romans 1:19–20). He speaks to everyone through His handiwork, and nature itself testifies of His power and plans.

Look around and pay attention to the world God has created. The main thing He says to us through nature is that He truly exists. He tries to reach us every day and He leaves clues about Himself everywhere, clues that say, "I am here! You don't have to worry or be afraid. I am here."

Every morning the sun comes up and every evening it goes down. The stars come out to sparkle against the night sky and the universe remains in order as a reminder that God is watching over us.

When we consider how some trees look totally dead during winter and come back to life each spring, we are reminded that God will bring our lives back into full bloom, even if we feel lifeless or hopeless because of our circumstances.

I enjoy simply looking at a tree and watching it blow in the wind. I have noticed that dead leaves sometimes cling to branches for a while, and then a big gust of wind comes along and blows them off, making room for new buds to grow and thrive. This reminds me that the wind of God's Spirit is faithful to blow away everything that is no longer needed in our lives and that He will protect all that needs to remain. He will bring new life and growth and times of refreshing.

Remember these examples of how God speaks through nature and look for His clues everywhere you go today!

GOD'S WORD FOR YOU TODAY: Look for one of the many clues God has left for you today.

God Wants to Take You to a New Level

Give instruction to a wise man and he will be yet wiser; teach a righteous man (one upright and in right standing with God) and he will increase in learning. (PROVERBS 9:9)

Even though God wants us to live joyful, contented lives, He sometimes causes discontent or a feeling that something is not right because He does not want us to continue doing the same old things anymore. He wants to prod us to seek Him so He can take us to new levels.

God always wants us to grow stronger, to go deeper, and to increase in intimacy with Him. Most of the time, He leads us into that process of maturity by leading us out of places where we have been comfortable in the past. Too much comfort for too long can mean that we are not growing. If you feel something stirring in your heart that you don't quite understand, just ask God what is happening and take time to wait on Him to answer.

Our time with God is vitally important to our growth and maturity, but we cannot do the same things all the time and experience all that God has for us. I have had times when reading the Bible became laborious and God simply led me to read a different translation for a few months. Just that little change brought new growth because I saw things in a different way. Satan tried to condemn me because I did not want to read the Bible, but God was just trying to get me to make a change in the translation I was reading. One day I felt a bit bored as I tried to read and pray so I moved to another chair in my office and suddenly I saw things that had been in my office for years, but I had not noticed them. A little adjustment caused me to see things from a whole new perspective and God taught me a spiritual lesson just because I sat in a different chair.

GOD'S WORD FOR YOU TODAY: Don't be afraid to move your chair.

Trust God Completely

In You, O Lord, do I put my trust. (PSALM 31:1)

I remember when God told me to quit my full-time job where I was making very good money. He began to deal with me, saying, "You're going to have to put that down and stay home and prepare for ministry."

I didn't obey quickly because I was afraid to leave my job. After all, how did I even know for sure that I was hearing from God? He continued dealing with me so I finally tried to make a deal with Him, saying, "I won't work full-time, but I'll work part-time."

So I went to work part-time because I was afraid to trust God completely. Dave and I didn't have as much income as we had before, but I found we could survive on less money than we had previously. We had to cut down on expenses, but we were able to pay our bills. I also had more time to prepare for ministry. This seemed like a good plan, but it was not God's plan.

I learned that God doesn't want to make "deals" and I ended up getting fired from my part-time job. I was a good worker and had never been fired from a job before. Even though I didn't like my circumstances, I was finally where God wanted me to be all along—totally dependent on Him.

Without a job, I had to learn to trust God for every little thing I needed. For six years, we needed divine intervention each month just to be able to pay our bills, but during that time I learned a lot about God's faithfulness. He always provided and what we learned through our experience enabled us to trust Him for the resources we now need to run an international ministry. I encourage you to obey God completely and don't try to make deals with Him because they never work.

GOD'S WORD FOR YOU TODAY: When we negotiate with God, we never win.

Like a Child

Truly I say to you, whoever does not accept and receive and welcome the kingdom of God like a little child [does] shall not in any way enter it [at all]. (LUKE 18:17)

God hears the simplest, faintest cry and receives the most child-like requests. I have raised four children and I now have nine grandchildren—and I can tell you that one thing children are *not* is complicated. Children have no trouble letting you know what they want, running into your arms when they are afraid, or giving you a big generous kiss, sometimes for no apparent reason. When they ask their parents a question, they fully expect to get an answer and we should have the same expectation when we talk to God. Children are not sophisticated enough to hide their hearts or feelings very well and as a result, communicating with them can be easy and refreshing.

That's the way God wants us to be when we talk to Him. We need to approach God with childlike simplicity and wait, eager to hear what He has to say to us. Just as children are naturally inclined to trust their parents completely, we also need to be innocent, pure, and free from doubt as we trust God's voice. When we pray with simple, childlike faith, we can experience God's miracle-working power and see things change.

––––––––––––

GOD'S WORD FOR YOU TODAY: When you pray today, call God "Daddy" and confide in Him completely.

Create the Right Atmosphere

If possible, as far as it depends on you, live at peace with everyone.
(ROMANS 12:18)

If we want to hear from God, we need to create an atmosphere conducive to His presence. By atmosphere I mean the environment or predominant mood that surrounds us. Atmosphere is created by attitudes and certain attitudes enhance or hinder our relationship with God. To hear from God we need an atmosphere of peace and we can maintain peace by our attitudes of faith in God and willingness to forgive those we might be upset with.

We can feel strife in the atmosphere when it is present. Likewise, we can sense peace in places where people and situations are at peace, and we should work to create and maintain peaceful atmospheres wherever we go because we cannot hear from God in the midst of turmoil. An attitude of strife and dissension does not create an atmosphere in which God will speak, but He will speak in peaceful atmospheres where hearts—and minds—are at peace and full of love.

To enjoy the fullness of God's presence we need to consistently maintain an atmosphere around us and in our hearts that allows us to honor Him. If we want to hear from God, we must yield all bad attitudes to the lordship of Jesus Christ so we can help create atmospheres in which we can sense His presence and hear His voice.

———————

GOD'S WORD FOR YOU TODAY: Make "peacemaker" your role.

Friendship Makes Us Bold

*Let us therefore come boldly to the throne of grace, that we may
obtain mercy and find grace to help in time of need.*

(HEBREWS 4:16 NKJV)

When we begin to understand our friendship with God and see ourselves as His friends, our prayers become more Spirit-led, more faith-filled, and much bolder. Jesus told a story in Luke 11, immediately after He taught His disciples to pray using what we call the "Lord's Prayer." We can surmise that He was using the story to illustrate His lesson on prayer. He said: "Which of you who has a friend will go to him at midnight and will say to him, Friend, lend me three loaves [of bread], for a friend of mine who is on a journey has just come, and I have nothing to put before him; and he from within will answer, Do not disturb me; the door is now closed, and my children are with me in bed; I cannot get up and supply you [with anything]? I tell you, although he will not get up and supply him anything because he is his friend, yet because of his shameless persistence and insistence he will get up and give him as much as he needs" (Luke 11:5–8).

Notice that the man who needs bread gets it only "because of his shameless persistence and insistence." We will only "shamelessly persist" with our friends—because friendship makes us bold, and the more we grow and progress in our friendship with God, the bolder and more confident we can be as we approach Him.

GOD'S WORD FOR YOU TODAY: Remember to pray with the same passion and intimacy that you reserve for your closest friends.

Keep Your Appointment

*You will seek Me, inquire for, and require Me [as a vital necessity]
and find Me when you search for Me with all your heart.*

                                                          (JEREMIAH 29:13)

We may have to deal sternly with our flesh to resist the spirit of passivity that tries to keep us from growing in the knowledge of God. A commitment to spend time with God is as serious a commitment as any we will ever make.

If I needed dialysis because of kidney disease and had to be at the hospital twice a week for treatment at 8:00 AM, I certainly would not accept an invitation to do anything else during those times, no matter how appealing it seemed or how much I wanted to do it. I would know my life depended on keeping my dialysis appointment. We should be that serious about our time with God. The quality of our lives is greatly affected by the time we spend with Him, so that time should have priority in our schedules.

Sometimes we become slack in keeping our appointments with God because we know He is always available. We know He will always be there for us, so we may skip or reschedule our time with Him so we can do something that seems more urgent. If we spent more "priority time" with God, we might not have so many "urgent" situations that tend to rob us of our time.

When we spend time with God, even if we don't feel His presence or think we are learning anything, we are still sowing good seeds that will produce good harvests in our lives. With persistence, you will reach the point where you understand more of God's Word, where you are enjoying fellowship with Him, and where you are talking to God and hearing His voice.

GOD'S WORD FOR YOU TODAY: Keep your appointments with God.

Pray and Obey

You have given me the capacity to hear and obey. (PSALM 40:6)

For many years, I wanted God to speak to me, but I wanted to pick and choose what things to obey. I wanted to do what He said to do if it was easy and I thought it was a good idea, but if I didn't like what I heard, I acted like it wasn't from God!

Some of what God says to you will be very exciting. Other things He says may not be so thrilling, but that doesn't mean they won't work out for your good if you will simply obey. For example, if God tells you that you need to apologize because you were rude to someone, it won't work for you to respond, "Well, that person was rude to me, too!" If you talk back to Him with excuses, you may have prayed and even heard God's voice, but you didn't obey.

Looking back at more than three decades of walking with God and being in ministry, I have to say that the simplest explanation for the success Dave and I have enjoyed is that we have learned to pray, hear from God, and then do what He tells us to do. Over the years, as I have sought God and pressed forward in what I feel He has told me to do, I can say that what I have done more than anything else is simply to pray and obey. Doing so has not always been popular, but it has worked.

If you want God's plan for your life, I can give you the recipe in its most basic form: pray and obey. God has given you the capacity to do both, and if you do it continually, you will be moving right along in His will for your life.

GOD'S WORD FOR YOU TODAY: Pray. Listen with your heart. Obey what you hear.

God Says, "You Can Trust Me"

Blessed ... is the man who fears (reveres and worships) the Lord ...
He shall not be afraid of evil tidings; his heart is firmly fixed, trusting
(leaning on and being confident) in the Lord. (PSALM 112:1, 7)

God sometimes speaks by giving us peace deep inside our hearts. You may face situations in which everyone around you is telling you to trust God and be at peace, but the "how to" evades you. Fears are screaming at you, unnerving you, and threatening you. Friends are saying, "Everything will be all right," but you find that hard to believe until God Himself speaks deep in your heart and says, "You can trust Me; I will take care of this. Everything really *is* going to be all right."

In 1989, I went to the doctor for a regular checkup. He discovered a fast-growing type of cancer, and recommended surgery immediately.

As a result of this news, I struggled with tremendous fear. I had trouble sleeping, and there were times when fear hit me so hard I felt I was going to fall down. No matter how many of my family members or friends reassured me, I still battled great fear until very early one morning, about 3:00, God spoke deep inside my heart and said, "Joyce, you can trust Me."

After that, I did not experience any sickening fear again. I was apprehensive as I waited for results on tests, but I was not terrified. I knew I was in God's hands and whatever happened, He would take care of me.

As it turned out, I did not need further treatment. I ended up thankful instead of fearful—and that's what can happen in any situation when we learn to hear God's voice.

GOD'S WORD FOR YOU TODAY: Trust God. He won't let you down.

Just Give It Time

Show me now Your way, that I may know You [progressively become more deeply and intimately acquainted with You].

(EXODUS 33:13)

When you spend time with God, it becomes evident. You become calmer, you're easier to get along with, you are more joyful, and you remain stable in every situation. Spending quality time with God is an investment that yields rich benefits. You begin to understand what He likes and what offends Him. As with any friend, the more time you spend with God, the more like Him you become.

Spending time with God causes you to become more sensitive to the love He wants to demonstrate to you and to others. Your conscience alerts you when you're talking to someone in a way that does not please Him. Your heart grieves when He grieves, and you quickly pray, "Oh, God, I'm sorry." You soon want to apologize to the person you have offended and discover that saying, "I'm sorry. I didn't mean to hurt you," isn't so difficult after all.

When God told Moses he had found favor in His eyes (see Exodus 33:12), Moses understood that God was telling him he could ask for anything his heart desired.

Moses responded by saying that he simply wanted to become more intimately acquainted with God. Moses had seen God perform history's most magnificent miracles, yet what he wanted most of all was to know God intimately.

I pray that knowing God is the desire of your heart. You can know Him and hear His voice as clearly and as intimately as you want to. All it takes is spending time with Him.

GOD'S WORD FOR YOU TODAY: God does not have favorites, but He does have confidantes.

God Speaks When We Worship

O come, let us worship and bow down, let us kneel before the Lord our Maker [in reverent praise and supplication]. (PSALM 95:6)

I believe that worship creates an atmosphere in which God can speak to us. Worship is difficult to define. It is more about Who God is rather than what He does for us. True worship comes from deep within us; it is precious and awesome and it is our attempt to verbalize how we feel about God. It is a powerful outpouring of our hearts toward the Lord and it represents a depth of love, gratitude, and devotion that we find difficult to put into words. Human language is not rich enough to describe everything that true worship is. In fact, worship is so personal and intimate that maybe we should not even attempt to limit or define it with our words.

Worship is much more than just singing songs. In fact, true worship is first and foremost a condition of heart and a state of mind. We can be worshipping passionately without singing a single note. Worship is born in our hearts; it fills our thoughts and then it is expressed through our mouths and through our bodies. If our hearts are filled with awe for God, we may want to sing, dance, clap, or lift up our hands in worship. We may also be reverently silent and still before God. We may desire to give offerings or offer other forms of outward expression of love for God. But any of these actions done without a right heart are simply formalism and meaningless to God.

I encourage you to sincerely worship God today. Do it because you love Him, and don't be surprised if He speaks to you while you are worshipping Him.

———————————

GOD'S WORD FOR YOU TODAY: Worship God from a heart of gratitude for Who He is.

A Simple Privilege

The law of the Lord is perfect, restoring the [whole] person; the testimony of the Lord is sure, making wise the simple. (PSALM 19:7)

I cannot imagine a higher honor than being able to talk to and hear from God, and I believe prayer is the greatest privilege of our lives. It's not something we *have* to do; it's something we *get* to do. Prayer is the way we partner with God to see His plans and purposes come to pass in our lives and in the lives of those we love. It is the means by which we human beings on Earth can actually enter into the awesome presence of God. It allows us to share our hearts with Him, to listen for His voice, and to know how to discover and enjoy all the great things He has for us. Communicating with God is indeed the greatest privilege I can think of, but this high and holy work is also the simplest privilege I know.

I do not believe talking to God or hearing His voice was ever meant to be complicated and that, from the very beginning, He intended it to be an easy, natural way of life by which we are connected with Him all day, every day.

———————

GOD'S WORD FOR YOU TODAY: Let prayer become like breathing; do it naturally and simply all throughout the day.

Practice Makes Perfect

You shall walk after the Lord your God and [reverently] fear Him …
and obey His voice. (DEUTERONOMY 13:4)

Once we begin listening to and hearing from God, it is important to obey whatever we hear Him say. Obedience increases our quality of fellowship with Him and strengthens our faith. We might say, "Practice makes perfect," when it comes to hearing and obeying Him. In other words, we become more and more confident as we gain experience. It takes a lot of practice to reach the point of complete submission to God's leading. Even knowing that God's ways are perfect and that His plans always work, we still act ignorant sometimes when He asks us to do something that requires personal sacrifice, or we might even be afraid that we are not hearing clearly and therefore too cautious to take action.

Don't be fearful of sacrifice or of making a mistake. There are many things in life that are worse than being wrong. Jesus said, "Follow Me." I firmly believe that when we have done our best to hear from God, then we must "step out and find out," if we truly are hearing His voice or not. Shrinking back in fear all of our lives will never allow us to make progress in our ability to hear from God.

He did not say, "You take the lead, and I will follow you." I have learned that we may as well do quickly whatever God says, because if we don't, I can guarantee that we will be miserable.

When our children are learning how to walk, we don't get angry when they fall down. We realize they are learning and we work with them. God is the same way and He will teach you how to hear from Him if you walk in faith and not fear.

———————

GOD'S WORD FOR YOU TODAY: Listen, discern, and obey boldly.

God Speaks in Many Ways

It is I, [the One] Who speaks in righteousness. (ISAIAH 63:1)

In the verse for today, God declares that He speaks, and when He does, He speaks in righteousness. We can always depend on what He says to be right. God speaks to us in many ways that include but are not limited to: His Word, nature, people, circumstances, peace, wisdom, supernatural intervention, dreams, visions, and what some call "the inner witness," which is best described as a "knowing" deep inside our hearts. He also speaks in what the Bible calls a "still, small voice," which I believe also refers to the inner witness.

God also speaks through the conscience, through our desires, and in an audible voice, but always remember that when He speaks, what He says is always right and it never disagrees with His written Word. We rarely hear God's audible voice, though it does happen. I have heard His audible voice three or four times over the course of my life. On two of these occasions, I was sleeping and His voice awakened me by simply calling my name. All I heard was "Joyce," but I knew God was speaking. He did not say what He wanted, but I knew instinctively that He was calling me to do something special for Him, although clarity did not come in that area for several years.

I want to encourage you to ask God to help you hear His voice in any way He chooses to speak to you. He loves you; He has good plans for your life; and He wants to talk to you about these things.

GOD'S WORD FOR YOU TODAY: God speaks in many ways; just remember—He will never contradict the Bible.

God-Given Desires

Delight yourself also in the Lord, and He will give you the desires and secret petitions of your heart. (PSALM 37:4)

One of the ways God speaks to us is through the sanctified desires of our hearts. God places right desires in our hearts and then He gives us those desires. I remember a time when I had a desire for homemade zucchini bread but had no talent or time to make it. I simply said, "Lord, I sure would like some fresh zucchini bread," and did not think about it again. About a week later a lady who knew nothing of my desire handed me a box and when I opened it, I found homemade zucchini bread. God delights in doing small and large things for us and we should never fail to appreciate all of them.

We need to ask God to give us sanctified, or holy, desires. We usually have desire for natural things such as success, finances, nice homes, and good relationships, but we should also desire spiritual things. We should desire to know God in a deeper and more intimate way, to always display the fruit of the Spirit, especially love, to serve God in ways that glorify Him, to always be obedient to God, et cetera. Let us ask God to take away fleshly desire and give us sanctified desire.

God puts in us desires that will bring His righteousness, peace, and joy to our lives (see Romans 14:17), and they never disagree with His Word.

Wrong desires torment us and we are impatient about receiving them, but sanctified desire comes with a willingness to wait on God's ways and timing.

GOD'S WORD FOR YOU TODAY: Place your desires before God, pray about them and trust God to give them to you if and when they are right for you.

Wait for Peace

I will listen [with expectancy] to what God the Lord will say, for He will speak peace to His people. (PSALM 85:8)

When God speaks, He gives us a deep sense of internal peace to confirm that the message we are hearing is truly from Him. Even if He speaks to chastise us, His Spirit of Truth leaves a calming sense of comfort in our souls.

When our enemy, the deceiver, speaks to us, he cannot give peace. When we try to solve things with our own reasoning, we cannot get peace because "the mind of the flesh [which is sense and reason without the Holy Spirit] is death [death that comprises all the miseries arising from sin, both here and hereafter]. But the mind of the [Holy] Spirit is life and [soul] peace [both now and forever]" (Romans 8:6).

Whenever you believe you hear God speak or make a decision based on something you believe He has said, use the scale of peace. If peace cannot hold its weight against the guidance you have heard, then don't proceed with it. You don't have to explain to others why you don't have peace about it; you may not even know that yourself. You can simply say, "I do not have peace about this right now; therefore, it's not wise for me to go ahead with it."

Always wait until peace about doing what you think God has instructed you to do fills your soul. Peace is confirmation that you are truly hearing from God and that your timing is right to take action. Peace gives us confidence and faith, which enable us to be obedient to God's instructions.

GOD'S WORD FOR YOU TODAY: Wait for peace before you act.

Be Filled at All Times

Do not get drunk with wine, for that is debauchery; but ever be filled and stimulated with the [Holy] Spirit. (EPHESIANS 5:18)

It is important for you to know that you are instructed in God's Word to "ever be filled" with the Spirit—that is, to be filled at all times.

To do that, it is necessary to give Him first place in our lives. Often this requires discipline, because many other things demand our time and attention. There are many things we want and need, but nothing is more important than God. Seeking God daily through His Word and spending time with Him is the key to staying filled with His presence. An attitude of gratitude is also very helpful, as is guarding our thoughts carefully.

The Holy Spirit never goes away; once He takes up occupancy, He settles in and refuses to leave. But it is important that we keep ourselves stirred up in spiritual things. Anything that is hot can grow cold if the fire goes out.

I went through a six-month period of time when God forbade me to ask for anything except more of Him. It was a great discipline in drawing near to Him on a deeper level of intimacy than I had known before. I would start to say, "God, I need_____," then I would stop myself as I remembered His instruction to me. I would finish my sentence with, "more of You."

God gives us everything we need; and He knows what we need before we ask for it. If we delight ourselves in Him and hunger for Him, He will also give us our hearts' desires. I encourage you, today and every day, to keep yourself filled with the Holy Spirit and to want more of God than anything else. He'll take care of the rest.

———————

GOD'S WORD FOR YOU TODAY: Be sure you're always "filled up" with the Holy Spirit.

Help Is Here

I will ask the Father, and He will give you another Comforter
(Counselor, Helper, Intercessor, Advocate, Strengthener, and
Standby), that He may remain with you forever. (JOHN 14:16)

Many people have received Jesus as Savior and Lord. They will go to heaven, but never draw on the full capacity of the Holy Spirit that is available to them or experience the true success God wants them to enjoy on Earth. Simply put, many will be on their way to heaven, but they won't enjoy the trip.

We often look at those who have wealth, position, power and we consider them "successful." But many people who are considered successful still lack peace, joy, contentment, and other true blessings. Such people have never learned to depend completely on the power of the Holy Spirit.

People who are self-sufficient often think depending on God is a sign of weakness. But the truth is that by drawing on the ability of the Holy Spirit, they can accomplish more in their lives than they ever could by working in their own strength.

God created us in such a way that although we do have strengths, we also have weaknesses and we need His help. We know He wants to help us because He sent a Divine Helper, the Holy Spirit, to live inside us.

We often struggle needlessly because we do not receive the help available to us. I encourage you to depend on Him, not on your own strength. Whatever you are facing, you don't have to go through it alone.

GOD'S WORD FOR YOU TODAY: Your worst day with God will be better than your best day without Him. The Holy Spirit is here to speak to you and help you in every way you need help today.

Out of Your Own Mouth

The plans of the mind and orderly thinking belong to man, but from the Lord comes the [wise] answer of the tongue. (PROVERBS 16:1)

God sometimes speaks to us out of our own mouths. I learned this when I was facing a major decision and needed a godly answer, but couldn't seem to find God's leading. My own thoughts left me confused, and I wasn't making any progress until I took a walk with a friend.

My friend and I discussed the matter for about an hour as we walked, enjoying the fresh air and each other's company. We discussed several possible solutions and their potential outcomes. We talked about how good it might be to handle the situation one way, and how bad it could be to handle it another way. As we continued to talk, suddenly a wise solution to my situation settled in my heart and came out of my mouth and I knew it was from the Lord. It didn't come from my mind; it rose from my spirit, my inner being.

What I decided I needed to do wasn't something I naturally wanted to do. Some of my struggle centered around wanting to convince God my situation should be dealt with differently. His voice was difficult to discern because my mind was already set against His plan. A stubborn mind-set is a great enemy of peace and can hinder our ability to hear God. We have to be willing to lay aside our own desires, or we may miss a clear word from Him. He always knows best, and we have to submit what we think to what He thinks in every circumstance.

God promises that if we seek Him, He will fill our mouths with the words we need to say (see Psalm 81:10). This is exactly what He did for me and what He will do for you as you continue to seek Him and surrender to His plans.

GOD'S WORD FOR YOU TODAY: Ask God to fill your mouth with the words you need to say today.

Keep a Tender Conscience

The [Holy] Spirit distinctly and expressly declares that in latter times some will turn away from the faith … through the hypocrisy and pretensions of liars whose consciences are seared (cauterized).

(1 TIMOTHY 4:1–2)

Today's verses speak of a person's conscience being "seared" or "cauterized." If a wound is cauterized, it becomes scar tissue and is unable to feel anything. Similarly, when people's consciences become cauterized, they become tough and numb, unable to feel what they should feel. Years of disobedience and personal pain can make us hard instead of gentle, but through God's grace we can change. We want to stay tender toward God so we can immediately sense when we are hurting others or disobeying Him in any way.

Ask God for a tender heart and conscience so you can be sensitive to Him and His dealings with you. If you know people who have hard hearts from years of personal pain and or disobedience to God, pray for them also. It is a beautiful thing to be able to discern immediately when our behavior does not please God. Thank God each time you sense Him dealing with you and keep working with the Holy Spirit to keep your conscience tender toward Him. We can ask for His forgiveness and immediately change our behavior: "Father, I pray for myself and my loved ones who have seared, hardened, cauterized consciences. I ask that You do a work to break that hardness off of us. Please soften our hearts toward You. Give us tender hearts that are responsive to Your leading, so we can immediately sense what You are saying to us and what You want us to do. In Jesus' name, amen."

GOD'S WORD FOR YOU TODAY: Be tough in your resolve but tender in your heart.

A Winning Combination

Happy (blessed, fortunate, enviable) is the man who finds skillful and godly Wisdom, and the man who gets understanding [drawing it forth from God's Word and life's experiences]. (PROVERBS 3:13)

One of my favorite ways to hear from God is through conventional wisdom and common sense. Wisdom discerns truth in a situation, while common sense provides good judgment regarding what to do with the truth. I consider wisdom supernatural because it isn't taught by men; it is a gift from God.

Many sophisticated, intelligent people lack wisdom and common sense. God's Word says, "If any of you is deficient in wisdom, let him ask of the giving God [Who gives] to everyone liberally and ungrudgingly, without reproaching or faultfinding, and it will be given him" (James 1:5).

I am amazed how many people think they must stop using common sense in order to be "spiritual." Spiritual people don't float around all day on clouds of glory; they live in the real world and deal with real issues in real ways. They need real answers, just like everyone else—and those answers are found in God's Word and revealed to us by His Spirit.

We do the seeking, and God does the speaking, but He is the Spirit of Wisdom and will not tell us to do anything that is unwise. Many times we ask God to speak to us and lead us, but if He does not give us a specific word from Scripture or speak a word in our hearts, we still have to live our daily lives and make decisions. God is not going to dictate every little choice we make, but He does give us wisdom and common sense—and those two make a winning combination.

GOD'S WORD FOR YOU TODAY: If you do the seeking, God will do the speaking.

First Response

O God, You are my God; early will I seek You. (PSALM 63:1 NKJV)

Sometimes I marvel at how long we can struggle in a situation before we think to talk to God about it and listen for His voice. We complain about our problems; we grumble; we murmur; we tell our friends; and we talk about how we wish God would do something about it. We struggle with situations in our minds and in our emotions, while we often fail to take advantage of the simplest solution there is: prayer. But worse than that, we then make perhaps the most ridiculous statement known to man: "Well, I guess all I can do is pray." I am sure you have heard that before and maybe you have even said it. We all have. We are all guilty of treating prayer as a last-ditch effort and saying things like, "Well, nothing else is working, so maybe we should pray." Do you know what that tells me? It tells me that we really do not believe in the power of prayer as we should. We carry burdens we do not need to bear—and life is much harder than it has to be—because we do not realize how powerful prayer is. If we did, we would talk to God and listen to what He says about everything, not as a last resort, but as a first response.

GOD'S WORD FOR YOU TODAY: Let prayer be your first response, not your last resort.

Be Still

Let be and be still, and know (recognize and understand) that I am God. (PSALM 46:10)

Talking has always come easily to me, but I have had to learn to listen. I once felt my husband did not want to spend time sitting and talking together, so I told him we needed to talk more. He responded, "Joyce, we don't talk. You talk and I listen." He was right, and I needed to change if I expected him to want to spend time with me.

I soon discovered that I treated God the same way I treated Dave. I did the talking and expected Him to listen. I complained that I never heard from God, but the truth is that I never took time to listen to Him. The verse for today teaches us to be still, and know that God is God. Many of us find being still difficult to do because our flesh likes to be busy and active doing things, but we must learn to spend time alone and to be still if we want to hear God's voice.

For many people, listening is an ability that must be developed and practiced. Sometimes this means sitting quietly in God's presence without saying anything. We should practice listening! One way to do this is to ask God if there is anyone He wants you to encourage or bless— and then be still and listen. You will be surprised at how quickly He responds by placing someone on your heart. He may give you specific things you can do to encourage them. As we listen for God's direction He gives us creative ideas that perhaps we have never considered. Take time to be still and listen carefully to Him and then be obedient and do what He shows you to do.

———————

GOD'S WORD FOR YOU TODAY: Take time out today. Be still and listen.

Keep Pressing On

I do not consider, brethren, that I have captured and made it my own [yet]; but one thing I do [it is my one aspiration]: forgetting what lies behind and straining forward to what lies ahead, I press on toward the goal to win the [supreme and heavenly] prize to which God in Christ Jesus is calling us upward. (PHILIPPIANS 3:13–14)

Our relationships with God are progressive and we all move from one level to another. No one ever "masters" communication with God because there is no limit to the depth of relationship we can have with Him; it just keeps growing, keeps going deeper, keeps getting stronger. Our ability to hear His voice develops and improves over time. Over time and with practice, we get better at sharing our hearts with God and we become more skilled and experienced at hearing His voice and understanding what He is saying to us. We never become certified experts in prayer and we never stop learning to communicate with God; our experiences just keep getting richer and better.

God has so much for you, and though you may not have arrived at your final destination, you can thank God you are on the pathway that will take you there. As long as you are making progress, it really doesn't matter if you are crawling, walking, or running. Just keep pressing on!

_____

GOD'S WORD FOR YOU TODAY: You're okay and you're on your way.

God Speaks Suddenly

You have turned my mourning into dancing for me; You have put off my sackcloth and girded me with gladness. (PSALM 30:11)

On a Friday morning in February 1976, I was frustrated and desperate. I was trying to do everything the church said I should do and everything I thought God required of me, but nothing seemed to be working and I was quite disheartened. I knew I needed change in my life, but I wasn't sure exactly what change I needed. I knew I was searching, but I wasn't sure what I was searching for.

That morning, I cried out to God and told Him I couldn't go on any longer. I remember saying, "God, something is missing. I don't know what it is, but something is missing."

To my surprise, He spoke to me in what sounded loud enough to be His audible voice, calling my name and talking to me about patience. From that moment on, I *knew* He was going to do something about my situation. Later that day, in my car, Jesus filled me with the presence of the Holy Spirit in a way I had never before experienced. The best way to describe the feeling is to say I felt someone had poured liquid love into me. I immediately noticed newfound peace, joy, and love resting inside me and flowing out of me, and everyone around me noticed positive changes in my behavior as I began to love others as I never had before.

I got up that morning feeling as though everything had come to a discouraging end. I went to bed that night knowing I was at a place of new beginnings. God often works this way; He speaks and moves suddenly in our lives. Don't grow weary of waiting on God because today may be your day for a "suddenly."

GOD'S WORD FOR YOU TODAY: Today may be your day for a "suddenly."

Find Friends Who Hear God

Iron sharpens iron; so a man sharpens the countenance of his friend.
(PROVERBS 27:17)

If we listen, God will speak to us about our relationships—our marriages, friendships, business associations, and even casual acquaintances. He may ask us to sever friendships or relationships with people who can tempt us to stray from His plan for our lives. We can easily become like those we spend time with. If we spend time with people who are selfish and self-centered, we may soon find ourselves often focused on ourselves, thinking about what we can do or get for ourselves. In contrast, God may encourage us to make friends with someone who is a giver. If we spend time with such a person, before long, we will be givers, too.

It is enjoyable and beneficial to spend time with someone who really hears from God, someone who truly senses what the Holy Spirit is saying and doing. It is not fun to spend time with people who are dull in their spiritual hearing, and we can tell when we are with someone like that. The verse for today says that "iron sharpens iron," and we can sharpen our ability to hear the right things by being with people who practice listening for God's voice and obeying Him.

GOD'S WORD FOR YOU TODAY: We become the company we keep; make "iron" choices.

God's Words Agree with His Word

Your word have I laid up in my heart, that I might not sin against
You. (PSALM 119:11)

I once sat down to do some writing on a book and sensed the Lord saying, "Take a few minutes and just wait on Me." I waited for a very short time and then started to make a phone call. The Lord gently said, "I didn't tell you to make phone calls; I told you to wait on Me." My desire to do something was not unusual; most people have a hard time being still and waiting on someone, something, or even God.

After I got quiet and waited for a period of time, the Lord began to speak to me about angels—something I certainly was not expecting. He led me to look up several Scriptures and I ended up having a mini–Bible study on the power and presence of angels. God has reasons for everything He does, and I believe He wanted me to be more aware of the angels working on my behalf—something I had not thought about for a long, long time.

You may wonder how I knew with certainty that God was speaking to me and that the whole subject of angels was not something I came up with in my own mind. The answer is that I had peace about what I heard. It felt "right" inside of me. My spirit confirmed it as a message from the Lord, and what I heard agreed with God's Word.

There have been other times I have waited on God and heard a similar voice, but knew intuitively that it was not God's. We must know God through His Word in order to safely know when He is speaking to us and when He isn't.

––––––––––

GOD'S WORD FOR YOU TODAY: Study God's Word so
you can recognize His voice.

He Will Tell You What's Ahead

He will announce and declare to you the things that are to come [that will happen in the future]. (JOHN 16:13)

One of the many benefits of hearing from God is that listening to His voice helps us prepare for the future. The Holy Spirit gives to us the messages the Father gives to Him, and He often tells us things that will happen in the future.

We find many instances in the Bible in which God spoke to people and gave them information about the future. He told Noah to prepare for a flood that would come to destroy the people of the earth (see Genesis 6:13–17). He told Moses to go to Pharaoh and ask for the release of the Israelites and that Pharaoh would not grant this request (see Exodus 7). Obviously, God does not tell us everything that will happen in the future, but His Word promises He will tell us some things.

There are times when I sense that something good, or perhaps something challenging, is going to happen. When a challenge awaits me and I have some prior knowledge of it, that knowledge helps to cushion the blow when the difficult situation comes. If an automobile with good shock absorbers hits a pothole, those absorbers protect passengers in the car from the jarring impact that would result and no one gets hurt. God's giving us information ahead of time works the same way.

Part of the Holy Spirit's ministry is to tell us things to come. He knows the mind of God and He knows God's individual plans for our lives. He will reveal what we need to know when we need to know it in order to fulfill the good plans God has for us.

GOD'S WORD FOR YOU TODAY: Trust the Holy Spirit to tell you what you need to know about the future.

The Real Thing

Seek, inquire for, and crave peace and pursue (go after) it!
(PSALM 34:14)

I teach a lot about following peace as we follow God, but I want to make sure you understand that there is such a thing as false peace and we need to beware of it. For example, when we have a strong desire to do something, it can produce a false sense of peace that actually comes only from our emotions. As time passes, this false peace disappears, and God's true will emerges. For this reason, we should never move too quickly to make important decisions. A little time of waiting is always wise and prudent.

Here is an example. Someone Dave and I love very much was in need, and we wanted to meet the need. Doing so would have given that individual great joy and fulfilled a long-held desire for that person. I got excited and went to Dave, who agreed we should help. We proceeded with our plan, but the further we went with it, the less peace I felt. This created a problem because we had committed to help and I didn't want to break my word. I didn't mind saying I had made a mistake, but I didn't want to disappoint the person who was counting on us.

A few weeks passed and I kept praying about the situation. Eventually, I lost my peace to the point that I went to the person and said, "Something is not right about our plan; I have absolutely no peace about it." To my great relief, the other person felt the same way. I had allowed my excitement over this plan to create a false sense of peace that dissipated over time.

GOD'S WORD FOR YOU TODAY: Don't make serious decisions without waiting to make sure true peace abides within you.

Study God's Word; Hear God's Voice

Study and be eager and do your utmost to present yourself to God approved (tested by trial), a workman who has no cause to be ashamed, correctly analyzing and accurately dividing [rightly handling and skillfully teaching] the Word of Truth. (2 TIMOTHY 2:15)

Anyone who wants to hear God's voice must be a student of the Word. Of all the other ways God may choose to speak to us, He will never contradict the written Word, which was originally referred to by the Greek word *logos*. His spoken word in the Greek language is referred to as *rhema*. God specifically brings to our remembrance His *logos* for every situation. His *rhema* (spoken word to us) may not be found word for word on the pages of the Bible, but its principles will always be supported by the written Word. In this way, the Bible confirms whether or not what we are hearing is from God.

For example, the *logos*, the written Word, doesn't tell us when to buy a new car or what kind to buy. We need the *rhema* word for that. Even though the Word doesn't give specific instructions on buying a car, it does say a lot about wisdom. If we think we have "heard" that we are supposed to buy a certain kind of car and then realize such a large purchase would put us into deep debt for several years, we can easily see that buying that car would not be wise and the voice we thought we heard was not God's.

———

GOD'S WORD FOR YOU TODAY: Logos + rhema = wisdom.

God Will Speak Wisdom to You

If you cry out for insight and raise your voice for understanding, if you seek [Wisdom] as for silver and search for skillful and godly Wisdom as for hidden treasures, then you will understand the reverent and worshipful fear of the Lord. (PROVERBS 2:3–5)

Today's verses urge us to seek wisdom and cry out for understanding. This is because God's wisdom far surpasses any human being's best ideas. God sees the end from the beginning, He sees people's hearts and motives, and He knows things we do not. Whether we find ourselves dealing with the everyday hassles of life or up against a full-scale attack of the enemy, God's wisdom will make the difference—and the only way to get that wisdom is to ask God for it.

Many times, when God speaks to us, He reveals wisdom. He may do so by sharing a particular insight into a situation or by clearly telling us what to do when we have decisions to make. He can make His wisdom known in a variety of ways, and we should always receive it as a precious gift.

I encourage you to value the wisdom of God as a priceless spiritual treasure and think of it as something you cannot do without—because you cannot, if you want to have a successful life. Make a habit of praying and asking God for His wisdom in every situation—large and small. He will give it to you and you will be thrilled with the results.

GOD'S WORD FOR YOU TODAY: No issue is so small that it doesn't require God's wisdom.

God Hears and Answers

He will surely be gracious to you at the sound of your cry; when He hears it, He will answer you. (ISAIAH 30:19)

Our friendship not only benefits us, it also benefits those around us. When people come to us with needs or concerns, we may be able to offer some help, or we may not be able to meet their needs at all. Even if we do not have what people really need, God does. When we are friends with God, we can say to people, "I don't have what you need, but I know Someone who does. I'll ask my friend! I will intercede before God for you."

We know that God has the power to intervene in people's circumstances, to help their children stop using drugs, to bring financial breakthroughs, to work medical miracles or to reconcile marriages. The more intimately we know God, the more confident we are in His willingness and ability to help people. When they come to us, we can go to Him and know He will come through for them. We can actually ask God to do us a favor and help someone we love even when we know that they don't deserve it. We can pray with compassion out of a heart of love—and God hears and answers.

God loves you and He loves the sound of your voice coming to Him in prayer and fellowship. Go to Him often not only for your needs, but also for the needs of others.

———

GOD'S WORD FOR YOU TODAY: Remember that God loves the sound of your voice.

A Home for God's Spirit

May Christ through your faith [actually] dwell (settle down, abide, make His permanent home) in your hearts! (EPHESIANS 3:17)

If you are born again, you hopefully know that Jesus lives on the inside of you through the power of the Holy Spirit. The question is, is God comfortable in you? Does He feel at home within you? Even though the Spirit of God lives within you, other things live in you, too—such as fear, anger, jealousy, or murmuring and complaining.

God once gave me an illustration of what it is like for Him to live in a heart where murmuring, complaining, and discord reside. Suppose you go to a friend's house and your friend says, "Oh, come on in. I'll get you a cup of coffee. Get comfortable and make yourself at home." Then, your friend begins yelling at her husband and the two of them rant and rave and carry on right in front of you. How comfortable would you be in the presence of such strife?

If we want to be a comfortable "home" for the Spirit of the Lord, we must give up things that cause us to forget about His presence or are offensive to Him. We must stop grumbling, allowing strife and unrest inside us, or harboring unforgiveness. Instead, we need to make sure our inner lives are engaged in things that please and honor God's presence. Our mouths should be full of praise and thanksgiving. We should wake up every day and say in our hearts, "Good morning, Lord. I want You to feel at home and be comfortable in me today."

We all need to take inventory of what goes in our hearts because they are the dwelling place of God. When we examine our inner lives, we are looking at holy ground where God has chosen to make His home. Let's commit to making Him comfortable in us.

GOD'S WORD FOR YOU TODAY: Make sure you are a comfortable home for the Spirit of the Lord.

All Access

Through Him also we have [our] access (entrance, introduction) by faith into this grace (state of God's favor) in which we [firmly and safely] stand. And let us rejoice and exult in our hope of experiencing and enjoying the glory of God. (ROMANS 5:2)

Everything in our spiritual lives depends on our personal faith in God and our personal relationship with Him, which certainly includes being able to hear His voice. We can enjoy that relationship because Jesus' death on the cross gives us free, unhindered access to our heavenly Father and our faith makes it possible for us to have an intimate, dynamic relationship with Him.

I love Ephesians 3:12 and have recently been studying it. It says: "In Whom, because of our faith in Him, we dare to have the boldness (courage and confidence) of free access (an unreserved approach to God with freedom and without fear)." As I meditated on this Scripture, I became quite excited to realize that as ordinary human beings we have free access to God at any time through prayer; we can hear His voice anytime we want or need to. We can approach Him boldly without reservations, without fear, and with complete freedom. How awesome is that! Personal faith in God opens the door to unlimited help from Him and to unhindered communication with Him.

Come to God with confidence that He loves you, desires your fellowship, and wants not only to hear from you, but He desires to talk to you.

GOD'S WORD FOR YOU TODAY: Expect to hear from God and to be led by His Holy Spirit.

A Lamp and a Light

Your word is a lamp to my feet and a light to my path.
(PSALM 119:105)

There is nothing more supernatural than the Word of God, which is given to us by divine inspiration of the Holy Spirit speaking through His prophets and disciples. The Bible has an answer for every question we might ever have. The Word of God is full of life principles, true stories of God's mercy toward human behavior, and rich parables filled with important truths for every person on Earth.

The Bible is a personal letter to you and me. It tells us everything we need to know. There may be times when God speaks something to us that is not in a specific chapter or verse, but if He is truly speaking, then what we hear will always be in agreement with His Word. God will speak to us and lead us in every situation as we seek Him through His Word. When I need to hear from God about something specific, He frequently reminds me of a Scripture that clearly gives me the answer I am seeking.

Hearing God's voice (being led by the Holy Spirit) throughout each day has become a natural way of life for me since I received the fullness of the Holy Spirit. God gives the gift of His Spirit to everyone who asks (see Luke 11:13), and the Holy Spirit helps us understand God's Word so we can apply its wisdom to our lives.

―――――――――――

GOD'S WORD FOR YOU TODAY: Read God's Word as a personal letter, written just for you.

Give Yourself a Gift

Become useful and helpful and kind to one another, tenderhearted (compassionate, understanding, loving-hearted), forgiving one another [readily and freely], as God in Christ forgave you.

(EPHESIANS 4:32)

Unforgiveness, bitterness, resentment, or offense of any kind can render us unable to hear from God. The Word of God is very clear on this subject. If we want God to forgive our sins and offenses against Him, we must forgive others their sins and offenses against us.

Ephesians 4:30–32, the passage that contains our verse for today, teaches that we grieve the Holy Spirit when we harbor negative emotions such as anger, resentment, and animosity in our hearts. When we hold unforgiveness against anyone for any reason, it hardens our hearts and prevents us from being sensitive to God's leading in our lives.

I once heard someone say that holding unforgiveness is like drinking poison and hoping your enemy will die. Why spend your life being angry and bitter toward someone who is probably enjoying his or her life and does not even care that you are upset? Do yourself a favor—forgive those who hurt you! Give yourself the gift of forgiveness. It will bring peace to your heart and enable you to hear God's voice and follow His leading in your life.

GOD'S WORD FOR YOU TODAY: Give yourself the gift of forgiving others.

Winning God's Way

Show me Your ways, O Lord; teach me Your paths. (PSALM 25:4)

Most of us are happy when we get what we want. That's human nature. But when we walk with God as we should, other things become more important than seeing our desires fulfilled—things like seeking God's desires for our lives, hearing His voice as we make decisions, and being obedient to His leading in every situation.

Dave and I once saw a picture in a store in the mall and I wanted to buy it. Dave didn't think we needed it, so I threw one of my silent temper tantrums; I simply became quiet because I was angry.

"You okay?" Dave asked.

"Fine. I'm fine, fine, just fine." I responded with my mouth while my mind was thinking, *You always try to tell me what to do. What can't you just leave me alone and let me do what I want to do? Neh, neh, neh—.*

I continued pouting for about an hour. I was trying to manipulate Dave. I knew that with his peaceful, phlegmatic personality, he would rather let me have my way than fight with me. I was too immature in the Lord to understand that my behavior was ungodly.

I began to push Dave to buy the picture and we finally bought it. As I placed it in my home, the Holy Spirit said to me, "You know, you really didn't win. You got your picture, but you still lost because you didn't do it My way."

The only way to win in life is to do things God's way. Then, even if we don't get what we want, we have the great satisfaction of knowing we have obeyed His voice—and that outlasts the satisfaction that comes with any earthly possession or achievement.

———————————

GOD'S WORD FOR YOU TODAY: When God's way becomes your way, you're on your way to great peace and joy.

Stay Safe in the Word

Test and prove all things [until you can recognize] what is good; [to that] hold fast. (1 THESSALONIANS 5:21)

Hearing from God clearly and avoiding the possibility of deception comes only from spending regular time with Him, learning His Word. Listening for God's voice without having knowledge of His Word is a mistake. Knowing God's written Word protects us from deception.

Trying to hear from God without knowing His Word is irresponsible and even dangerous. People who want to be led by the Spirit but are too lazy to spend time in the Word and in prayer set themselves up for deception because evil spirits are eager to whisper to listening ears. The devil tried to say things to Jesus and He always replied, "It is written," and then quoted Scripture to refute the lies of the enemy (see Luke 4).

Some people seek God only when they are in trouble and need help. But if they are not used to hearing from God, they will find recognizing His voice difficult when they really need Him.

We need to compare any idea, prompting, or thought that comes to us with God's Word. If we don't know the Word, we won't have anything against which to measure theories and arguments that rise up in our thoughts. The enemy can present wild ideas that make sense to us. The fact that thoughts are logical doesn't mean they are from God. We may like what we hear, but the fact that something appeals to us doesn't mean it is from God. We may hear something that feels good to our emotions, but if it fails to give us peace it is not from God. God's advice to us is to always follow peace and let it be an umpire in our lives (see Colossians 3:15).

GOD'S WORD FOR YOU TODAY: Test everything you hear against the Word of God, because that is the only standard of truth that exists.

God Speaks So He Can Help Us

The yoke shall be destroyed because of the anointing.
(ISAIAH 10:27 KJV)

When God speaks to you about an issue that needs to be dealt with in your life, you should not put it off. You can trust that the anointing, which is the power and ability of the Holy Spirit, is present to break its grip on you. If you put off confronting the problem until you want to deal with it, you may have to face trying to change without God's power or anointing.

We often want to do things in our own timing, and we struggle and struggle because it is not anointed by God at the time we are trying to deal with it. For example, there are times when I feel like I want to confront an issue with an employee, but I know that it would be wiser for me to pray about it for a while and let God prepare that person's heart. When I follow God's timetable, I always have His anointing to get it done. I have learned to deal with issues when God wants to deal with them and leave them alone when He wants me to wait. I have also had the frustrating experience of trying over and over to change myself without waiting on God's help and timing. God's anointing must be present for anything to work right in our lives.

When God convicts us of something that needs to change in our lives that means He has prepared us to face it. We may not feel that we are ready, but we can trust that His timing is perfect and His anointing is present to break the yoke that is hindering our full freedom. I have learned to say, "Lord, I may not feel ready, but if You say the time is now then I trust that Your power is with me and I am willing to be obedient to You." As you step out in faith to deal with issues you will find that the wisdom, grace, power, and ability that you need are present.

GOD'S WORD FOR YOU TODAY: Don't put off until another day what He wants you to deal with today.

Only God Gives Peace

The Lord will give [unyielding and impenetrable] strength to His people; the Lord will bless His people with peace. (PSALM 29:11)

One of the greatest ways God speaks to us and leads us is through the inner witness. In other words, we just know inside what is right or wrong. It is a deeper level of knowing than "head knowledge." This type of knowing is in the spirit—we simply have peace or a lack of peace. By the presence or absence of peace, we know what we should do.

I once spoke with a woman who needed to make a serious decision. Her family and friends were giving her advice, but she needed to know within herself what the right answer was because she was the one who would have to live with it. She had been in a certain business all of her life and was feeling that she wanted to get out of it and stay home with her children. Of course, this would require drastic financial adjustments and personal changes for her, things that could even affect her emotionally. She needed to know from God, not from other people, what the right decision was.

The woman went to a retreat with a relative. During the course of that weekend, as she praised and worshipped God and listened to the speaker, a knowing and a peace came into her heart that she was indeed right about closing the business. She said a moment just came when she knew what was right. She has had peace about her decision ever since.

It is amazing how well-meaning people can tell us things, yet they really don't affect us. But when God speaks to us about a matter, it has a great impact on us. Ask God for the inner witness that only He can give.

GOD'S WORD FOR YOU TODAY: Only God can give you peace.

You're an Original

He fashions their hearts individually. (PSALM 33:15 NKJV)

Psalm 33:15 speaks about us as individuals. Because God has fashioned our hearts individually, our prayers need to flow naturally out of our hearts and be consistent with the way He has designed us. As we develop our individual styles of communication with God, we can learn from people who may be more experienced than we are, but we need to be careful not to imitate them or allow them to set standards for us. I hope to be an example to many, but I want Jesus to be their standard. There is nothing at all wrong with incorporating something someone else is doing into your own prayer life if you truly feel God's Spirit is leading you to do so, but it is wrong to force yourself to do what others do if you are not comfortable with it in your spirit.

I encourage you to develop your own style of talking to God and listening to His voice. Don't try to keep up with others or copy their prayer styles—and don't feel compelled to work every "prayer principle" you have ever learned every time you pray. Just be who you are, remembering that God has fashioned you just the way He wants you to be, that He takes pleasure in who you are, and that He wants to speak to you in unique and personal ways.

GOD'S WORD FOR YOU TODAY: God loves who you are and how you talk. Don't be shy with Him.

Be Steadfast

Let endurance and steadfastness and patience have full play and do a thorough work, so that you may be [people] perfectly and fully developed [with no defects], lacking in nothing. (JAMES 1:4)

Today's verse speaks of being steadfast. To be steadfast is to be stable; a steadfast person is steady, calm, and even-tempered, no matter what happens. A steadfast believer can give the devil a nervous breakdown! When we mature spiritually to the point that we can maintain a level of steadfastness, then we do not react to every little harassing thing the enemy sends against us. Regardless of what he hurls our way, we will not be impressed, we will not be afraid, we will not be easily upset, we will not give up, and we will not be moved—if we are steadfast.

In order to be steadfast and immovable, we must know God and know Him intimately. We must be able to hear His voice when the storms of life are swirling around us. We must also know the overcoming power that belongs to us in the name of Jesus and through the blood of Jesus. We will remember that "this, too, shall pass" and keep our sights set on the victory that is sure, rather than allow ourselves to be tossed and turned by everything the devil assaults us with. As we do, God's power is released in our lives. Whatever you might be facing today, let patience do the work that God desires in you.

GOD'S WORD FOR YOU TODAY: Be steadfast in God, and give the devil a nervous breakdown!

Soft and Sensitive

I will give them one heart [a new heart] and I will put a new spirit within them; and I will take the stony [unnaturally hardened] heart out of their flesh, and will give them a heart of flesh [sensitive and responsive to the touch of their God]. (EZEKIEL 11:19)

In the verse for today, God promises to replace hearts of stone with hearts of flesh. In other words, He can transform a hard-hearted person into a softhearted, sensitive person.

When we give our lives to God, He puts a sense of right and wrong deep within our conscience. But if we rebel against our conscience too many times, we can become hard-hearted. If that happens, we need to let God soften our hearts so that we can be spiritually sensitive to the leadership of the Holy Spirit.

I was very hard-hearted before I began really fellowshipping with God. Being in His presence regularly softened my heart and made me much more sensitive to His voice. Without a heart sensitive to the touch of God, we will not recognize many of the times He is speaking to us. He speaks gently, in a still, small voice, or with gentle conviction about a matter.

A hard-hearted person is also in danger of hurting other people and not even being aware that they are doing so, and this grieves the heart of God. Those who are hard-hearted and busy "doing their own thing" will not be sensitive to God's will or voice. God wants to soften our hearts with His Word, because a hardened heart cannot hear His voice or receive the other many blessings He longs to give.

GOD'S WORD FOR YOU TODAY: Keep your heart soft and sensitive to God's voice.

Lord, Teach Me to Pray

He was praying in a certain place; and when He stopped, one of His disciples said to Him, Lord, teach us to pray. (LUKE 11:1)

One of the most important, life-changing prayers a person can ever utter is: "Lord, teach me to pray." It's not simply, "Lord, teach me to *pray*," but "Lord, teach *me* to pray." You see, simply knowing about prayer is not enough; we have to know how to pray—to talk and listen to God—as individuals who are in an intimate, dynamic personal relationship with the God to Whom we pray. Although there are principles of prayer that apply to everyone, we are individuals and God will lead each of us to pray and communicate with Him in uniquely personal ways.

There was a time when I attended many "prayer seminars," and then attempted to duplicate in my prayer experience what I heard others say about the way they prayed. Eventually, though, I realized God had a personalized prayer plan for me—a way for me to talk to Him and listen to Him most effectively—and I needed to find out what that was. I started by saying, "Lord, teach *me* to pray." God answered me in a powerful way and brought wonderful improvements to my prayer life.

If you want to enjoy a deeper, intimate, powerful relationship with God through prayer, I encourage you to say, "Lord, teach *me* to pray." He'll do it, and you'll soon find greater freedom and effectiveness in your prayer life. God will lead you in a unique, fresh plan that works wonderfully for you.

GOD'S WORD FOR YOU TODAY: Let God teach *you* to pray.

God Speaks Through Promptings

I am speaking the truth in Christ. I am not lying; my conscience [enlightened and prompted] by the Holy Spirit bearing witness with me. (ROMANS 9:1)

In today's verse, Paul writes about being "prompted" by the Holy Spirit. Such promptings or nudges from the Holy Spirit are one way God speaks to us.

Let me be practical about this. Sometimes God prompts me to do something as menial as picking up a piece of clothing in a store that has fallen off of a hanger. I don't hear His audible voice telling me to do so, but I feel a nudge on the inside, a desire to leave the place where I am better than I found it. The Lord uses my obedience to teach me more about His character. He says to me, "Everything you do in life is an act of sowing seeds that will return to you. You will reap whatever you sow." If I sow seeds of excellence, then I can expect excellent things to happen in my life.

As another example, I was recently prompted by the Holy Spirit to send an e-mail of encouragement to a woman I know who is in ministry. I have known her for years and never felt that urge, but I followed the prompting and received a quick reply telling me that my encouragement at that particular time was confirmation to her about some decisions she was making.

Being led by the inner promptings of God is an adventure that makes every day exciting and fresh. In learning to hear from God we must learn to follow these gentle, inner promptings.

GOD'S WORD FOR YOU TODAY: Be sensitive to "nudges" from the Holy Spirit, no matter how small they may be.

The Holy Spirit Knows What to Do

When He, the Spirit of Truth (the Truth-giving Spirit) comes, He will guide you into all the Truth (the whole, full Truth). (JOHN 16:13)

When God sends His Holy Spirit to work in people's lives, He condemns sin, not sinners. Throughout His Word, we see clear proof of His love for individuals and His desire to nurture people so they can leave their sin behind and move on in His great plans for their lives. We never need to be afraid to let Him show us and speak to us about what we are doing wrong.

The Holy Spirit lives within us. His job is to lead us, teach us, help us with prayer, comfort us, convict us of sin, and lead us as we fulfill God's plan for our lives.

We can trust the Holy Spirit because He knows exactly what needs to be done in our lives and the right timing for it. You might say we are broken and He knows how to "fix" us.

I am sure the Holy Spirit is working in and with you on some area of your life just as He is with all of us. I encourage you to submit to Him completely because He knows what He is doing and will do it exactly right. If people try to fix us or we try to fix ourselves we often only make things worse, but the Holy Spirit works in mysterious ways His wonders to perform. We may not always understand or even like what He is doing, but the end result will be glorious. Relax, enjoy the day, and thank God that He is working in you.

GOD'S WORD FOR YOU TODAY: Let go, and let God.

Live God's Way

Teach me Your way, O Lord, that I may walk and live in Your truth;
direct and unite my heart [solely, reverently] to fear and honor Your
name. (PSALM 86:11)

If we listen to God's voice and live God's way, if we choose to serve
Him, we can avoid long wrestling matches with Him. Wisdom tells us
to let God do with us what He wants, so we don't keep going around
and around the same "mountain" all the time (see Deuteronomy 2:3). I
have met people who have been dealing with the same obstacles and
issues for twenty or thirty years. If they had simply obeyed God in the
beginning, they would have moved on with their lives long ago.

No matter how much we may enjoy where we are when God finds
us, He will not let us stay there and become stagnant. He has new
places to take us and new lessons to teach us. He wants to keep us full
of life, full of growth, and full of His purposes and plans.

God has said to us, "If you don't pay attention to Me, if you ignore
Me and do not give heed to My reproof, I am going to cry out to you.
I will try to help you, but if you continue to give Me a deaf ear, you will
come to Me in a panic when you get in trouble" (see Proverbs 1:24–28).
God is merciful and long-suffering, but there comes a time when we
must realize that we just need to be obedient to Him. The sooner we
obey and start living God's way, the sooner we can get on with our lives
and move forward in God's good plans.

***

GOD'S WORD FOR YOU TODAY: Pray, obey, and don't
delay!

God Cares About Every Detail

Are not two little sparrows sold for a penny? And yet not one of them will fall to the ground without your Father's leave (consent) and notice. But even the very hairs of your head are all numbered. Fear not, then; you are of more value than many sparrows.

(MATTHEW 10:29–31)

Through the power of the Holy Spirit, God wants to speak to you every day. He wants to lead you step-by-step away from trouble and into the good things He has in store for you. He cares about the tiniest details of your life. According to the verses for today, He even keeps track of how many hairs you have on your head. He cares about the desires of your heart, and He wants to reveal to you truth that will set you free from worry and fear.

God's plan to share an intimate relationship with you existed before you were even born, as you can read in Psalm 139:16: "Your eyes saw my unformed substance, and in Your book all the days [of my life] were written before ever they took shape, when as yet there was none of them." God knows all of our days and has a plan for each one. If we will ask Him what we are to do each day and believe that He is guiding us, we will find ourselves fulfilling His plan for our lives.

It seems incomprehensible that God could have a plan for every person on Earth, but it also brings great peace to know He can take chaos and turn it into something meaningful and worthwhile. Spend time getting to know God because His plan is unveiled through intimate relationship with Him.

GOD'S WORD FOR YOU TODAY: Remember that God even keeps track of the sparrows—He is surely in control of whatever life brings you today.

True Satisfaction

He satisfies the longing soul and fills the hungry soul with good.
(PSALM 107:9)

Hopefully, you have experienced times with God that were extremely satisfying to you. He is the only One Who can truly satisfy the longing soul, so don't waste your time on empty pursuits.

No matter what we own, where we go, or what we do, nothing apart from God can truly satisfy us. Money, travel, houses and furniture, clothes, great opportunities, marriage, children, and many other blessings all can certainly be exciting and cause happiness. But happiness is based on what is happening in a given moment, while true joy, which God wants us to have, is based on an internal assurance that is completely independent of outward circumstances.

We will never be consistently satisfied unless we put God first in everything, and when we do, then He will add the things we desire (see Matthew 6:33).

We spend time and money, and make careful plans to feed ourselves physically each day. Sometimes we may know one day what we are going to eat the next! Just as we must feed our natural bodies, we must also nourish ourselves spiritually. We often seem to think we can have a great relationship with God without feeding ourselves on His Word and filling ourselves with His presence. Seek Him at least as diligently as you seek physical food.

We were created to enjoy a living, vital relationship with God, and something will always be missing for each of us until we do enjoy that. If we take time to feast on His Word and enjoy His presence every day, we will experience deep and continual satisfaction.

GOD'S WORD FOR YOU TODAY: Feed your soul as well as you feed your body.

From the Inside Out

The King's daughter in the inner part [of the palace] is all glorious; her clothing is inwrought with gold. (PSALM 45:13)

During the Christmas season, department store windows often feature bright, shiny presents with perfectly tied bows. These gifts may look desirable, but if we were to open them, we would find nothing inside. They are empty, just for "show." Our lives can be the same way, like beautifully wrapped packages with nothing of value inside. On the outside, our lives may look attractive or even enviable to others, but on the inside we may be dry and empty. We can look spiritual on the outside, but be powerless within if we do not allow the Holy Spirit to make His home in our hearts.

The verse for today emphasizes the importance of the inner life. God puts the Holy Spirit inside us to work on our inner lives—our attitudes, our responses, our motivations, our priorities, and other important things. As we submit to Christ's Lordship in our inmost beings, we will sense when He is speaking to us, and we will experience His righteousness, peace, and joy rising up from within us to empower us for abundant living (see Romans 14:17).

The Holy Spirit lives inside us to make us more and more like Christ and to fill us with His presence and guidance, so we will have something to share with others, something that comes from deep in the core of our being and is valuable, powerful, and life giving to everyone with whom we interact.

GOD'S WORD FOR YOU TODAY: Focus on your inner life more than your outer life.

Let the Spirit Take the Lead

*I am the Lord your God, Who teaches you to profit, Who leads you in
the way that you should go.* (ISAIAH 48:17)

Most people are afraid not to be like everyone else. Many people are
more comfortable following specified rules than daring to follow the leading of God's Spirit. When we follow man-made rules, we please people,
but when we step out in faith and follow God's Spirit, we please Him. We
do not need to feel pressured to pray a certain way for a certain length
of time or to focus on specific things because other people are doing so.
Instead, we need to be free to express our uniqueness as we pray the way
God is teaching us. God uses each of us to pray about different things
and that way all the things that need to be prayed about get covered.

Somehow we feel safe when we are doing what everyone else is
doing, but the sad thing is that we will feel unfulfilled until we learn to
"untie the boat from the dock," so to speak, and let the ocean of God's
Spirit take us wherever He wills. I spent many years tied to the dock following specified rules and regulations of prayer that others had taught
me and it was a good beginning, but eventually my prayer experience
became very dry and boring. When I learned to untie my boat from the
dock and give myself to the leadership of the Holy Spirit, a freshness
and creativity came and it has been wonderful. I find that the Holy
Spirit leads me differently almost every day as I pray and I no longer do
it according to rules, regulations, and time clocks.

Start right now asking God to show you who you are in the uniqueness He has given you and to help you hear and follow His voice according to the one-of-a-kind, wonderful way He has created you.

GOD'S WORD FOR YOU TODAY: Untie your boat from
the dock, and let God do the steering.

Intimacy Brings Freedom

*I do nothing of Myself (of My own accord or on My own authority),
but I say [exactly] what My Father has taught Me.* (JOHN 8:28)

I have asked God on several occasions what He wanted me to do in specific situations and He has responded, "Do whatever you want to do." The first time I heard Him say that, I was afraid to believe God would give me that kind of liberty, but I now know He gives more and more freedom to us as we grow and mature spiritually.

As I thought about this, I realized all I needed to do was think about my own children. When they were young and inexperienced, I made all their decisions for them. As they got more mature, I let them do more of what they wanted to do. They had been around Dave and me for a long time and were beginning to know our hearts. Now all four of our children are grown, and most of the time they do what they want to do and rarely ever offend us because they know our hearts and act accordingly.

After we walk with God for a number of years, we get to know His heart, His character, and His ways. If we are committed to following them, He can give us greater liberty because we have become "one" with Him. As we grow spiritually, we desire more and more to honor God and reflect His heart in everything we do. Our spirits become filled with His Spirit, and our desires begin to merge with His.

In the verse for today, we read that Jesus does and says only what the Father has taught Him. I encourage you to seek such oneness with God that you, too, will do nothing of your own accord, or out of your own desires and strength, but that you will enjoy such intimacy with God that your desires become one with His.

GOD'S WORD FOR YOU TODAY: Let God's desires be your desires.

Checks and Balances

Great peace have they who love Your law. (PSALM 119:165)

I have written several times in this devotional about the fact that God sometimes leads us through circumstances. This is certainly true, but we must be balanced as we seek to hear and obey His voice through circumstances. I do not recommend using circumstances *alone* to discern God's will. We should also consider peace and wisdom, which I have also addressed in this book. These are major ways in which we hear from God, and we should never ignore them. A circumstance might look like an open door, but we should not go through the door unless we have peace.

Following circumstances alone can get us into real trouble. Satan can arrange circumstances as well as God can, because he has access to the natural realm in which we live. Therefore, if we follow circumstances alone, without considering other ways we hear from God, we can fall into deception.

We know we cannot go against God's Word. We must be led by peace and walk in wisdom. It is easy to do a quick "inner check" to test the level of peace in our hearts before allowing circumstances to lead us. The safest way to hear from God is to combine biblical methods of being led by the Spirit and allow them to serve as checks and balances for one another. It is always best to consider the whole counsel of God's Word and never merely try to find portions of it that agree with what you would like.

———

GOD'S WORD FOR YOU TODAY: Always follow peace when making decisions.

God Knows You Intimately

There is not a word in my tongue [still unuttered], but, behold, O Lord, You know it altogether. (PSALM 139:4)

Because we relate to God as individuals—and that's the way He wants it—we also pray as individuals. Even when we pray corporately with others, we are still individuals; we simply join our hearts with others as one voice. During these corporate prayer times, I believe God wants our hearts to be in unity much more than He wants our methods to be the same.

When we say, "Lord, teach me to pray," we are asking Him to teach us to pray in a distinctly personal way and to enable our prayers to be easy, natural expressions of who we are. We are not supposed to check our individuality at the door of the prayer closet. We need to go to God just the way we are and give Him the pleasure of enjoying the company of the "original" He has made each of us to be. We need to approach God with our strengths, weaknesses, uniqueness, and everything else that so wonderfully distinguishes us from all the other people in the world. God enjoys meeting us where we are, developing a personal relationship with us, and helping us grow to become everything He wants us to be. It is refreshing to realize that we can come to God just as we are and be relaxed in His presence.

GOD'S WORD FOR YOU TODAY: There's no need to "put on your makeup" before you approach God.

Be Strong and Courageous

Only you be strong and very courageous, that you may do according to all the law which Moses My servant commanded you. (JOSHUA 1:7)

God wants us to be totally free from fear. He doesn't want us to live in torment, and He doesn't want fear to stop us from confidently doing what He tells us to do. God moves on our behalf when we focus on Him instead of on our fears, when we listen to His voice instead of the voice of fear. When we have fearful thoughts or feelings, our enemy, Satan, is simply trying to distract us from God and His will for our lives. We may feel fear at various times in our lives, but we can choose to trust God and, if we need to, "do it afraid."

God spoke to my heart about "doing it afraid" many years ago. When He told Joshua to "fear not," He was warning him that fear would try to stop him from doing what God wanted him to do. God told Joshua not to allow fear to control him, but to keep moving forward, strong and full of courage.

When we feel afraid, the first thing we should do is pray. We should determine to seek God until we know we have emotional and mental victory over fear. As we do this, we are focusing on God instead of on our fears. We are worshipping Him for Who He is and expressing our appreciation for the good He has done, is doing, and will continue to do.

Next time you face fear in your life, remember to be strong and full of courage and to keep moving forward in God's will. Even if you have to do something afraid, go ahead and do it while staying focused on God instead of your fear.

GOD'S WORD FOR YOU TODAY: Follow the voice of God, not the voice of fear.

God Speaks a Fresh Word

Seek, inquire of and for the Lord, and crave Him and His strength.
(PSALM 105:4)

When King Jehoshaphat heard that a huge army was amassing to attack Judah, he knew what to do. He needed to set himself to seek not the advice of the people, but to seek God and hear directly from Him.

No doubt, Jehoshaphat had been involved in other battles before this one, so why couldn't he use the same methods he had employed in previous situations? No matter how many times something has worked in the past, it may not work to solve a current crisis unless God anoints it afresh. He may anoint an old method and choose to work through it, but He may also give us brand-new direction, instructions we have never heard before. We must always look to God, not to methods, formulas, or ways that have worked in the past. Our focus, our source of strength and supply, must be God and God alone.

Jehoshaphat knew that unless he heard from God, he was not going to make it. The Amplified Bible calls his need to hear God's voice "his vital need." It was something he could not do without; it was vital. It was essential to his life and the survival of his people.

You may be in a situation similar to Jehoshaphat's. You, too, may need a fresh word from God. You may feel that, like a drowning man or woman, you are going under for the last time. You may be desperate for a personal word from God in order to survive.

God wants to speak to you even more than you want to hear from Him. Seek Him by giving Him your time and attention, and you won't be disappointed.

GOD'S WORD FOR YOU TODAY: Be open to hear a fresh word from God today.

Hear and Obey

*Simon (Peter) answered, Master, we toiled all night [exhaustingly]
and caught nothing [in our nets]. But on the ground of Your word, I
will lower the nets [again].* (LUKE 5:5)

God has blessings and new opportunities in store for us. To receive
them we must hear His voice so we can perceive them and then take
steps of faith toward them. This often means doing things we don't feel
like doing, may not think will work, or may not feel are important. But
our trust and reverence toward God must be greater than what we personally want, think, or feel.

We see a perfect example of this in Luke 5. Peter and some of the
other disciples had been fishing all night; they had caught nothing.
They were tired; in fact, they were exhausted. They needed a good
night's sleep and probably wanted a good meal. They had just finished
washing and storing their nets, which was a big job.

Then Jesus appeared on the shore of the lake and told them that if
they wanted to catch a haul of fish, they should cast their nets again,
this time in deeper water. Peter explained that they had worked hard
all night and had caught nothing, and that now they were tired. But he
also agreed to try again because Jesus had told them to do so.

This is the kind of attitude the Lord wants us to have. We may not
feel like doing something; we may not want to do it; we may not think
it is a good idea; we may be afraid it will not work, but we need to be
willing to hear and obey God when He speaks to us.

GOD'S WORD FOR YOU TODAY: Be willing to obey
God even if you don't feel up to it. He has great things in
store for you!

Are the "-ites" After You?

The Moabites, the Ammonites, and with them the Meunites came against Jehoshaphat to battle. (2 CHRONICLES 20:1)

In today's verse, the Moabites, the Ammonites, and the Meunites were after King Jehoshaphat and the people of Judah. In other places in the Old Testament, the Jebusites, the Hittites, and the Canaanites were troublemakers for God's people.

But with us, it is the "fear-ites," the "disease-ites," the "stress-ites," the "financial problem–ites," the "insecurity-ites," the "grouchy neighbor–ites," and so on.

I wonder, which "-ites" are chasing you right now? Whatever they are, you can learn from King Jehoshaphat's response to the "-ites" who were after him. The first thing he did was fear, but then he quickly did something else: he set himself to seek the Lord. Determined to hear from Him, Jehoshaphat even proclaimed a fast throughout his kingdom for that very purpose. He knew he needed to hear from God. He needed a battle plan, and only God could give him one that would succeed.

Like Jehoshaphat, we should develop the habit of running to God instead of to people when we have trouble. We should seek Him rather than consulting our own wisdom or asking for other people's opinions. We need to ask ourselves whether we "run to the phone or run to the throne" when faced with trouble. God may use a person to speak a word of advice to us, but we always need to seek Him first.

Hearing God's voice is a great way to fight fear. When we hear from Him, faith fills our hearts and drives fear away. Jehoshaphat knew he needed to hear from God centuries ago and we have the same need now. Be sure to seek God and listen to His voice today.

GOD'S WORD FOR YOU TODAY: Ask God to protect you from the "-ites" in your life.

Your All-the-Time, Everyday Friend

Evening and morning and at noon I will pray, and cry aloud, and He shall hear my voice. (PSALM 55:17 NKJV)

Developing your friendship with God is similar to developing a friendship with someone on Earth. It takes time. The truth is that you can be as close to God as you want to be; it all depends on the time you are willing to invest in your relationship with Him. I encourage you to get to know Him by spending time in prayer and in His Word. Your friendship with God will also deepen and grow as you walk with Him over time on a regular basis and as you experience His faithfulness. The difference between developing a relationship with God as a friend and building relationships with people is that with God, you end up with a friend Who is perfect! One Who will never leave you nor forsake you. One Who is faithful, dependable, loving, and forgiving.

Make a priority of developing a great friendship with God and inviting Him to be a vital part of everything you do, every day. Include Him in your thoughts, in your conversation, and in all your everyday activities. Don't just run to Him when you are desperate; talk to Him in the grocery store, while you are driving your car, combing your hair, walking the dog, or cooking dinner. Approach Him as your partner and friend, and simply refuse to do anything without Him. He really wants to be involved in your life! Let God out of the Sunday-morning box so many people keep Him in and let Him invade your Monday, Tuesday, Wednesday, Thursday, Friday, Saturday, and all day Sunday as well. Don't try to keep Him in a religious compartment, because He wants to have free access to every area of your life. He wants to be your friend.

GOD'S WORD FOR YOU TODAY: God is your Lord, but He also wants to be your friend.

The Key to God's Anointing

This shall be a holy anointing oil…It shall not be poured on man's flesh. (EXODUS 30:31–32 NKJV)

I do not have anything to offer people except the anointing (presence and power) of God that is on my life. I am not fancy; I do not sing or do other things that might thrill people. I simply speak the truth of God's Word. I offer biblical insight on living in victory and obeying God in practical ways. I tell people how to change so they can enjoy their lives more and I tell them how to grow spiritually. I teach God's Word in ways that help them in their everyday lives. By God's grace, this ministry reaches millions of people around the world, but I *must* have God's anointing in order to do what He has called me to do—or I am of no value to anyone. I have learned that I will not carry God's anointing if I do not walk in love, because God does not anoint the flesh (our own desires and selfish attitudes or behaviors).

We read in today's verse that when the anointing oil was poured on the priests in the Old Testament, none of it could be put on their flesh. God does not anoint carnal behavior. We really must walk in love because that aids and increases the anointing on our lives, and the anointing is what empowers us to do what God has called us to do. God's anointing is His presence and power and it enables us to do with ease what we could never accomplish with any amount of struggle on our own. We all need God's anointing. A person does not have to work at a so-called "spiritual" job to need God's anointing. We need it to be good parents, to have successful marriages, to be good friends, and literally in everything we do.

GOD'S WORD FOR YOU TODAY: God's presence and power (anointing) is what you need to be successful at anything.

God Will Restore Your Soul

He restores my soul. (PSALM 23:3 NKJV)

For a period of time in my life, I rebuked whatever I didn't want because I thought it must be from the devil. I say that I rebuked until my "rebuker" was just totally worn out. But then I discovered that a lot of what I was trying to rebuke was from God. Many of the things I did not like or want were things God had allowed for my growth and development.

The writer of Hebrews said that we must submit to the discipline of God. He chastises us only because He loves us. Don't try to resist what God intends to use for your good. Ask the Lord to do a deep and thorough work in you so you can be all He wants you to be, do all He wants you to do, and have all He wants you to have. During my years of resisting anything that was painful or difficult, the simple truth is that I did not grow spiritually. I kept going around and around the same old mountains (problems). Finally, I realized that I was trying to avoid pain, but I had pain anyway. The pain of staying the way we are is much worse than the pain of changing.

Our personality is our soul (mind, will, and emotions), but often it has been wounded by our experiences in the world. God promises to restore our souls if we will cooperate with the work of the Holy Spirit in us. I had a broken soul, one that had no peace or joy, but God has made me whole and He wants to do the same for you.

GOD'S WORD FOR YOU TODAY: Open your soul to God and ask Him to heal every wound and bruise.

Don't Resist; Receive What God Says

Search me [thoroughly], O God, and know my heart! Try me and
know my thoughts! And see if there is any wicked or hurtful way in
me, and lead me in the way everlasting. (PSALM 139:23–24)

Often, when we are convicted of sin, we become grouchy because God
is dealing with us. Until we admit our sin, become ready to turn from
it, and ask for forgiveness, we feel a pressure that makes us uncomfortable. As soon as we come into agreement with God, our peace returns
and our behavior improves.

The devil attacks with condemnation and shame to keep us from
approaching God confidently in prayer so our needs can be met and we
can once again enjoy fellowship with God. Feeling bad about ourselves
or thinking God is angry with us separates us from His presence. He
never leaves us, but our fears can make us doubt His presence.

That's why discerning the truth and knowing the difference between
conviction and condemnation is so important. If you heed conviction,
it lifts you up and out of sin; condemnation only makes you feel bad
about yourself and often causes the problem to get worse.

When you pray, ask God regularly to speak to you and convict you
of your sin, realizing that conviction is a blessing, not a problem. When
I begin my prayer times, I almost always ask my heavenly Father to
reveal anything I am doing wrong and cleanse me of all sin and unrighteousness. Conviction is vitally necessary in order to walk with God
properly. The gift of conviction is one way of hearing God. Don't make
the mistake of letting it condemn you, but let it lift you to a new place of
freedom and intimacy with God. Don't resist it; receive it.

GOD'S WORD FOR YOU TODAY: Let God lift you up
and out.

God Has an Answer Before We Ask

I call on the Lord, Who is worthy to be praised, and I am saved from my enemies. (2 SAMUEL 22:4)

In the face of a daunting battle, Jehoshaphat approached God by first praising Him and telling Him how great, awesome, powerful, and wonderful He is. He then began to recount specific mighty acts the Lord had performed in the past to protect His people and uphold His promises. After all that, he presented his request to God. He began by expressing his total confidence that the Lord would handle the problem. Then he simply said, "Oh, by the way, God, our enemies are coming against us to try to take away the possession You gave us for our inheritance. I just thought I would mention this little problem. But You are so great: I know You already have this situation under control."

When we ask God for help, we should realize He hears us the first time we ask. We don't need to spend our prayer time asking for the same thing over and over again. I think it is best to ask God for what we want or need and then, when it comes to our mind again, thank Him that He is working. We need to tell Him we trust Him and know His timing will be perfect.

God has a plan for your deliverance before your problems ever appear. God is never surprised! Continue focusing on Him; worship, praise, and thank Him that help is on the way; and continue listening for His voice as He leads you through your battles all the way to victory.

GOD'S WORD FOR YOU TODAY: God doesn't need our reminders, but He does need our praise.

God Wants to Bless Us

The Lord God is a Sun and Shield; the Lord bestows [present] grace
and favor and [future] glory (honor, splendor, and heavenly bliss)!
No good thing will He withhold from those who walk uprightly.

(PSALM 84:11)

Through our conscience, the Holy Spirit lets us know if we're doing something wrong, something that grieves Him, interferes with our fellowship with Him, or would cause us not to sense His presence in our lives. He also helps us get back to the place we need to be. He convicts us and convinces us, but He never, never condemns us.

God loves us even more than we love our own children, and in His love He disciplines us. I remember how I hated to take privileges away from my children when they were small. But I knew they were bound for trouble if they didn't learn to listen to me. God has the same kind of concern for us, but He is patient. He tells us and tells us, again and again, what we ought to do. He may tell us fifteen different ways, trying to get our attention, wanting us to obey Him for our own good.

God's message of convicting love is everywhere. He wants us to listen to Him because He loves us. If we persist in our own ways, He withholds privileges and blessings from us. But He does so only because He wants us to mature to a place where He can pour out His full blessings upon us. If God freely gave us His Son, Jesus, surely He won't hold back anything else we need. We can count on Him to meet our needs and to bless us abundantly.

GOD'S WORD FOR YOU TODAY: Remember that God
wants to bless you, even when He disciplines you.

Alive to God

Consider yourselves also dead to sin and your relation to it broken,
but alive to God [living in unbroken fellowship with Him] in Christ
Jesus. (ROMANS 6:11)

People who are not saved are spiritually dead. This means they are not able to enjoy communion with God or perceive and follow the intuitive promptings of the Holy Spirit. These people are limited to their natural or intellectual knowledge and to their common sense; they cannot enjoy the privilege and power of living by revelation. But, when we have been born again and are alive spiritually, God can speak to us and show us things we could not know without divine revelation.

In the past, I have held jobs and positions of responsibility in which I did not have all the natural knowledge to carry out the assignments given to me. But, I had an intimate, personal relationship with the Lord, so He led me and enabled me to do things I was not fully trained to do.

I never studied how to lead a ministry or how to use mass communications effectively. But God has equipped me and the team at Joyce Meyer Ministries with everything we need to minister in various ways, including mass media, all around the world. God leads us, step-by-step, by His Spirit. With each step of faith we take, He continues to teach us and show us what to do next.

God will also equip you to do what He has called you to do if you are in fellowship with Him. If you will be diligent to seek Him and listen to His voice, He will lead you supernaturally. He will teach you how to fulfill His purposes for your life—and they may be far greater than anything you are currently trained to do or could ever imagine.

———————

GOD'S WORD FOR YOU TODAY: God will equip you with everything you need.

Sometimes God Whispers

A great and strong wind rent the mountains and broke in pieces the rocks before the Lord, but the Lord was not in the wind; and after the wind an earthquake, but the Lord was not in the earthquake; and after the earthquake a fire, but the Lord was not in the fire; and after the fire [a sound of gentle stillness and] a still, small voice.

(1 KINGS 19:11–12)

I was fascinated when I learned several years ago that some horses have what their trainers call a "reining ear." While most horses need to be led by a strap fastened to the bit in their mouth, some horses keep one ear tuned to their master's voice. One ear is open for natural warnings; the other is sensitive to the trusted trainer.

The prophet Elijah had a reining ear. When natural circumstances gave him every reason to be frightened and he desperately needed to hear from God, he was able to do so, even with the noise and confusion around him. You see, he had just defeated 450 false prophets in a duel of power between their silent Baal and the one true God. Now the wicked Queen Jezebel threatened to kill him within a day. He needed to know what to do!

He stood on a mountain before God. A strong wind tore through the mountains; a terrible earthquake took place; and fire broke out all around him. After the fire came "a still, small voice." God's voice to Elijah wasn't in the power of the wind, the earthquake, or the fire, but in the whisper. Elijah had a reining ear, one that was trained and sensitive toward his Master, so he did what God said to do, which saved his life.

God still speaks softly and in whispers deep in our hearts today. Ask Him to give you a hearing ear so you can hear His still, small voice.

GOD'S WORD FOR YOU TODAY: Listen for God with a "reining" ear.

The Spirit vs. the Flesh

Walk and live [habitually] in the [Holy] Spirit [responsive to and controlled and guided by the Spirit]; then you will certainly not gratify the cravings and desires of the flesh [of human nature without God].

(GALATIANS 5:16)

Like a horse that has been trained to keep his ear always tuned to the voice of its master, we must be willing to follow the Lord in *all* His leadings, not just those we feel good about or happen to agree with. We won't always like what we hear Him tell us to do.

We must realize that in order to follow God, the flesh must be told no at times, and when that happens, the flesh suffers. There are times when we are galloping full speed ahead in one direction when suddenly the Master tells us to stop and instructs us to go in another direction. It is painful to us when we don't get our way, but ultimately we understand that God's ways are always best.

In the verse for today, the apostle Paul writes about the conflict between the Spirit and the flesh. If we follow the leading of the Spirit, we won't satisfy or fulfill the desires of the flesh that lead us away from God's best. This verse doesn't say that the desires of the flesh will disappear; we will always have to wrestle with them. But if we choose to be led by the Spirit, we won't fulfill fleshly desires—and the devil won't get his way.

We will sense a war going on in us as we choose to follow God's leading. Our flesh and God's Spirit usually disagree and we are tempted to keep the flesh comfortable. But, we all must learn to submit to God's Spirit and overcome fleshly desires and temptations. Determine today that you will not let your flesh lead you, but that you will be led by the Spirit of God.

GOD'S WORD FOR YOU TODAY: God wants to give you His best.

Listen with Your Spirit

The wind blows (breathes) where it wills; and though you hear its sound, yet you neither know where it comes from nor where it is going. So it is with everyone who is born of the Spirit. (JOHN 3:8)

When we are born again, we are made alive in our spirits and we become sensitive to the voice of God. We hear His whisper even though we cannot tell where it comes from. He speaks softly to convict, correct, and direct us with a still, small voice in our hearts.

We can communicate with human beings using our mouths, facial expressions, gestures, and all kinds of body language, but when we want to communicate with God, we have to do so with our spirits.

God speaks to our inner beings through direct communion, through intuition (a sense of unexplainable discernment), and through our conscience (our base convictions of right and wrong), and through peace. Our spirits can know things our natural minds do not understand and cannot grasp.

For example, when we are sensitive to God's voice, we can look at a situation that appears to be right, but we know intuitively that something is wrong about it. That "check" in our spirits is intended to keep us from getting involved with someone we should not align with or becoming involved in something we should not participate in.

Pay attention to the things you feel in your heart and sense in your spirit because that is where God will speak words of direction, encouragement, warning, and comfort to you.

GOD'S WORD FOR YOU TODAY: Pay attention to the "checks" in your spirit.

Talk to God About Himself

O Lord, God of our fathers, are You not God in heaven? And do You not rule over all the kingdoms of the nations? In Your hand are power and might, so that none is able to withstand You.

(2 CHRONICLES 20:6)

When King Jehoshaphat had a problem, he went to the Lord. But he didn't go to the Lord and just talk about his problem; he went to the Lord and talked about Who He is. Instead of simply talking to God about our problems, we also need to talk to Him about Himself. We need to talk to Him about how wonderful He is, how good He has been to us, what He has done in the past, and what we know He is able to do because of His greatness. After we have praised and worshipped Him in this way, then we can talk about the problem.

I can think of a few people who call me only when they have problems, and that hurts me because I feel they are not interested in me, but only in what I can do for them. I am sure you have experienced this and felt the same way. These people may call themselves my friends, but in reality they are not. Certainly, friends are for times of trouble, but those are not the only times they are for. Friends are for good times, too. We need to spend time not only talking to our friends about our problems, but also encouraging them, showing appreciation to them, and supporting them with words and actions.

When you spend time with God today, be sure to talk to Him about Himself and all the good He does for you before you mention your problems.

Abraham was a friend of God. I want to be God's friend also, and I believe you do, too. God is not simply our problem-solver; He's our everything.

GOD'S WORD FOR YOU TODAY: Talk to God about Himself before you talk to Him about yourself.

In Comparison, It's Nothing

*I consider that the sufferings of this present time (this present life)
are not worth being compared with the glory that is about to
be revealed to us and in us and for us and conferred on us!*

(ROMANS 8:18)

What does it mean to share Christ's suffering? The bottom line is that anytime our flesh wants to do one thing and the Spirit of God wants us to do something else, our flesh will suffer if we choose to follow the Spirit. We don't like that, but the verse for today says that if we want to share Christ's glory, we must also be willing to share His suffering.

I can still remember suffering through my early years of walking in obedience to God's Spirit. I thought, *Dear God, am I ever going to get over this? Am I ever going to get to the point where I can obey You and not hurt while I'm doing it?*

Once the fleshly appetite is no longer in control, we reach the point where obeying God is easy, where we actually *enjoy* obeying Him. There are things that are easy for me now that were once very difficult and painful, and the same thing happens to everyone who is willing to go through the difficulties to get to the glory.

In Romans 8:18, Paul basically said, "We suffer a little now, but so what? The glory that will come from our obedience far outshines the suffering we endure now." That is good news! Whatever we may suffer, whatever we may go through, is absolutely nothing compared to the good things God is going to do in our lives as we continue to press on with Him.

———————

GOD'S WORD FOR YOU TODAY: God will do great things in your life as you continue to move forward with Him.

Pray and Give Thanks

When Daniel knew that the writing was signed, he went into his house, … he got down upon his knees three times a day and prayed and gave thanks before his God, as he had done previously. (DANIEL 6:10)

Giving thanks is so important to being able to hear God's voice because, like praise and worship, it is something God *responds* to. It's something God loves, something that warms His heart. Anytime we give God pleasure like that, our intimacy with Him increases—and that makes for a better relationship with Him.

If we are not thankful for what we have, why should He give us something else to murmur about? On the other hand, when God sees that we genuinely appreciate and are thankful for the big and little things, He is inclined to bless us even more. According to Philippians 4:6, everything we ask God for should be preceded and accompanied by thanksgiving. No matter what we pray for, thanksgiving should always go with it. A good habit to develop is starting all of our prayers with thanksgiving. An example of this would be: "Thank You for all You have done in my life. You are awesome and I really love and appreciate You."

I encourage you to examine your life, to pay attention to your thoughts and your words, and see how much thanksgiving you express. If you want a challenge, just try to get through an entire day without uttering one word of complaint. Develop an attitude of thanksgiving in every situation. In fact, just become outrageously thankful—and watch as your intimacy with God increases and as He pours out greater blessings than ever before.

GOD'S WORD FOR YOU TODAY: Speak words of thanksgiving, not words of complaint.

Love Your Neighbor as Yourself

The whole Law [concerning human relationships] is complied with in the one precept, You shall love your neighbor as [you do] yourself. (GALATIANS 5:14)

God wants to speak to us about many things, but one of the important things He wants to speak to us about is our relationships with other people. God loves us; and He wants us to love ourselves in a healthy, balanced manner and let His love flow through us to other people.

In your quest to hear from God, I urge you to pray that He will speak to you regularly concerning any wisdom He has for you in your relationships. Relationships are a large part of life and if they are not good, the quality of our lives deteriorates.

Just this morning I was praying for my husband and asked God what I might do for him. I had a thought to leave him a note that he would find on the kitchen counter when he came to eat breakfast. The note simply said, "Good morning, Dave . . . I LOVE YOU!!!" I put a smiley face at the bottom and signed the note. I believe the idea to leave the note was God speaking to me and my obedience to do that *little* thing enhanced our relationship.

Start praying about all of your relationships. Take them one by one and ask God what you can do to make them better. We usually think about what others need to do for us, but if we follow the law of love, we will be more concerned for them than we are for ourselves.

GOD'S WORD FOR YOU TODAY: Ask God to show you how you can make your relationships better.

God Speaks to Us Individually

Your ears will hear a word behind you, saying, This is the way; walk in it, when you turn to the right hand and when you turn to the left.
(ISAIAH 30:21)

One reason God speaks to us is to help us know the difference between right and wrong so we can make good choices. Some things may be wrong for one person and right for another, or vice versa, so we all need individual direction from God. Of course, certain general guidelines of right and wrong apply to everyone; for example, we all know that lying, cheating, and stealing are wrong, just as many other things are. But, there are also things specific to us as individuals. My son was on a trip and had planned to extend it one day, but he woke up in the morning and had no peace about staying, so he returned home. God has different and unique plans for everyone, and He knows certain things about us that we don't even know about ourselves.

We may not understand why God tells us not to do something when everyone around us is doing it, but if our hearts are tender, we trust and obey Him even when we don't understand why. The bottom line is, we don't have to know the why behind everything He asks or requires of us—we simply need to learn to hear His voice and obey.

Soldiers in training for battle are sometimes required to do ridiculous exercises, things that don't seem to make sense. They learn to do those things promptly and obey orders quickly and without question, even when they don't understand. If they are on the front lines of battle and their leaders issue a command, they could be killed if they stop and ask, "Why?" In the same way, God wants us to trust His loving guidance in our lives and obey Him without delay and without question.

GOD'S WORD FOR YOU TODAY: Obey God's voice even when you don't understand.

God Leads Us Gently

He will feed His flock like a shepherd: He will gather the lambs in His arm, He will carry them in His bosom and will gently lead those that have their young. (ISAIAH 40:11)

When God speaks to us and guides us, He doesn't scream at us or push us in the direction in which He wants us to go. No, He leads us, like a gentle shepherd, inviting us to follow Him to greener pastures. He wants us to get to the point where we are so sensitive to His voice that even a little whisper of caution is enough to cause us to ask, "What are You saying here, Lord?" The minute we sense Him directing us to change what we are doing, we should promptly obey Him. If we sense a lack of peace concerning something we are doing, we should stop and seek God for His direction.

Proverbs 3:6 says that if we will acknowledge God in all our ways, He will direct our paths. Acknowledging God simply means having enough respect for Him, enough reverential fear and awe of Him, to care what He thinks of our every move.

A good way to start each day would be to pray:

"Lord, I care about what You think, and I don't want to be doing things You don't want me to do. If I start to do anything today that You don't want me to do, please show me what it is so I can stop it, turn away from it, and do Your will instead. Amen."

GOD'S WORD FOR YOU TODAY: Care more about what God thinks than anything else.

Seek God All the Time

It was told Jehoshaphat, A great multitude has come against you …
Then Jehoshaphat feared, and set himself [determinedly, as his vital
need] to seek the Lord; he proclaimed a fast in all Judah.

(2 CHRONICLES 20:2–3)

When King Jehoshaphat needed to hear from God, he proclaimed a fast throughout his entire kingdom of Judah. All the people gathered to seek the Lord for help, longing for Him with all their hearts.

Jehoshaphat proclaimed a fast to demonstrate his sincerity to God and his need for God. If you need to hear from God, consider missing a few meals and taking that time to seek God. Turning the television off and spending time with God instead of watching it is not a bad idea either, nor is spending a few evenings at home seeking God instead of going out with friends asking for their advice and opinions. These disciplines and others prove that you understand the importance of hearing from God.

Some people seek God earnestly only when they are in trouble, but we need to seek Him intensely all the time. God once impressed upon me that the reason so many people have so many problems is that the only time they seek Him is when they are in trouble. He showed me that if He removed some people's problems, they would not seek Him at all. He said, "Seek Me as if you were desperate all the time and then you won't find yourself desperate so often in reality." I think this is good advice and I encourage you to follow it every day.

GOD'S WORD FOR YOU TODAY: Don't wait until you are in trouble to seek God; seek Him all the time.

Want to Hear More?

You shall walk after the Lord your God and [reverently] fear Him, and keep His commandments and obey His voice, and you shall serve Him and cling to Him. (DEUTERONOMY 13:4)

If we expect to hear from God, we must listen for His voice. We must also be quick to obey if we want to hear from Him often. Our sensitivity to His voice in our hearts can be increased by obedience and reduced by disobedience. Disobedience breeds more disobedience, and obedience leads to more obedience.

There are some days when we know as soon as we awake that we're going to have a "flesh day." We start the day feeling stubborn and lazy, frustrated and touchy. Our first thoughts are: *I want everyone to leave me alone today. I'm not cleaning this house, I'm going shopping. I'm not staying on my diet either; I will eat what I want to eat all day long—and I don't want anyone to say anything about it.*

On days like these, we have a decision to make. We can follow those feelings or we can pray, "God, please help me—and do it quickly!" Our feelings can come under the Lordship of Jesus Christ if we simply ask Him to help us straighten out our attitudes.

I know all about flesh days; I know we can start out acting bad and then get worse. It seems that once we give in to a selfish attitude and follow our flesh, it's downhill the rest of the day. But every time we obey our conscience, we open the window that God can use to lead us by His Spirit. Every time we obey God's voice, it lets in more light for the next time. Once we know the joy of following God, we will be unwilling to live without it.

GOD'S WORD FOR YOU TODAY: Don't let yourself have a "flesh day" today.

The Narrow Path Is a Good Place

The gate is narrow (contracted by pressure) and the way is strait-ened and compressed that leads away to life, and few are those who find it. (MATTHEW 7:14)

Perhaps you can think of something you did a few years ago that would bother your conscience if you tried to do it now. It may not have bothered you five years ago, but because God has now revealed to you that it is wrong, you would not think of doing it anymore.

God speaks to us about issues, works with us to bring correction, and then lets us rest for a while. But eventually, as long as we're still listening, He will always talk to us about something new.

If you are anything like I was, you once walked through life on a wide and reckless path, but you are now on a narrow path. I remember saying to God once, "It seems like my path gets narrower and narrower all the time." I remember feeling that the path God was leading me on was getting so narrow that there was no room on it for me! No wonder Paul said, "It's no longer I who live, but Christ who lives in me" (see Galatians 2:20). When Jesus comes to live in us, He takes up permanent residence and slowly expands His presence in our lives until there is more of Himself and less of our old selfish nature.

If you feel you are on a narrow path—as though you cannot do what you used to do or as though the restrictions on you are very tight—then be encouraged; your old selfish nature is getting squeezed out so more of God's presence can dwell in you.

GOD'S WORD FOR YOU TODAY: Embrace your restrictions, knowing that they will make more room for God.

Stay Balanced

Be well balanced (temperate, sober of mind), be vigilant and cautious at all times; for that enemy of yours, the devil, roams around like a lion roaring [in fierce hunger], seeking someone to seize upon and devour. (1 PETER 5:8)

Listening to the Holy Spirit will keep us balanced in every area of our lives. The Spirit will tell us when we're spending too much money or not spending enough, when we're talking too much or not talking enough, or even when we're resting too much or not resting enough. Anytime we are doing too much or too little of something, we are out of balance.

The verse for today states that we are to be well-balanced so Satan cannot take advantage of us. For years, he took advantage of me because I was not balanced in my approach to work. I felt that my whole life should be arranged around work. As long as I was working and accomplishing something, I didn't feel the guilt that the devil used against me. But that urge to work all the time was not from God; it did not push me toward godly balance in my life. Work is a good thing, but I also needed to rest and have enjoyment.

Each day as you seek to hear from God, ask Him to show you any area in your life that is out of balance and work with Him to make adjustments. We have many things in life to juggle and therefore it is easy to get out of balance, but God is always available to help us in this area. Simply ask Him if you are doing too much or too little of anything and make the changes He recommends.

GOD'S WORD FOR YOU TODAY: Stay in balance with God's help.

The Best Friend You'll Ever Have

There is a friend who sticks closer than a brother. (PROVERBS 18:24)

If I had to identify the most important key to effective prayer and an intimate relationship with God, I would say that it is approaching God as His friend. When we go to God believing He sees us as His friends, new wonders are opened to us. We experience freedom and boldness, which are both necessary to effective prayer.

If we do not know God as a friend and if we are not confident that He thinks of us as His friends, we will be reluctant to tell Him what we need or to ask Him for anything. If we have a stiff, distant relationship with God, our prayers can be legalistic. But if we go to Him as our friend, yet without losing our reverence and awe of Him, our communication with Him will stay fresh, exciting, and intimate.

A natural friendship involves loving and being loved. It means knowing that someone is on your side, wanting to help you, cheering you on, and always keeping your best interest in mind. A friend is someone you value, a comrade, a partner, someone who is dear to you, someone you want to spend time with, and someone you enjoy. You become someone's friend by investing time in them and with them, and by sharing your life with that person. I encourage you to see God as your friend. Treat Him with respect and honor, but treat Him as your friend and learn to communicate with Him as openly and easily as you would with an earthly companion. He's the best friend you'll ever have.

GOD'S WORD FOR YOU TODAY: You are a friend of God.

One Step at a Time

The Lord said to Abram, Go for yourself [for your own advantage] away from your country, from your relatives and your father's house, to the land that I will show you. (GENESIS 12:1)

Abram learned to trust God to lead him one step at a time. His story begins in Genesis 12:1, the verse for today. Notice in this verse that God gave Abram step one, not step two. He basically told him that he would not get step two until he had accomplished step one. This is so simple, but so profound and insightful about how God speaks: He gives us direction one step at a time.

Many people refuse to take step one until they think they understand steps two, three, four, and five. If you are like this, I hope you will be inspired today to go forward in God's plan for your life by trusting Him with the first step. After the first few steps, your faith will grow because you will realize there is always a sure foundation beneath each step God instructs you to take.

God asked Abram to take a difficult step by leaving everything and everyone familiar to him. But, God promised him that taking such a step would be to his advantage.

When we obey God we are blessed. God has a good plan for our lives, a plan that is to our advantage. All we have to do is walk in it—one step at a time.

GOD'S WORD FOR YOU TODAY: Obey God's voice one step at a time.

Don't Be a Know-It-All

As for God, His way is perfect! The word of the Lord is tested and tried; He is a shield to all those who take refuge and put their trust in Him. (PSALM 18:30)

Truth from God's written Word keeps us stable in the storms of life. We can expect to hear from God through His written Word. It never changes or wavers in its intent for us. Even if His Word does not speak specifically to the details of our situation, it does speak of God's heart and character and it assures us He will always take care of us and make a way for us.

The Word teaches that our knowledge is fragmented, incomplete, and imperfect. According to 1 Corinthians 13:9, we know only "in part"(NKJV). This tells me there will never be a time in our lives when we can say, "I know everything I need to know." Go to God in humility and be hungry to learn from His Word. Ask Him daily to teach you what you should do in every situation.

Receive the Holy Spirit as your Teacher so He can daily lead you into all truth (see John 16:13). He will reveal things to you that you could never figure out on your own. I have decided to be a *lifetime learner* and I highly recommend the same for you.

———————————

GOD'S WORD FOR YOU TODAY: Don't be a know-it-all; ask God to teach you what you need to learn today.

Don't "Just" Pray

Bring all the tithes (the whole tenth of your income) into the store-house … and prove Me now by it, says the Lord of hosts, if I will not open the windows of heaven for you and pour you out a blessing, that there shall not be room enough to receive it. (MALACHI 3:10)

One of the prayers I hear people pray often, and have prayed many times myself, is what I call a "just" prayer, which sounds something like this: "Now Lord, we *just* thank You for this food," "God, we *just* ask You to protect us," "Father, we *just* come to You tonight …" "Oh, God, if You would *just* help us in this situation we would be so thankful …" Do you see what I mean? We sound as if we are afraid to ask God for very much.

The word *just* can mean "righteous" or "fair," but it can also mean "barely enough to get by" or "by a narrow margin." God wants to give us exceedingly, abundantly, above and beyond all that we can dare to hope, ask, or think (see Ephesians 3:20). He wants to open the windows of heaven and pour out blessings, so why should we approach Him asking for barely enough to get by on? Why should we approach God as if we are afraid to ask for too much? When we approach Him that way, it seems as if we do not believe He is generous and good. We must realize that He is not a God who gives "just" enough to barely get by, but He desires to bless us abundantly, as the verse for today promises.

God does not want to hear fearful, insecure "just" prayers. He wants to hear bold, confident, faith-filled prayers prayed by people who are secure in their friendship with Him.

GOD'S WORD FOR YOU TODAY: When it comes to prayer, "just" just isn't enough.

There's a Treasure Within You

*We possess this precious treasure [the divine Light of the Gospel]
in [frail, human] vessels of earth, that the grandeur and exceeding
greatness of the power may be shown to be from God and not from
ourselves.* (2 CORINTHIANS 4:7)

More than anything else, I want to clearly hear God's voice and be
aware of His abiding presence all the time and I believe you are reading this book because that is also your desire. I have written previously
about many years when I believed in Jesus Christ as my Savior, but did
not enjoy close fellowship with God. I felt I was always reaching for Him
and falling short of that goal. One day, as I stood before a mirror combing my hair, I asked Him a simple question: "God, why do I consistently
feel as though I am reaching out for You and coming up short of finding
You?" Immediately, I heard these words in my heart: "Joyce, you are
reaching *out* and you need to be reaching *in*." Let me explain: God's
Word says that He lives in us, but some people find this truth difficult
to understand. The verse for today explains that we have the treasure of
God's presence within us; but many who believe in Jesus never experience the joy of His presence or of continual fellowship with Him.

I was working trying to get to God, but the truth was that in His grace
and mercy He had come to me and made His home in me. The same is
true for you as a child of God. He is with you all the time, and He is your
strength, peace, joy, and help. He wants to talk to you, so start listening
in your heart and you will find that He is closer than you think.

GOD'S WORD FOR YOU TODAY: Don't reach out for God;
reach in.

Say "Thank You"

O give thanks to the Lord, for He is good; for His mercy and loving-kindness endure forever! (1 CHRONICLES 16:34)

Thanksgiving should be a regular part of our lives. It is something that creates an atmosphere where God can speak; it is a type of prayer, and it should flow out of us in a natural way that is pure and easy. We can take time each evening and thank God for the things He helped us with that day, but we should also continually breathe out simple prayers of thanksgiving every time we see Him working in our lives or blessing us. For example, "Lord, thank You for a good night's sleep," or "God, I thank You that my visit to the dentist didn't hurt as much as I thought it might," or "Father, thank You for helping me make good decisions today," or "Lord, thank You for keeping me encouraged."

God is always good to us, always faithful, and always working diligently in our lives to help us in every possible way. We need to respond by letting Him know we appreciate Him and everything He is doing for us. We should thank God silently in our hearts and we should also voice our thankfulness aloud because that helps us stay conscious and aware of God's love, which He demonstrates through His goodness to us.

GOD'S WORD FOR YOU TODAY: Thank God for twenty things today before you ask Him for anything.

Attitude Determines Destiny

Keep and guard your heart with all vigilance and above all that you guard, for out of it flow the springs of life. (PROVERBS 4:23)

Attitude is very important; our attitudes become the behavior that we display. Attitude, good or bad, begins with thoughts.

A well-known quotation says, "Sow a thought, reap an action; sow an action, reap a habit; sow a habit, reap a character; sow a character, reap a destiny."

Destiny is the outcome of life; character is who we are; habits are subconscious patterns of behavior. Our destiny, or the outcome of our lives, actually comes from our thoughts. That is where the entire process begins. No wonder the Bible teaches us to entirely renew our minds, developing new attitudes and ideals (see Romans 12:2; Ephesians 4:23). We are to be good students of God's Word and by it develop new thinking patterns, which will ultimately change our entire destiny, the outcome of our lives.

We can hinder the Holy Spirit with bad attitudes such as bitterness, anger, unforgiveness, mean-spiritedness, disrespect, seeking revenge, or being ungrateful—and the list could go on. The Holy Spirit flows through a godly attitude, not an ungodly one.

Examine your attitude regularly and guard it with all diligence, as today's verse instructs. If you need to change your attitude; all you have to do is change your thoughts.

Satan will always try to fill our minds with wrong thoughts, be we do not have to receive what he tries to give us. I would not take a spoonful of poison simply because someone offered it to me, and neither would you. If we are smart enough to refuse poison, we should be intelligent enough not to allow Satan to poison our thoughts, our attitudes, and ultimately our destiny.

GOD'S WORD FOR YOU TODAY: Do a daily attitude inventory to make sure yours is in good condition.

A Consecrated Life

Unto You, O Lord, do I bring my life. (PSALM 25:1)

I love to lift up my hands in the morning and pray the prayer of consecration found in the verse for today. I actually say the words, "Unto You, O Lord, do I bring my life." This really defines consecration— complete, voluntary surrender to the Lord. In a prayer of consecration, you are saying to Him: "Here I am, God. I give myself to You. Not just my money, but myself. Not just one hour on Sunday morning, but myself. Not just a portion of my day, but myself. Unto You, O Lord, do I bring my *entire* life. I lay it before You. Do what You want to do with me. Speak to me and through me today. Touch people through me today. Make a difference in my world through me today. I am not an owner of anything; I'm a steward. Everything I am and everything I have has come from You and is available to You today."

When we consecrate something, we set it apart for God's use. Therefore, when we consecrate our lives, we turn our backs on our fleshly desires, worldly values, carnal thinking, undisciplined living, bad habits, and everything else that does not agree with God's Word. We close our ears to the noise of the world and open them to the voice of God. We intentionally put distance between ourselves and ungodly things, so we are prepared and available for God to use us. Consecration is not easy, but it is worth the discipline and the sacrifice it requires.

GOD'S WORD FOR YOU TODAY: Say to God, "Here I am," today.

Selective Hearing Not Allowed

Today, if you would hear His voice and when you hear it, do not harden your hearts. (HEBREWS 4:7)

When we are unwilling to hear God's voice in one area of our lives, we are often unable to hear His voice in other areas. Sometimes we hear only what we want to hear, and this is called "selective hearing." When this happens, people eventually believe they can't hear from God anymore, but this is not true. The fact is that He has already spoken to them and they have failed to respond. Let me share a story to illustrate.

A woman once told me that she asked God to give her direction concerning what He wanted her to do: He wanted her to forgive her sister for an offense that had taken place months earlier. The woman was not willing to forgive, so she soon stopped praying. When she did seek the Lord again for something, all she heard in her heart was, "Forgive your sister first."

Over a two-year period, every time she asked for God's guidance in a new situation, He gently reminded her to forgive her sister. Finally, she realized she would never get out of her rut or grow spiritually if she did not obey, so she prayed, "Lord, give me the power to forgive my sister." Instantly she understood many things from her sister's perspective—things she hadn't considered before. Within a short time her relationship with her sister was completely restored and quickly became stronger than ever.

If we really want to hear from God, we have to be open to hear whatever He wants to say and willing to respond to it. I encourage you to hear and obey today.

GOD'S WORD FOR YOU TODAY: Do you have selective hearing in a particular area of your life? Be willing to hear God's voice.

Sincere Faith

The object and purpose of our instruction and charge is love, which springs from a pure heart and a good (clear) conscience and sincere (unfeigned) faith. (1 TIMOTHY 1:5)

We do not want to be child*ish* in our faith or in our praying; we want to be child*like*. The Lord does not want us to complicate our relationship with Him. He searches for sincere hearts, because He is a God of hearts. He wants us to pray in faith, which is not an emotion, but a spiritual force that impacts the unseen realm. God is a God of order, but not a God of rules and regulations and laws; and He does not want us to wear ourselves out trying to pray long, drawn-out prayers that are not Spirit-led or that follow a formula and require a certain posture. That would be legalistic and it always takes the life of our relationship with God. "The Spirit makes alive, but the law kills" (see 2 Corinthians 3:6).

When we follow the leading of the Holy Spirit, our communication with God will be filled with life. We will have no need to watch the clock making sure we put the right amount of time in, as many people do. When we approach talking and listening to God as an obligation and a work of our own flesh, five minutes can seem like an hour, but when our prayer is energized by the Holy Spirit, an hour can seem like five minutes. I like to pray and fellowship with God until I feel full and content. Try to relax and enjoy your time with God and it will be very rewarding.

GOD'S WORD FOR YOU TODAY: Strive to be childlike; not childish.

You Can't Drive a Parked Car

Establish my steps and direct them by [means of] Your word.
(PSALM 119:133)

People often ask, "How do I know what God wants me to do with my life?" Some spend many years being totally immobile because they are waiting to hear a voice from heaven telling them what to do.

My best advice to anyone in this position is to simply do *something*. Do what you think God might be calling you to do and if you make a mistake, He will help you correct it. Don't spend your life so afraid of making a mistake that you never try to obey what you believe God has spoken to you. I like to say, you can't drive a parked car. You need to be moving if you want God to show you which way to go. He has no need to say to you, "Turn left," if you are not going anywhere. But if you are moving, He can give you directions.

Let me insert a word of wisdom here. There are certainly times when we need to be still, wait on God, pray, and not take immediate action. But that does not apply to every situation. There are times when the only way we can discover God's will is to get moving in a certain direction and let Him speak to us and lead us as we go. If you are going in the wrong direction, He will close that door and open another one.

GOD'S WORD FOR YOU TODAY: Make sure you're in gear when you pray.

Keep It Simple

I fear, lest somehow, as the serpent deceived Eve by his craftiness, so your minds may be corrupted from the simplicity that is in Christ.

(2 CORINTHIANS 11:3 NKJV)

God really wants our relationships and communication with Him to be simple, but the devil has twisted our thinking about prayer because he not only knows how powerful it is, he also knows how easy it should be for us.

Just ask yourself, *Why would God create us for communication and fellowship with Him and then complicate it?* God has not complicated anything; He has made a simple and enjoyable way for us to pray and enjoy spending time with Him. Satan wants us to believe that prayer has to take a long time and that we must follow a specific formula. He surrounds prayer with rules and regulations and steals the creativity and freedom God desires us to enjoy as we pray. He tries to keep us from having faith and to convince us that we really are not worthy enough to be talking to God anyway and that we cannot hear God's voice.

When we do pray the devil always tries to condemn us by telling us that we do not pray enough or the right way, and that our prayers do not make a difference. He also attempts to distract us when we are praying. For these reasons, people often feel that prayer is so difficult and unfruitful that they rarely do it.

In general, many people seem to be frustrated and dissatisfied with their prayer lives, but that can change. We can pray simple, heartfelt prayers in faith and be assured that God hears and answers.

GOD'S WORD FOR YOU TODAY: A "kiss" for you: Keep It Simple, Sister (or Brother)!

Wait on God

Be still and rest in the Lord; wait for Him and patiently lean yourself upon Him. (PSALM 37:7)

I need to hear from God every day, and I want to hear from Him about everything. To hear God, we must be willing to wait on wisdom out of a passion for wanting God's will more than anything else. We will hear from God much more clearly if we are determined not to take action based on our fleshly desires or emotions. We will be blessed if we wait until we are confident that we have direction from God before we take any steps at all. Then we should do what God is leading us to do, even if it is difficult for us.

Several years ago I started collecting classic movies because there wasn't anything decent to watch on television. One day a magazine listing many good, clean movies arrived at our house. It seemed God had dropped into my lap an opportunity to get more movies. I got excited and decided to order about fifteen movies. But then I put the order form aside for a few days and when I looked at it again, my emotions and excitement had subsided and I ended up ordering only two movies. This is a simple example, but the principle applies to many areas of life.

When we act on enthusiastic emotions alone we often make mistakes. I say, "Let emotions subside and then decide." It is amazing what a difference a good night's sleep makes in the way we feel about things.

I encourage you to learn to wait. Emotions will rise and fall; and emotional energy will come and go, rarely leading us to the destination God has for us. God will always lead us to a good place if we will simply allow His Word and His wisdom, rather than our emotions, to lead us.

GOD'S WORD FOR YOU TODAY: Put your emotions aside, then decide.

Don't Miss a Blessing

Blessed (happy, fortunate, and to be envied) is the man who rever-
ently and worshipfully fears [the Lord] at all times [regardless of
circumstances], but he who hardens his heart will fall into calamity.

(PROVERBS 28:14)

God may speak to us in a dozen different ways, but if we harden our hearts and refuse to obey what He says, we will miss out on blessings He wants to give us. I can remember a time when every little thing God wanted me to do, or everything I was doing that He *didn't* want me to do, became a wrestling match between us. It took days, weeks, months, and sometimes even years of God's dealing with me before I finally accepted the fact that He wasn't going to change His mind about what He was asking of me.

When I finally gave in to His way, things always worked in ways that blessed me beyond anything I could imagine. Had I simply done what God asked me to do the first time He asked me to do it, I could have saved myself a lot of trouble.

Most of us are stubborn and set in our ways, even if our ways don't work. We can, however, learn to be tender toward God and become sensitive to His voice and the leading of His Spirit. Our spirits are designed for communion with God. He speaks through both our intuition and our conscience to keep us out of trouble and to let us know what is right and what is wrong. Then, by His Spirit, He helps us do what is right.

I encourage you today to turn from any stubbornness you might have toward God and to walk with Him with a tender heart that seeks to hear and obey His voice.

GOD'S WORD FOR YOU TODAY: Better to be set in God's ways than in your own.

Are You Listening to Him?

We have much to say which is hard to explain, since you have become dull in your [spiritual] hearing and sluggish [even slothful in achieving spiritual insight]. (HEBREWS 5:11)

Have you ever met someone who asks questions, but never bothers to listen to the answers or perhaps answers their own questions? It is hard to talk to someone like that, someone who doesn't listen. I am confident that God does not bother to try to speak to people with that kind of an attitude. If we won't listen to Him, He will find someone who is eager to hear what He has to say.

Hebrews 5:11 warns us that we will miss learning rich life principles if we don't have a listening attitude. A listening attitude will keep our hearing from becoming dull. A person who has a listening attitude is not one who wants to hear from God only when he or she is in trouble or needs God's help, but one who wants to hear what He has to say about every aspect of life.

When we expect a human being to say something, we pay attention to that person; our ears are ready to hear his or her voice. The same is true in our relationship with God; we should live every day fully expecting to hear from God and listening for His voice.

Jesus said that people have ears to hear, but they hear not, and that they have eyes to see, but they see not (see Matthew 13:9–16). He was not talking about physical hearing and sight capacities, but about spiritual ears and eyes, which we receive when we are born into the Kingdom of God. Our spiritual ears are the ears we use to hear God's voice. We are equipped to hear from God, but we must believe that we can hear from Him. All of God's promises become a reality in our lives through faith, so start believing today that you can and do hear from God.

GOD'S WORD FOR YOU TODAY: Use your spiritual ears.

We're All Adopted

*Even as [in His love] He chose us [actually picked us out for Himself as
His own] in Christ before the foundation of the world … For He foreor-
dained us (destined us, planned in love for us) to be adopted (revealed)
as His own children through Jesus Christ.* (EPHESIANS 1:4–5)

When I met my husband Dave, I was twenty-three years old with a
nine-month-old baby from a marriage that ended in divorce because of
my first husband's adultery and abandonment.

When Dave asked me to marry him, I responded, "Well, you know I
have a son, and if you get me, you get him."

Dave said something wonderful to me: "I don't know your son that
well, but I do know that I love you, and I will also love anything or anyone that is a part of you."

People are absolutely amazed when they discover that David is
adopted. They continually tell him how much he looks like his dad,
which is physically impossible because he has none of Dave's genes.

When God adopts us as His own, He wants to help us resemble
Him in remarkable ways. We don't resemble Him at all prior to our
adoption, but just as adopted children begin to take on traits of their
adoptive parents, we begin to take on characteristics of God as we grow
in our relationship with Him.

When I was adopted into God's family, I acted nothing like my heavenly Father, but I have changed over the years and hopefully people can
now see aspects of my Father in me. I have grown in love, patience,
grace toward others, thankfulness, and many other things. God wants
to bring about the same changes in your life and in the lives of those
you love.

———————

GOD'S WORD FOR YOU TODAY: You are daily being
molded into the image of God.

Go Ahead and Ask!

*This is the confidence (the assurance, the privilege of boldness) which
we have in Him: [we are sure] that if we ask anything (make any
request) according to His will (in agreement with His own plan), He
listens to and hears us.* (1 JOHN 5:14)

I want to encourage you to be filled with confidence as you approach
God in prayer. God wants us to enjoy prayer and that won't happen as
long as we are afraid of making mistakes. He promises to hear us and
answer if we have prayed according to His will, but what if we ask for
something that is not His will? We do need to pray according to God's
will to the best of our ability, but we should not allow the enemy to
ensnare us in so much fear that we are afraid to ask God for the things
that are on our hearts.

The worst that can happen if we pray outside of God's will is that we
won't get what we ask for—and that will be for our ultimate good! God
knows our hearts and He will not become angry if we make a mistake
and ask for something that is not His will. We don't need to approach
Him with the fear that we might make a mistake or that He will not be
pleased if we ask for too much. My way is to ask God for what I want and
need, always sticking to His Word as best I can, and then say, "God, if
anything I have asked for is not right for me, then I trust You not to give
it to me." Go to Him in faith, with boldness, expecting to receive His
answer.

GOD'S WORD FOR YOU TODAY: Go ahead and ask.

Resist Fear; Embrace Faith

Without faith it is impossible to please Him. (HEBREWS 11:6 NKJV)

Satan works overtime attempting to fill our lives with fear. Since we hear from God by faith, we must resist fear aggressively. The Bible says that God's Word reveals a righteousness that leads us from faith to faith (see Romans 1:17). If we learn who we are in Christ Jesus and understand how much He loves us, we can approach everything and anything in an attitude of faith. God has said repeatedly that we do not need to fear because He is with us.

The prayer that is of faith will help us and others in amazing ways; therefore, I encourage you to keep your faith strong. We receive God's will through prayers of faith, but we can also receive Satan's will through fear. Job said that the thing he feared came upon him (see Job 3:25), so be sure to live from faith to faith. Approach everything you do believing that God is good and expecting to receive His best.

Prayer is one of the most important things we must approach with a heart full of faith. This opens the windows of heaven and releases the power of God in our lives and circumstances. Be very watchful that fear doesn't sneak into your prayers and hinder you from receiving what God wants for you. If you are having a serious problem with fear I recommend that you begin your prayers by saying, "I approach God in faith today and I resist all fear." Now pray boldly, expecting to hear from God, and remember that God answers your prayers because He is good, not because you are perfect.

GOD'S WORD FOR YOU TODAY: Keep your heart full of faith.

God Understands

Great is our Lord and of great power; His understanding is inexhaustible and boundless. (PSALM 147:5)

I do not think I speak with much eloquence, and you may not think your way of communicating is very sophisticated either. I no longer worry about the way I sound when I talk to God; I simply tell the Lord what is on my heart—and I tell it the way it is—plain, simple, and straightforward. That is the way I talk to my husband; that's the way I talk to my children; that is the way I talk to people I work with; so that is the way I talk to God and that's the way He talks to me. I am not trying to impress Him; I am trying to share my heart with Him—and I can do that best when I am simply being myself.

God made us the way we are, so we need to approach Him without pretense and without thinking that we have to sound a certain way in order for Him to hear us. As long as we are sincere, He will hear. Even if what is on our hearts cannot be articulated, He still hears and understands what it is. A heart lifted up to Him is precious in His sight and He hears even words that cannot be uttered. Sometimes we hurt too badly to pray and all we can do is sigh or groan—and God understands even that. You can be comforted today by knowing that God understands and hears everything you say to Him.

GOD'S WORD FOR YOU TODAY: God loves authenticity; be yourself as you pray.

Humility Before God

Everyone who exalts himself will be humbled, but he who humbles himself will be exalted. (LUKE 18:14)

In Luke 18:10–11, we read about two men who went up to the temple to pray. One was a Pharisee and the other was a tax collector. Jesus said, "The Pharisee took his stand ostentatiously and began to pray thus before and with himself: God, I thank You that I am not like the rest of men—extortioners (robbers), swindlers [unrighteous in heart and life], adulterers—or even like this tax collector here." Then he went on to list all of his good works.

What I like about this passage is that the Bible does not say the Pharisee was praying to *God*. It says he went into the temple to pray, but he prayed "thus before and with *himself.*" Here we read about a man who appeared to be praying, and yet the Bible says he was not even talking to God; he was talking to himself! I think sometimes we also pray to impress people, maybe even to impress ourselves. Let's be honest: we can be impressed with our own eloquence. When we are talking to God and trying to hear from Him in agreement with someone else or with a group of people, we have to be very careful that we are not preaching to the other people and that we are not simply trying to sound superspiritual, but that we are really sharing our hearts with God. Agreement is incredibly powerful, but it has to be pure, and it has to come from a place of humility.

GOD'S WORD FOR YOU TODAY: God sees all the good works you have done in secret and He will reward you.

Be a Relational Believer

Now in Christ Jesus, you who once were [so] far away, through (by, in) the blood of Christ have been brought near. (EPHESIANS 2:13)

I was once what I call a "religious believer," and during that time, I asked God for help only when I was confronted with what I felt was a desperate situation, a crisis, or a serious problem for which I could not find a solution on my own. Also during that time, I prayed—not much—but I did pray because that was the "religious" thing to do.

After I became what I call a "relational believer," I quickly learned that the Holy Spirit was living in me to be my Comforter, my Teacher, my Friend, and my Helper—and I discovered that I needed help with everything from getting my hair fixed properly, bowling with a good score, and choosing the right gift for a friend, to making right decisions and getting through the desperate circumstances and serious problems of life.

When I really understood this truth and realized that Jesus did not die to give me a specific brand of religion but to bring me into a deep personal relationship with God, I made the transition from a "religious believer" to a "relational believer." My faith was no longer based on what I considered my good works but on Jesus' works. I saw that God's mercy and goodness opened up a way for me to be in close fellowship with God to receive His help in every area of my life, to hear His voice, and to enjoy intimate communion with Him.

GOD'S WORD FOR YOU TODAY: Be relational, not religious.

Our Best Help

I will lift up my eyes to the hills—from whence comes my help? My help comes from the LORD, who made heaven and earth.

(PSALM 121:1–2 NKJV)

We should be maturing in our faith to the point that we don't run to someone else every time we need to know what to do. I am not implying that asking for a word of counsel from people we feel are wiser than we are is wrong, but I do believe asking for people's opinions excessively and relying on them too heavily is wrong and insulting to God.

As you can tell from today's verses, David sought God first and knew God was his only help. The same is true for us, so we must be like David and always look to God first. We need to develop a habit of seeing God as our "first choice" for advice, not as our last resort.

God may use a person of His choice to clarify things, offer additional insight, or confirm what He has already told us, so seek Him first and if He leads you to a person, follow His leading.

In Numbers 22:22–40, God even used a donkey to speak to someone. He wants to speak to us so much that He will use whatever means is necessary. You can be assured that if you are trusting God to speak that He will find a way to get His message through to you.

GOD'S WORD FOR YOU TODAY: Ask for God's help first.

God Lives in You

Dwell in Me, and I will dwell in you. [Live in Me, and I will live in you.] (JOHN 15:4)

Why would God want to live in us? And how can He do so? After all, He is holy, and we are weak, human flesh with frailties, faults, and failures.

The answer is simple: He loves us and chooses to make His home in us. He does that because He is God; He has the ability to do what He wants, and He elects or chooses to make His home in our hearts. This choice is not based on any good deed we have done or ever could do; it is based solely on God's grace, power, and mercy. We become God's home by believing in Jesus Christ (as God instructs us in the Bible).

The verse for today emphasizes the fact that we must believe in Jesus Christ as the One God sent in order to experience intimacy with Him. Believing in Him enables us to hear His voice, receive His Word in our hearts, and feel His presence.

In addition to believing in Jesus as God's heaven-sent gift to human-kind, we are to simply believe that Jesus' sacrifice for our sins was enough to allow us into the presence of God. We become the home of God when we receive Jesus as our Savior and Lord. From that position, by the power of the Holy Spirit, He begins a wonderful work in us.

———

GOD'S WORD FOR YOU TODAY: Make sure God feels at home in your heart.

Go to God First

He shall call upon Me, and I will answer him; I will be with him in trouble, I will deliver him and honor him. (PSALM 91:15)

One time, a member of my extended family did something that really hurt me, and I felt rejected as a result. After it happened, I was sitting in the car in a lot of emotional pain and I said, "God, I need You to comfort me. I don't want to feel like this. I don't want to get bitter or develop resentment. I've experienced this same kind of pain from this person before and I don't want my day to be ruined by it. But I'm having trouble handling it and I have to have Your help."

Do you know what happened? God took the pain and all my bad feelings went away! But how many times, instead of turning to Him in prayer, do we turn to other people, mistakenly thinking that telling them all about what happened will comfort us, but it doesn't. The truth is that talking about something that hurt us only stirs up the pain in our emotions more and makes it more difficult to overcome. We tend to do everything we can think of before turning to God, and nothing ever changes the situation. We would be so much better off if our first response to every emergency and every kind of emotional pain were to pray. If we will depend totally on God, letting Him know that we need Him more than anyone or anything, we will experience major breakthroughs in our lives.

GOD'S WORD FOR YOU TODAY: Make God your "first responder."

Peace

*God's peace ... which transcends all understanding shall garrison
and mount guard over your hearts and minds in Christ Jesus.*

(PHILIPPIANS 4:7)

I have written several devotionals on the subject of God's leading His
people through peace, but I want to mention it one more time because it
is so important. People who do things they don't have peace about have
miserable lives and don't succeed at anything. We must follow peace.

Today's verse assures us that God leads us through peace. If you are
doing something, such as watching television, and you suddenly lose
your peace about it, you have heard from God. A lack of peace in that
situation is God saying to you, "Turn it off. What you are watching is
not good for you."

If you lose your peace when you say something, God is speaking to
you. Apologizing right then will save you a lot of trouble. You can say,
"I am sorry I said that. I was wrong to say it; please forgive me." God
wants to be involved in all of our decisions. One of the ways that He
lets us know how He feels about what we are doing is by either giving
peace as approval or withdrawing it as disapproval.

If we don't have peace, we are not obeying God because we are to let
the peace of God rule as an umpire in our hearts (see Colossians 3:15).
Anytime we lose our peace, we must stop and be sensitive to what God
is saying to us. Peace serves as a compass in our hearts, pointing us in
the right direction. This is why God in the Bible says: "Strive to live in
peace with everybody and pursue that consecration and holiness without which no one will [ever] see the Lord" (Hebrews 12:14).

GOD'S WORD FOR YOU TODAY: Following peace will
keep you out of trouble.

Sometimes You Just Stand

All Judah stood before the Lord, with their children and their wives.
(2 CHRONICLES 20:13)

I especially like the verse for today and the fact that an entire nation stood still before God. You see, in God's economy, standing still in faith is action. It isn't physical action, of course; it is spiritual action. Often in our lives, we take action naturally and do little or nothing spiritually. But when we discipline ourselves to be still and wait on the Lord, we are engaging in powerful spiritual activity. Our willingness to be still says to the Lord, "I am going to wait on You until You do something about this situation. In the meantime, I am going to be peaceful and enjoy my life while I wait on You."

The people of Judah, who stood still before God, had every reason to try to do something—*anything* other than standing still. Faced with an overwhelming force descending on them and threatening to destroy their land and enslave them, they must have been tempted to revolt or at least defend themselves. But they didn't. They simply stood still, waiting on God, and He miraculously delivered them.

Waiting on God brings strength (see Isaiah 40:31). We may need the strength we gain while waiting in order to do what God will instruct us to do when He gives us direction. Those who wait on the Lord hear His voice, receive answers, get direction, and gain strength to obey what He speaks to them.

GOD'S WORD FOR YOU TODAY: Standing still before the Lord is faith in action.

Anytime, Anywhere

Be unceasing in prayer. (1 THESSALONIANS 5:17)

We can pray anytime, anywhere. Our instructions are to "pray at all times, on every occasion, in every season" and to "be unceasing in prayer," but we know that we cannot spend all day long in a corner talking and listening to God. If we did, we could not live our lives. Prayer needs to be like breathing—regular, easy—and we need to just pray our way through life as part of the way we live. In fact, just as our physical lives are sustained by breathing, our spiritual lives should be maintained by praying. We can pray out loud or we can pray silently. We can pray sitting down, standing up, or walking. We can talk and listen to God while we are moving or while we are being still. We can pray while we are shopping, waiting for an appointment, participating in a business meeting, doing household chores, driving, or taking a shower. We can pray things like, "Thank You, Lord, for everything You're doing," or "God, I need You to help me," or "Oh, Jesus, help that lady over there who looks so sad." Actually, this approach to prayer is God's will. Satan wants us to procrastinate, hoping we will forget to pray. I encourage you to pray right away when something comes to your heart. This will help you stay close to God all day.

GOD'S WORD FOR YOU TODAY: Make a habit of constant communication with God.

An Unfolding Relationship

The path of the [uncompromisingly] just and righteous is like the light of dawn, that shines more and more (brighter and clearer) until [it reaches its full strength and glory in] the perfect day [to be prepared].

(PROVERBS 4:18)

One of the best things about learning to hear God's voice is that it is progressive. It is not a skill we master; it is an unfolding relationship we enjoy. As the relationship unfolds, we learn to communicate with Him more often, more deeply, and more effectively; we learn to follow the Holy Spirit more closely; we learn to pray with more confidence; and we learn to hear His voice more clearly.

Have you ever been happy in your relationship with God, feeling it was going well for a while and then, for no apparent reason, you start to feel restless, bored, distracted, or unsatisfied? Have you ever felt a nagging that something just was not right about your fellowship with God, or a stirring to do something differently? Most of the time, when you have such impressions, the Holy Spirit is trying to tell you something.

Your inner man (your spirit, the part of you that communes with God) knows when something is not right in your prayer life, because the Holy Spirit lives in your spirit and will let you know when something needs to change in your relationship with God. You just need to be bold enough to follow the Spirit. God knows we are ready for more and is urging us on to a deeper place of communing with Him and hearing His voice. God is always on the move and He wants us to move with Him. Never be afraid to leave one way or method of doing something to press toward something new.

GOD'S WORD FOR YOU TODAY: Remember, hearing God's voice is not a skill; it's a relationship.

We Wait; God Speaks

From of old no one has heard nor perceived by the ear, nor has the eye seen a God besides You, Who works and shows Himself active on behalf of him who [earnestly] waits for Him. (ISAIAH 64:4)

The Holy Spirit will lead us into amazing exploits in prayer if we will simply ask Him what to pray, wait for Him to answer, and then obey.

We are unwise if we say we don't have time to wait on God and allow Him to speak to us and lead us as we pray. We will wait forty-five minutes for a table at a restaurant, but say we do not have time to wait on God. When we wait on God, turning our hearts toward Him for direction, we honor Him. By our willingness to wait He knows that we want His will and that we are dependent upon Him for guidance.

We save a lot of time by turning our hearts toward God and waiting on Him. As the verse for today says, God shows Himself active on behalf of those who wait on Him. Start your prayers by simply saying, "I love You, Lord, and I wait on You for direction in my prayers today." Then begin to pray what is in your heart rather than what is in your own mind or will.

I was recently praying for someone to do a certain thing that I knew they needed to do, but God showed me that I needed to pray for them to develop discipline because the lack of it was affecting many areas of their life. I would have prayed for the one area I saw, but God saw much more deeply than I did.

Another time I was praying for someone concerning some problem behavior that I saw, but God showed me that the root of their problem was self-rejection and that I needed to pray for them to know how much God loved them. You can see that we often pray for what we see, but God will lead us deeper if we will wait on Him.

———

GOD'S WORD FOR YOU TODAY: Time spent waiting on God is never wasted.

Praying God's Prayers

As the heavens are higher than the earth, so are My ways higher than your ways and My thoughts than your thoughts. (ISAIAH 55:9)

I think one of the reasons we sometimes feel unfulfilled in prayer or sense that we are not "finished" praying about a matter is that we spend so much time just praying *our* prayers. But I tell you, there is a better, higher, more effective way: praying *God's* prayers. To be honest with you, if I am praying my prayer, I can pray about something for fifteen minutes and still feel unfinished; but if I am being led by the Holy Spirit and praying God's prayer, I can pray two sentences and feel completely satisfied.

I find that when I pray Spirit-led prayers, they are usually simpler and shorter than mine would be. They are direct, straightforward, and to the point. I feel satisfied that the task is complete when I pray God's way instead of my own way. When we pray our own way, we often focus on praying for carnal things and circumstances, but if we are led by God we will find ourselves praying for eternal things like the purity of our thoughts and motives and a deeper relationship with God. Ask God to teach you how to pray His prayers instead of your own and you will enjoy prayer much more.

———————————

GOD'S WORD FOR YOU TODAY: Pray God's prayers, not your prayers.

The Thoughts of God's Heart

The counsel of the Lord stands forever, the thoughts of His heart through all generations. (PSALM 33:11)

I know that you want to hear from God daily and I sincerely believe that is possible if you form a habit of listening. His counsel has been available to all generations, but few take the time to listen. Waiting on God does not mean that we sit for hours trying to hear from Him, but it means that we acknowledge that we cannot do anything right without Him. We don't run in the strength of our flesh, doing what we want to do, but we ask Him for His leadership.

I trust that when I ask God to lead me, He does. As I go through my day I am not hearing God's audible voice telling me what to do, but I do have a sensing in my heart concerning what direction I should take. For example, I woke up this morning with a plan for my day. I was going to stay home all day even though our son had invited us to go to lunch with him and his family. As I prayed, I began sensing that my time with him would be valuable and that I needed to do it. God changed my heart and I knew my day would be better if I followed His leading rather than my own plan.

Trust God to lead you today and don't be stubborn about your plan. God may have a surprise for you or an adventure that you don't want to miss.

GOD'S WORD FOR YOU TODAY: If God changes your heart, be willing to change your plans.

Fear Not

I the Lord your God hold your right hand; I am the Lord, Who says to you, Fear not; I will help you! (ISAIAH 41:13)

We sometimes encounter resistance as we seek to follow the Holy Spirit, and many times that opposition comes in the form of fear—not just major fears, such as fear of a natural disaster or a terrible disease or some other catastrophe—but a nagging sense of anxiety and unrest about common, ordinary things. The devil even tries to make us afraid of praying boldly. He wants us to approach God in fear rather than in faith.

Some people live every day with a constant undercurrent of little fears, making comments like, "I'm afraid I won't get to work on time with all this traffic," or "I'm afraid I'll burn the roast," or "I'm afraid it's going to rain out the ball game on Saturday." These everyday fears really are minor ones, but they are still fears and they still hinder a lifestyle of hearing from God by keeping people focused on their worries. Instead of allowing the enemy to pick at us with little things and infect our lives with these low-level, ongoing fears, we need to pray and trust God.

My motto is "Pray about everything and fear nothing." When we are developing a lifestyle of talking and listening to God, we will need to aggressively resist the little fears, habits, and thought patterns that do not promote or support prayer. The Holy Spirit wants to help us do that, so we need to ask Him to lead us out of negative habits and into a positive attitude that keeps us regularly connected to God in faith throughout the day. As we continue to allow the Holy Spirit to lead us in this way, our prayers and ability to hear from God will become as easy and habitual as breathing.

GOD'S WORD FOR YOU TODAY: Pray about everything; fear nothing.

God Answers the Prayers of the Righteous

The earnest (heartfelt, continued) prayer of a righteous man makes tremendous power available [dynamic in its working]. (JAMES 5:16)

When people struggle in their prayer lives, they often think it is because they are unholy and unrighteous so they try to behave better, hoping that then their prayers will be answered.

The truth is that if we are born again, we are righteous. We may not *do* everything right; but we *are* 100 percent righteous through Christ. Second Corinthians 5:21 tells us, "He made Him who knew no sin to be sin for us, that we might become the righteousness of God in Him" (NKJV). There is a difference between righteousness and "right" behavior. Righteousness describes our standing—our position or condition before God—*because of the blood of Jesus.* We cannot make ourselves righteous; only the blood of Jesus makes us righteous, as if we had never sinned at all. God views us as righteous even though we still make mistakes. Because He sees us as righteous, we have a God-given right to pray and expect God to hear and answer us. Always do the best you can to behave properly and do it because you love God, but remember that He hears and answers your prayers because He is good, not because you are.

GOD'S WORD FOR YOU TODAY: You have been made righteous by the grace of God.

Prayer Doesn't Have to Be Long to Be Powerful

When you pray, do not heap up phrases (multiply words, repeating the same ones over and over) as the Gentiles do ... Do not be like them, for your Father knows what you need before you ask Him.

(MATTHEW 6:7–8)

One of the biggest lies Satan tells people about prayer is that it needs to take a long time. He will make you think you have to pray for hours before you have really prayed, but I know from God's Word and my personal experience that prayers do not have to be long in order to be powerful. They don't have to be short to be powerful either. The length of our prayers really makes no difference to God. All that matters is that our prayers are Spirit-led, heartfelt, and accompanied by true faith.

I believe we can get so tangled up in the *words* of our prayers that we begin to lose the *power* of our prayers. I want to stress again that there is certainly nothing wrong with praying for an extended period of time. As previously stated, I do believe we should all set aside times for prolonged fellowship with God and prayer and that our willingness or lack of willingness to spend time with God determines our level of intimacy with Him. But, I do not believe we need to labor to put in a certain number of hours trying to talk and listen to God apart from the leading of the Holy Spirit, out of a sense of obligation, or as a work of the flesh. If issues in our lives really require us to pray at great length and take an extended period of time to hear God's voice, then we need to invest the time needed, but we do not have to pray prolonged prayers just for the sake of logging time.

GOD'S WORD FOR YOU TODAY: Let your prayer be Spirit-led, heart-filled, and spoken in true faith.

Be Humble When God Speaks

This is the man to whom I will look and have regard: he who is humble and of a broken or wounded spirit, and who trembles at My word. (ISAIAH 66:2)

When we hear from God, we have the choice to respond with humility and trust, or to harden our hearts and ignore Him. Regrettably, when some people don't get what they want, or when they go through trials and tests, they harden their hearts.

That's exactly what happened to the Israelites when they were making their trip through the wilderness. God had great things planned for them, but He tested them first to see if they were really going to believe Him. He led them the long, hard way on purpose—to see if they would keep His commands or not. In His Word, He tells us not to harden our hearts as they did (see Hebrews 3:7–8).

Their problems made them bitter instead of better. They hardened their hearts and would not learn the ways of God. They had many wrong attitudes and were prevented from making progress because they refused to trust God.

Don't let your heart get hard during difficult times. People with hard hearts are rebellious and refuse correction. They have difficulty hearing from God, and they have difficulty in relationships. They are not willing to see other people's viewpoints; they don't understand other people's needs and usually don't care about them. They are self-centered and unable to be moved with compassion.

Let us aggressively seek God to soften our hearts and help us be tender and sensitive to His touch and His voice.

———————

GOD'S WORD FOR YOU TODAY: When things don't work out the way you want them to, trust God and keep a good attitude.

God Speaks to Correct Us

The Lord corrects and disciplines everyone whom He loves.
(HEBREWS 12:6)

We all need to be corrected at times and I believe God's desire is to speak to us and do the correcting Himself before using other people or situations to correct us. Correction is one of the most difficult things to receive, especially when it comes through others, so God prefers to first help us deal with matters privately. But, if we do not know how to let Him correct us privately or will not receive it, He may correct us in more public ways.

One time we were ministering in a foreign country. I was in a restaurant trying to convey to the waiter what I wanted to eat, but he did not speak much English and I did not speak his language at all. Frustration soon became evident in my attitude and tone of voice. I was behaving poorly in front of people who knew I was in that country to minister and, of course, my example to them was important.

I knew I had behaved badly, but God wanted me to *really* know, so when Dave and I returned to our hotel room, Dave mentioned the incident and said I had not set a good example for others.

Although I knew he was right, and I knew God was using him to make sure I fully realized how important my behavior is, my inclination was to point out that Dave had acted similarly before. Had I done that, I would not have genuinely received the word of correction and then God would have had to correct me some other way—perhaps in a way that would have been more embarrassing or painful.

Begin to pray and ask God to help you receive correction from Him and to help you recognize when He is sending correction through others, knowing it is always for your good.

GOD'S WORD FOR YOU TODAY: Don't resist God's correction.

Power for Your Life

God has spoken once, twice have I heard this: that power belongs to God. (PSALM 62:11)

I believe that prayer—simply talking to God and listening to Him speak to us—is one of the greatest powers available in the entire universe. That's a bold statement, given the other kinds of power that are available today, but I am convinced beyond the slightest doubt that it is true. When we think of nuclear power or atomic power, we think of forces greater than we can imagine. When we think of an automobile or a motorcycle, we realize they have power.

But even the strongest earthly power is nothing compared to God's power. The power we know in the physical world is natural, but prayer power is spiritual. Prayer releases the power of almighty God into our daily lives and the power of prayer connects us to the power of God—and that is why it is a greater force than anything else.

The power of prayer can move the hand of God. God can change an individual heart, free a person from bondage and torment, overturn disappointments and devastations, break the power of an addiction, or heal a person's emotions. God's power can restore a marriage, impart a sense of value and purpose, bring peace and joy, grant wisdom, and work miracles. And the awesome, tremendous power of God—the greatest power in the universe—is released in our lives through simple, believing prayer.

GOD'S WORD FOR YOU TODAY: Use prayer to release God's power in your life.

God Speaks Wisdom

If any of you is deficient in wisdom, let him ask of the giving God [Who gives] to everyone liberally and ungrudgingly, without reproaching or faultfinding, and it will be given him. (JAMES 1:5)

One reason hearing God's voice is so powerful is that it releases God's wisdom into a situation—and God's wisdom can completely turn things around. When His wisdom comes into any circumstance—whether it is a decision, a relationship, a financial question, a medical crisis, a professional matter, a personal issue, or a choice that may affect the course of your life for years to come—it will give you insight and direction you probably would not have ever thought of on your own. The wisdom of God can save you money, time, energy; it can even save your life. It can result in blessings you never imagined; it can give you favor where you were once despised; it can heal division between people; and it can bring total restoration out of complete devastation. God's wisdom can make you so much smarter than you naturally are and lead to wonderful things!

Today's verse says God gives us wisdom, but what does it mean to be wise? Simply put, wise people make decisions now that they will be happy with later. Unwise people, on the other hand, do what feels good at the moment and almost always end up unhappy with their choices. Unwise people operate out of their emotions instead of asking God for His wisdom—and they usually regret the impulsive, emotional decisions that result. Wise people, on the contrary, look back on a situation and marvel at the grace and guidance God has given them as they have sought Him. They realize that they have been incredibly blessed by God as they experience the kind of fruitfulness that comes from making wise choices. As you seek God today, ask for His wisdom.

GOD'S WORD FOR YOU TODAY: Make decisions now that you'll be happy with later.

God Speaks Through Gifts and Abilities

A man's mind plans his way, but the Lord directs his steps.
(PROVERBS 16:9)

People often wonder, *What am I supposed to do with my life? What is my purpose for being alive? Does God have a plan for me?* One way God answers these questions is through our natural gifts and abilities. He leads us to understand our purpose through the skills and talents He gives us.

A God-given talent, or what we often call "a gift," is something we can do easily, something that comes naturally. For example, many great artists know just how to put shapes and colors together, so they enjoy painting, sculpting, or designing buildings. Many songwriters hear music in their heads, and they simply write down these melodies and/or lyrics to make beautiful music. Some people have natural abilities to organize or administrate, while others are gifted as counselors, helping people sort out their lives and relationships. No matter what our talents are, we derive great pleasure from doing what we are naturally good at doing.

If you are not sure of your purpose in life, just do what you are good at and then watch God confirm your choices by blessing your endeavors. Don't spend your life trying to do what you are not gifted to do. When people work in jobs where they are not gifted, they are miserable—and so is everyone around them. But when people are in their proper places, they will excel in their jobs and be a blessing to their employers and coworkers.

If we do what we are good at doing, we will sense God's anointing (presence and power) on our efforts. We will know we are operating in our gifts and that doing so honors God and ministers life to others. God speaks to us through this anointing, giving us peace and joy to know we are fulfilling His plan for our lives.

GOD'S WORD FOR YOU TODAY: Do what you're good at—it's God's gift to you.

Confess and Pray

Confess to one another therefore your faults (your slips, your false steps, your offenses, your sins) and pray [also] for one another, that you may be healed and restored [to a spiritual tone of mind and heart]. (JAMES 5:16)

Sin separates us from God. It causes us to feel far away from Him; it can cause us to want to hide from Him or to not want to talk to Him; and it can keep us from hearing His voice. When we know we have sinned, we must ask for God's forgiveness and then receive it, because He promises to forgive us when we repent. Hidden things can have power over us and so there are times when it is very helpful to confess our sins to other people, according to the verse for today.

Confessing our faults to someone and asking for prayer requires first of all that we find someone we truly trust and second that we be willing to put aside our pride and humbly share our struggles. If you find that challenging, ask God to help you grow in humility because the results are amazing if you find a friend you can trust, and you share with that person, "I'm struggling in this area and I want to be free. I'm hurting and I need you to pray for me."

I remember once having a real struggle with feeling jealous of a friend. I had prayed, but was still being tormented by the jealousy so I confessed it to Dave and asked him to pray for me. Getting it out in the open broke its power over me and I was set free from it. Always go to God first, but if you need the help of a friend or spiritual leader, don't let pride stand in your way.

———————

GOD'S WORD FOR YOU TODAY: Don't let pride stop you from confessing to others when you need to.

A Friend of God

I do not call you servants … But I have called you My friends.
(JOHN 15:15)

In Genesis 18:17, God called Abraham His friend and then shared with him His plan to destroy Sodom and Gomorrah. Just as He shared those intentions with Abraham, He will share things with you—His heart, His desires, His purposes, His plans—as His friend. He will give you understanding and insight into what is happening in your life and tell you what to do about it. He will lead you and help you be prepared for the future. As God's friend, you do not have to be caught off guard or ambushed by your circumstances. You can be informed and ready—because you are a friend of God and you hear His voice. He may not reveal everything you would like to know exactly when you would like to know it, but He will guide you and give you strength as you patiently trust Him.

You may be asking, "How do I become God's friend?" According to today's verse, you already are. In this verse, Jesus said to His disciples, "I have called you My friends." If you are a follower of Jesus, you are a modern-day disciple and you are His friend. As is the case in any friendship, you can be a casual acquaintance or you can be a close, intimate personal friend. Your friendship with God grows and develops just as your friendships with other people grow and develop. Just as a natural friendship requires time and energy to develop, so does your relationship with God.

I encourage you to invest time and energy in your relationship with God today by giving your attention to Him through reading and meditating on His Word and by talking and listening to Him as His friend.

GOD'S WORD FOR YOU TODAY: Make room in your schedule to invest time and energy in your relationship with God.

Crisis Management

Surely I know that it will be well with those who [reverently] fear God, who revere and worship Him, realizing His continual presence.

(ECCLESIASTES 8:12)

God has taught me some valuable lessons about crisis management. Jesus said, "Come to Me" (Matthew 11:28); He didn't say run to the phone and call three friends when we face an emergency. I am not against asking people to pray for us, but if we run to people, we won't find a cure; we will find only a bandage.

We face many challenges and crises in life. Sometimes the crises are major; sometimes they are minor. To avoid living in a constant state of emergency, the Lord impressed on me to seek Him continuously, or diligently. I used to seek time with God once in a while or when my life was in big trouble. Eventually, I learned that if I ever wanted to get out of crisis mode, I needed to seek God as if I were in desperate need of Him all the time—during hard times and during seasons of great blessing.

We often give God low priority when things are going well for us. But I have observed that if the only time we seek God is when we are desperate, He often keeps us in desperate circumstances in order to keep us in fellowship with Him.

God will always rescue and help us when we come to Him. But if we want to stay in a place of *constant* peace and victory, we must diligently seek Him at all times, as the verse for today urges us to do.

GOD'S WORD FOR YOU TODAY: Practice good crisis management by staying in fellowship with God at all times.

Are You Really Trusting God?

My beloved brethren, be steadfast, immovable, always abounding in the work of the Lord. (1 CORINTHIANS 15:58 NKJV)

The ability to be steadfast indicates trust in the Lord. Think about it: if I were to say, "I am trusting God," but then I stay anxious and upset, then I am not really trusting God. If I were to say, "I'm trusting God," but I sink into depression and despair, then I am not really trusting God. If I say I trust God and worry or lose my joy, then I am not really trusting God. When we truly trust God, we are able to enter into His rest and allow our hearts to settle into a place of unshakable confidence in Him. The enemy will not completely go away, but he will become more of a nuisance than a major problem to us.

As long as we are on Earth, doing our best to love and serve God, the enemy will be on the prowl around us. Part of God's design for our spiritual growth includes developing spiritual muscles as we learn to resist the enemy. The apostle Paul understood this well, so he did not pray that people would never have trouble; he prayed that they would have perseverance, that they would be steadfast and immovable, *really* trusting the Lord. God wants you to enter His rest and He will work on your behalf.

GOD'S WORD FOR YOU TODAY: *Really* trust the Lord.

Pray at All Times

Pray at all times (on every occasion, in every season) in the Spirit, with all [manner of] prayer and entreaty. (EPHESIANS 6:18)

In the verse for today, Paul is basically saying that we are to pray in every circumstance, following the Holy Spirit's direction, using different types of prayer in different situations. But how do we "pray at all times," as the Bible instructs? We do it by keeping an attitude of thanksgiving and total dependence upon God as we go about our everyday lives, turning our thoughts toward Him in the midst of doing all the things we have to do and listening for His voice in every situation. I believe God really wants us to live a lifestyle of prayer and that He wants to help us stop thinking about prayer as an event and begin to see it as a way of life, as an internal activity that undergirds everything else we do. He wants us to talk to Him and listen to Him continually—to pray our way through every day with our hearts connected to His and our ears attuned to His voice.

We often hear about a prayer need or think about a situation and say to ourselves, *I need to pray about that later when I pray.* That thought is a stall tactic of the enemy. Why not pray right that minute? We do not pray right away because of the wrong mind-sets we have about prayer. It would be easy if we just followed our hearts, but Satan wants to complicate prayer. He wants us to procrastinate in the hope that we will forget the matter entirely. Praying as we sense the desire or need to pray is simple, and it is the way we can pray continually and stay connected to God in every situation throughout the day.

GOD'S WORD FOR YOU TODAY: Don't put off talking to God.

Not by Bread Alone

Man does not live by bread only, but man lives by every word that proceeds out of the mouth of the Lord. (DEUTERONOMY 8:3)

During the years when my ministry didn't grow as I wanted it to, I became frustrated and dissatisfied. I fasted, prayed, and tried everything I knew to try to get more people to come to my conferences.

I remember complaining and being upset often when God would not give me the increase I wanted. God often tested me by allowing the attendance and enthusiasm of the people to be less than I desired. When I left those meetings, I questioned: "What am I doing wrong, God? Why aren't You blessing me? I'm fasting; I'm praying. I'm giving and believing, and You're not moving on my behalf!" I became so frustrated I felt I would explode. I asked, "God, why aren't You answering my prayers?"

He spoke to me and said, "Joyce, I am teaching you that man does not live by bread alone." He had spoken these same words to the Israelites as they traveled through the desert toward the Promised Land at a much slower pace than they had hoped for. He told them this was designed to humble them, to test and prove them. To teach them that man does not live by bread alone but by the word of God.

I did not like thinking that God was humbling me and testing me, but I realized that what God was saying by telling me that "man does not live by bread alone" was that He wanted my desires to be purely for more of Him, not for more of anything else. My ministry did grow in time, but only after God was first in my life. When you can be satisfied with God alone, then He can give you the other things you would like to have. He is our true bread in life and the true nourishment of our souls.

GOD'S WORD FOR YOU TODAY: Refuse to live by bread alone; want God more than anything else.

You Don't Have to Pray Perfectly

He is always living to make petition to God and intercede with Him and intervene for them. (HEBREWS 7:25)

I would like to share with you a truth that has really encouraged me in my relationship with God. Like many people, it seemed that no matter how much I prayed I had a feeling that something was not right with my prayer, so I finally asked the Lord one day, "Why do I feel like this? I'm praying every day. I'm spending a good amount of time in prayer. Why is it that when I come to the end of my prayer time, I feel so unsatisfied, and as if I didn't get through to You?" God answered me and said, "Because you don't feel like you're praying perfect prayers. You have doubts about yourself and that makes you doubt the power of your prayers."

I realized that was true; I did not feel that I was all that I should be. I had always had a nagging fear that caused me to say to myself, "I'm not praying with enough faith or I'm not praying long enough or I'm not talking to God about the right things."

God delivered me from that fear and doubt when He said to me, "You know what, Joyce? You're right. You're not praying perfect prayers. You're not perfect. That's why you have Jesus as your Intercessor and that is why you pray in His name."

You may not feel you pray "right" prayers either, but be encouraged. By the time your prayers get to God, He hears perfect prayers because you have prayed in Jesus' name, not your own name. When we pray in Jesus' name we present to God all that Jesus is, not what we are; therefore, our prayers are accepted by God.

GOD'S WORD FOR YOU TODAY: Let Jesus pray perfect prayers for you.

Frustrate the Enemy

*Consider it wholly joyful, my brethren, whenever you are enveloped
in or encounter trials of any sort or fall into various temptations. Be
assured and understand that the trial and proving of your faith bring
out endurance and steadfastness and patience.* (JAMES 1:2–3)

One of the mistakes many Christians make is that, when trials come,
they pray for their troubles to stop. I believe that, instead, we need to
pray for strength and endurance; we need to ask God to make us steadfast. If the enemy is aiming his biggest guns at us—doing everything
he can to upset our lives, ruin our businesses, tear apart our families,
or otherwise steal our peace—and we stay steadfast and patient, he
will be exceedingly frustrated, and ultimately defeated, because we are
not cooperating with him.

Philippians 1:28 says: "Do not [for a moment] be frightened or intimidated in anything by your opponents and adversaries, for such [con-
stancy and fearlessness] will be a clear sign (proof and seal) to them of
[their impending] destruction, but [a sure token and evidence] of your
deliverance and salvation, and that from God." This verse encourages
us not to be frightened or intimidated when the devil comes against us,
but to remain steadfast. As we do, we not only show the devil that he
cannot handle us, we also demonstrate to the Lord that we have faith
in Him. The fact that our actions affirm our trust in Him is God's signal
to release His power into our situations and deliver us. I believe God
wants you to hear Him telling you to stand firm and not be afraid.

GOD'S WORD FOR YOU TODAY: Let your trust in God be
so steadfast that it frustrates the enemy.

A New Heart

A new heart will I give you and a new spirit will I put within you, and I will take away the stony heart out of your flesh … And I will put My Spirit within you and cause you to walk in My statutes, and you shall heed My ordinances and do them. (EZEKIEL 36:26–27)

The verses for today contain a promise God spoke thousands of years ago, a promise that a day would come when He would give people new hearts and put His Spirit within them. When God spoke these words, people were living under the Old Covenant, the time before Jesus' birth, death, and resurrection. Under that Old Covenant, the Holy Spirit was with people and came upon them for special purposes, but He did not live in their hearts.

You and I are living in the New Covenant, the time God was talking about through the prophet Ezekiel when He promised to send His Spirit to live within us. No one could be born again and become a dwelling place for God's Spirit until Jesus died and rose from the dead. Now that He has come, we can receive Him as Lord and Savior and we can receive the Holy Spirit in our hearts. When He lives in us, He can speak to us, enable us to hear His voice, and give us power to obey what He says to us.

I encourage you to meditate on the amazing blessing of being chosen as a home for God. That means you and God are very close and you can expect to enjoy wonderful fellowship with Him.

GOD'S WORD FOR YOU TODAY: You are very close to God.

Faith Is Active

The apostles said to the Lord, Increase our faith (that trust and confidence that spring from our belief in God). (LUKE 17:5)

Many people, maybe even you, pray to have "great faith," but it doesn't come through prayer alone. It is built little by little as we step out in obedience to what God has asked us to do. He may even ask us to do things we have not had any experience doing or may not totally understand, but as we step out, we experience God's faithfulness and our faith grows.

God sometimes gives people a gift of faith for a certain situation in their lives, but normally faith becomes great through experience. Our faith grows deeper, stronger, and greater as we exercise it.

In the verse for today, the disciples asked Jesus to increase their faith. He responded by telling them in Luke 17:6 that they needed to act on their faith in order for it to increase. The same is true for us today. One way we demonstrate our faith is by doing things; faith often requires action. Certainly, there are times when God wants us to wait on Him to act on our behalf, but there are other times when we need to prove that we have faith by doing something. When we want to grow in our faith, we need to be willing to wait expectantly or take action according to God's Word to us, but our faith will not increase while we do nothing.

GOD'S WORD FOR YOU TODAY: Act in ways that demonstrate your faith.

Seasons Change

He changes the times and the seasons. (DANIEL 2:21)

Years ago, I enjoyed a good job as part of a church staff. I had a thriving ministry, a regular paycheck, and plenty of opportunities to do what I loved and felt called to do. Then there came a time when God spoke to me about leaving that job and taking my ministry "to the north, south, east, and west." I heard Him say, "This season in your life is complete; I am finished with you in this place."

In my heart, I knew God had spoken. Nevertheless, I had a mixture of excitement and fear about starting my own ministry. I wanted to venture beyond what I had known to that point, but I was afraid of making a mistake and losing what I had. I wanted to see what God would do, but I was afraid to take such a big step into unknown territory.

Sometimes God gets finished with something and we keep hanging on to it. My spirit wanted to step out, but my flesh wanted to stay. I had a lot of security in the position God was calling me to leave, and I didn't want to give it up. But, eventually I did obey Him and today I enjoy ministry around the world. Remember that God changes things and when He does we must be willing to follow His leading.

———————

GOD'S WORD FOR YOU TODAY: Listen for God's voice to lead you when you need to make changes in your life.

Expect Big Things from God

*To Him Who, by (in consequence of) the [action of His] power
that is at work within us, is able to [carry out His purpose and] do
superabundantly, far over and above all that we [dare] ask or think
[infinitely beyond our highest prayers, desires, thoughts, hopes, or
dreams].* (EPHESIANS 3:20)

Some people are so afraid of receiving bad news that they never think
to pray for good news! That's not a godly attitude. If we want to hear
God's voice and see His power released in our lives, we need to have
attitudes that are pleasing to Him. We need to have positive expectations instead of negative ones. Our basic approach to life needs to be
full of faith and hope and good expectations, because the Bible says
that without faith it is impossible to please God (see Hebrews 11:6) and
that hope will never disappoint us (see Romans 5:5). There is nothing
negative about God; there is nothing in Him or in His actions that will
ever disappoint us; everything He does is for our good—so that's what
we need to expect as we pray. We should not pray and then *wonder* if
God will do anything at all; we should pray *expecting* God to do even
more than we have asked.

The verse for today says that God can do "superabundantly, far
over and above all" that we would ever dare to ask or even *think* to ask
and *infinitely beyond* our "highest prayers, desires, thought, hopes, or
dreams." Now that is amazing—and it should give us all the confidence
we need in order to pray expectantly. Personally, I would rather pray
big prayers with great expectations and receive half of what I prayed for
than to pray little puny prayers without any faith and get it all!

GOD'S WORD FOR YOU TODAY: Expect big things
from God.

God Will Find You

Behold, the Lord's eye is upon those who fear Him [who revere and worship Him with awe], who wait for Him and hope in His mercy and loving-kindness. (PSALM 33:18)

I remember a time when I was trying so hard to hear from God and was so afraid I would make a mistake. At the time, I was just beginning to learn to hear God's voice. Being led by the Spirit was new to me, and I was afraid because I didn't have enough experience hearing from God to know whether I was truly hearing or not. I didn't understand that God redeems our mistakes if our hearts are right.

He was speaking to me and trying to get me to step out in faith and do something, but I kept saying, "Lord, what if I miss You? What if I'm not really hearing You and I do the wrong thing? I'm scared I will miss You, God!"

He spoke to me and said simply, "Joyce, don't worry. If you miss Me, I will find you." Those words gave me the courage to do what God was calling me to do and brought great peace to my heart. They have encouraged me to step out in faith many, many times since I first heard them. I share them with you today to encourage you, too, to take the steps of faith you need to take in response to what God is saying to you right now.

If you want God's will in your life more than anything else and if you've done everything you know to do to hear from God, then you have to take a chance, step out, and believe. Even if you do make a mistake, God will fix it and work it out for your good.

———————————

GOD'S WORD FOR YOU TODAY: Take a chance on what you believe you've heard from God and don't be afraid of missing Him.

In the Spirit, with the Word

Let my cry come before You, O Lord; give me understanding according to Your word. (PSALM 119:169 NKJV)

Whatever type of prayer we pray—whether it is a prayer of consecration or commitment, petition or perseverance, intercession or agreement, praise, worship, or thanksgiving, God's Word is an essential ingredient. Our prayers are always effective when we remind God of His Word and pray in faith that He is able to perform what He has spoken. I also believe that to be most effective, prayer needs to be "in the Spirit."

We need both the Word and the Spirit in our prayers in order to stay balanced and strong in our spiritual lives. If people seek supernatural experiences or become excessive in spiritual matters, they may become deceived and be too emotional or even flaky. At the same time, if we focus on the Word without also being sensitive to the Spirit, we can become legalistic and dry. When we have the Spirit and the Word together, we can live solid lives that are balanced—grounded in truth and graced with joy and power. We need the solid foundation of the Word of God and we need the enthusiasm and excitement of the Spirit. Praying in agreement with the Word and praying in the Spirit keeps us praying according to God's will. It also causes our prayers to be effective and bears great fruit in our lives. Whatever you do, I encourage you to fill your prayers with the Word and let the Holy Spirit lead. You will see tremendous results.

GOD'S WORD FOR YOU TODAY: The Word of God is the sword of the Spirit; it is your weapon against Satan. Use it aggressively!

Get to the Point

Do not fret or have any anxiety about anything, but in every circum-
stance and in everything, by prayer and petition (definite requests),
with thanksgiving, continue to make your wants known to God.

(PHILIPPIANS 4:6)

I recall a time during my journey with God when He challenged me to make an effort to ask Him for what I wanted and needed in as few words as possible. I had a bad habit of talking too much when I prayed. I would go on and on because I had the mistaken idea that short prayers were not good prayers. Of course, long prayers are good prayers, too, if they are sincere and necessary.

When God challenged me to make my requests of Him in as few words as possible, He simply asked me to be concise and to-the-point and then wait on Him for a little while before going to the next thing I needed to pray about. When I did, I could not believe the increased power that came to my prayer life. To this day, when I pray that way, I sense more of the Holy Spirit's power and presence than I do if I go on and on and on and on. I have learned that some of the most powerful, effective prayers I can pray are things like, "Thank You, Lord," "Oh, God, I need Your wisdom," "Give me strength to keep going, Lord," or "I love You, Jesus." And perhaps the most powerful of all: "Help!!!!!!!" See? Just a few words will connect us with heaven as we call upon the Lord to act on our behalf. It is not the length of our prayers that makes them effective, but the sincerity and faith behind them.

GOD'S WORD FOR YOU TODAY: Quality always bests quantity, even in prayer.

Always Available

The upright shall dwell in Your presence (before Your very face).
(PSALM 140:13)

The fact that the Holy Spirit lives inside of us proves His willingness to always be available to speak to us and help us when we need Him. As we continue to grow spiritually, we will experience temptation, but God has given us the Holy Spirit to enable us to resist it and make right choices instead of wrong ones.

Nevertheless, no human being is perfect and we will make mistakes. But God's forgiveness is always available to us through Jesus Christ. Receiving this forgiveness strengthens us and enables us to keep moving forward with God. It also puts our hearts at peace, sets us free, and helps us hear God's voice clearly.

Feeling defeated and condemned by every mistake we make weakens us. Instead of using our energy to feel bad about ourselves, we should use it to make sure our hearts are tuned to God's voice as He leads us into greater strength and deeper relationship with Himself. His forgiveness and His presence are always available to us through the Holy Spirit. As you seek God today, I encourage you to receive His love and mercy. His arms are open and He is waiting to spend time with you.

GOD'S WORD FOR YOU TODAY: Remember that the Holy Spirit is always available to you.

Time for a Change

*All of us ... are constantly being transfigured into His very own image
in ever increasing splendor and from one degree of glory to another;
[for this comes] from the Lord [Who is] the Spirit.*

(2 CORINTHIANS 3:18)

The verse for today teaches us that we need both the Word of God and
the Spirit of God working in our lives in order for us to experience the
changes God wants to bring to our lives.

Everyone who comes to Christ needs change. We certainly don't
want to stay the same as we were before we knew Him, do we? We can
and should desire change, but we must also realize we cannot change
ourselves. We must lean entirely on the power of the Holy Spirit to
speak to us about the changes that are needed and then to bring them
about in our lives. As believers, we certainly have to cooperate with the
work He does within us, but we also have to remember that He is the
One Who does the changing. Many times, He will speak to us about
changes He wants to make in our lives, so we need to keep our hearts
sensitive to His voice so we can readily work with Him as He changes
us "from one degree of glory to another."

As God works in our lives, one of the ways we hear from Him is that
we become uncomfortable in our spirit when we are doing something
that displeases Him. Anytime the Holy Spirit wants to make a change
in us or our behavior, all we need to do is surrender and He will go to
work. Just say, "Your will be done, Lord, not mine."

GOD'S WORD FOR YOU TODAY: Lean on the Holy Spirit
to bring about the changes needed in your life.

Praise Your Way into God's Presence

Enter into His gates with thanksgiving and a thank offering and into His courts with praise! Be thankful and say so to Him, bless and affectionately praise His name! (PSALM 100:4)

There are ways to make ourselves available to hear God's voice and one of them is to enter into respectful, heartfelt praise and worship. God delights to manifest His presence and power to people who are truly praising and worshipping Him. And when His presence and power come, we hear His voice, we see miracles, people are healed, lives are changed, and transformation takes place from the inside out.

Isn't that part of what you desire in your relationship with God? When you talk to Him and listen for His voice, aren't you praying primarily because you want some kind of change or transformation in some area of your life? If you are asking Him to provide a new job, that's change. If you are praying for a loved one to come to know the Lord, that's change. If you are asking God to reveal Himself more to you and to help you grow in spiritual maturity, that's change. If you are praying for the teenager who lives down the street to stop using drugs, that's change. If you are asking God to help you not lose your temper so easily, that's change.

Whatever you are praying for, one of the best ways to start is with praise and worship. They will keep your heart right before God and make a way for you to hear His voice and for change to take place.

GOD'S WORD FOR YOU TODAY: When you need to hear God's voice, praise and worship Him.

Renew Your Mind

Be transformed (changed) by the [entire] renewal of your mind ...
so that you may prove [for yourselves] what is the good and
acceptable and perfect will of God, even the thing which is good
and acceptable and perfect [in His sight for you]. (ROMANS 12:2)

I accepted Jesus Christ as my Savior at the age of nine. I became aware of my sinful state and sought forgiveness from God through Jesus. I was born of the Spirit at that time, but I did not really understand what had taken place in my life. I had no teaching, therefore I remained in darkness experientially even though the Light was living in me.

As a young adult, I went to church faithfully, was baptized, took confirmation classes, and did everything I understood I needed to be doing, yet I never enjoyed closeness and intimacy with God. I believe multitudes of people are in that same position today and many others have been in centuries past.

Although I did my best to be "religious," I learned that Jesus did not die to give us religion; He died to give us a personal relationship with God through Himself and through the power of the Holy Spirit Whom He would send to dwell in each believer.

As I mentioned, I was born of the Spirit but lacked revelation of what that truly meant. People can be very wealthy, but if they believe they are poor, their lives will be no different from the lives of those who live in poverty. If people have a great inheritance but do not know it, they cannot spend it.

Today's verse tells us that God has a plan in mind for us. His will toward us is good and acceptable and perfect, but we must completely renew our minds before we will ever experience this good thing God has planned (see Romans 12:1–2). We renew our minds and we get new attitudes and new ideals by studying God's Word. We must learn to think like God thinks!

GOD'S WORD FOR YOU TODAY: Think like God thinks!

Be Spiritually Alive

The law of the Spirit of life [which is] in Christ Jesus [the law of our new being] has freed me from the law of sin and of death.

(ROMANS 8:2)

When we try to have relationship with God by keeping all of the laws of religion we fail miserably and always feel defeated. Jesus kept the law perfectly for us and paid the debt we owed to God for our sin and unrighteousness. He opened up a way for us to approach God through faith in Him rather than through our own works.

Jesus said that if we love Him we will keep and obey His commandments (see John 14:15). He did not say that if we kept them all, He would love us. God already loves us, and He wants us to respond to His love by willingly doing our best to obey Him. He also wants us to know that when we make mistakes we can be instantly and completely forgiven.

Under the Old Covenant, sin produced spiritual death, but the law of love that we now live under produces life in us. God's love is amazing and realizing that we are not under pressure to perform perfectly all the time enables us to relax in His presence and hear His voice.

———————————

GOD'S WORD FOR YOU TODAY: Jesus' work on the cross makes it possible for you to enjoy intimate fellowship with God.

Mind and Mouth

Out of the fullness (the overflow, the superabundance) of the heart the mouth speaks. (MATTHEW 12:34)

Today's verse reminds me of a woman who came to one of my conferences and shared with me that she never stopped thinking and talking about her problems, even though she was being taught not to focus on them. She knew she needed to stop thinking about negative things, but she seemed powerless to do so.

This woman had been abused, and she met several other women who shared that pain. As they talked, she realized God had told her everything He had told them, but they had obeyed while she had disobeyed. They had renewed their minds with the Word of God while she had kept driving her problems deeper into her soul by refusing to get them off of her mind.

Whatever we set our minds on eventually comes out of our mouths. Because this woman refused to obey God and stop thinking and talking about her problems, she was in a prison she could not escape. We seek things by thinking and speaking about them. She could have used her thoughts and words to seek God, but she used them to seek more of the very things she was trying to overcome.

I encourage you to seek God by thinking and speaking about the things of God and by asking the Holy Spirit to fill your mind and your mouth with the things He wants you to focus on.

GOD'S WORD FOR YOU TODAY: Think about things today that make you happy, not things that make you sad.

God Moves In

Guard and keep [with the greatest care] the precious and excellently adapted [Truth] which has been entrusted [to you], by the [help of the] Holy Spirit Who makes His home in us. (2 TIMOTHY 1:14)

In Old Testament times, Adam and Eve walked with God in the Garden of Eden and Moses met Him on Mount Sinai. Today, God does not meet us in our gardens or on nearby mountains where we can interact with Him by invitation only. He does not choose to live in a tent, as He did when the children of Israel traveled through the wilderness. And He does not live in a building made by human hands.

When we accept Christ, the Holy Spirit comes to dwell in us (see John 14:17 KJV). God chooses to move into our spirits—into the core center of our lives—where He can be closer to us than any other living thing. When God's Holy Spirit moves into our hearts, our spirits become a dwelling place for Him (see 1 Corinthians 3:16–17) and is made holy because God is there.

The holy state into which we as believers are placed is then worked out in our souls and in our bodies and God wants this working out to be evident in our everyday lives. It occurs as a process, and the phases of change we go through actually become our testimony to those who know us. We are actually learning how to live inside out! God has done an amazing work in our spirits and the Holy Spirit is teaching us how to live in such a way that we can be a witness to the world that needs Him.

GOD'S WORD FOR YOU TODAY: Live from the inside out!

Our Greatest Desire

They will not hunger or thirst, neither will mirage [mislead] or scorching wind or sun smite them; for He Who has mercy on them will lead them, and by springs of water will He guide them.

(ISAIAH 49:10)

God doesn't want us to desire anything more than we desire Him. It's not that we shouldn't want things, it's just that we shouldn't want them more than we want Him. He desires for us to live in the reality of His presence every day of our lives and to be thoroughly satisfied with Who He is.

The verses for today speak of a mirage. We actually thirst for God, but if we do not realize that He is the One we crave, we can be easily misled, the way a mirage misleads thirsty travelers in the desert. Satan can deceive us by making us focus on things that will never truly satisfy. Nothing can satisfy us apart from God, so we must set our minds to seek Him. If we give Him first place in our desires, thoughts, conversations, and choices, our thirst will truly be quenched and we will not be led astray.

We have legitimate needs, and God wants to meet them. If we seek His face (presence), we will find that His hand is always open to us. However, if we seek things we can be easily deceived, and may find that we have wasted a great deal of our lives being led by mirages—things that appeared to be what we needed but were nothing at all.

GOD'S WORD FOR YOU TODAY: God has everything you need.

Be Refreshed

Repent (change your mind and purpose); turn around and return [to God], that your sins may be erased (blotted out, wiped clean), that times of refreshing ... may come from the presence of the Lord.

(ACTS 3:19)

God manifests His presence in many ways. Most of the time we can't see Him, but, like the wind, we can see the work He does in us. If I'm tired, weary, frustrated, or bothered about something, and I become refreshed after spending time with God, then I know the wind of the Spirit has blown on me.

God wants to bring a refreshing into your life. Don't be frustrated or worn-out in your soul when the answer is living inside of you. If you are too busy to spend time with God, you are simply too busy, so make some adjustments to your schedule. Don't be burned out, upset, weary, and stressed out when times of refreshing are available to you.

Learn to come away from the busyness of life to spend time with God the way Jesus did. You can't wait for the people around you to approve of the time you need to spend with God. Somebody will always find something they think you need to do! Set aside time first thing in the morning if at all possible and then try taking several "mini spiritual vacations" throughout the day. Stop what you are doing for two or three minutes; take a deep breath to help you relax and simply tell God how much you love and need Him. Be quiet in His presence for the remainder of the time and you will be refreshed in an amazing way.

GOD'S WORD FOR YOU TODAY: Don't get burned out or stressed out; take time to be refreshed in the presence of the Lord.

Do Good Works

We are God's [own] handiwork (His workmanship), recreated in
Christ Jesus, [born anew] that we may do those good works which
God predestined (planned beforehand) for us. (EPHESIANS 2:10)

Years ago, when I first started walking more intimately with God, I used to wait for some special confirmation from Him for everything I wanted to do—until I learned that His Spirit abides in me to do good works. In the early years of walking with God, it was in my heart to give ten dollars to a woman in need. I carried that desire in my heart for three weeks until I finally prayed, "God, is it really You telling me to give this person the money? I'll do it if it's *really* You!" Ten dollars was a lot of money back then and I did not want to part with it unless I had clear direction from God.

He spoke to me so clearly and responded, "Joyce, even if it isn't *really* Me, I won't get mad at you if you bless somebody!"

One of the fruits of the fact that God's Spirit lives within us is goodness (see Galatians 5:22–23). Therefore, we have desires to be good to people. God told Abraham that He was going to bless him so he could be a blessing to others (see Genesis 12:2). Imagine how awesome it would be to reach the point where we simply live to make others happy as a service to God.

The world is full of people with needs. There is always someone, somewhere, who needs a word of encouragement. Someone needs a babysitter, help with transportation, or financial help. I find that when I spend time with God I feel a strong desire to help somebody and I have learned that desire is God speaking to me. God is good and when we spend time with Him we want to do good things for others.

Ask God each day to show you whom you can bless and remember that where love is, God abides (see 1 John 4:12).

GOD'S WORD FOR YOU TODAY: Take advantage of every opportunity you have to do something good.

Anyone Can Enter

By this fresh (new) and living way which He initiated and dedicated and opened for us through the separating curtain (veil of the Holy of Holies), that is, through His flesh. (HEBREWS 10:19–20)

When Jesus died, the temple veil that separated the Holy Place from the Most Holy Place was torn from the top to the bottom (see Mark 15:37–38). That opened a way for anyone to go into God's presence. Prior to Jesus' death, only the high priest could go into God's presence and then only once a year with the blood of slain animals, to cover and atone for his sins and the sins of the people.

It is significant that the tear in the veil of the temple was from top to bottom. The veil, or curtain, was so high and so thick that no human could have torn it—it was torn supernaturally by the power of God, showing that He was opening a new and living way for His people to approach Him, as we read in today's verses.

From the beginning, God has desired fellowship with man; that was His purpose in creating us. He never wanted to close people off from His presence, but He knew that His holiness was so powerful that it would destroy anything unholy that came near it. Therefore, the way for sinners to be completely cleansed had to be provided prior to man's having access to God's presence.

We are in the world, but we are not to be of the world (see John 17:14–16). Our worldliness and earthly ways separate us from God's presence and can keep us from hearing His voice. Unless we are constantly receiving by faith the sacrifice of Jesus' blood to keep us clean, we cannot enjoy intimacy and come into proper fellowship with God.

GOD'S WORD FOR YOU TODAY: God wants to fellowship with you; enter His presence freely today.

Help!

I the Lord your God hold your right hand; I am the Lord, Who says to you, Fear not; I will help you! (ISAIAH 41:13)

No matter how well we may think we run our lives, the truth is that we need help with everything. We need all kinds of help in our everyday lives. Often, realizing how much help we need takes a long time. We like to believe we can do whatever needs to be done independently and without assistance. However, the Lord sent us a Divine Helper; therefore, we must need help. Jesus Himself continually intercedes for us as He sits at the right hand of God (see Hebrews 7:25; Romans 8:34), and that tells us that we continually need God's intervention in our lives. We are actually very needy and totally unable to handle life properly on our own.

Although we may seem to manage ourselves and our lives well for a while, sooner or later something happens and things begin to fall apart if we are living in our own strength instead of receiving divine help.

Many times, we do fine until trouble comes. It may come in the form of a broken marriage, the death of a loved one, the loss of a job, or something else that is important to us. But eventually, we all reach a point where we have to recognize our neediness.

If we want to live life the way God intended—filled with righteousness, peace, and joy (see Romans 14:17), we have to admit that we need help and we have to receive it from the Holy Spirit, the One God sent to help us.

———————

GOD'S WORD FOR YOU TODAY: Admit your need for help and trust the Holy Spirit to help you.

God Speaks to His Friends

*The Lord said, Shall I hide from Abraham [My friend and servant]
what I am going to do?* (GENESIS 18:17)

Perhaps no one is more often referred to as "God's friend" than Abraham. While the Bible refers to David as "a man after God's own heart" and to John as "the disciple Jesus loved," Abraham has the distinct honor of being called the *friend* of God in more than one place in Scripture.

When God decided to execute judgment on the wickedness of the people of Sodom and Gomorrah, He told Abraham what He planned to do.

In a friendship, people tell each other about what they are going to do. Because God considered Abraham His friend, He told him what He was going to do—just like you would tell your friend what you are going to do. When Abraham heard about the devastation God intended to release against Sodom and Gomorrah, he "came near and said, 'Would You also destroy the righteous with the wicked?'" (Genesis 18:23 NKJV). Just as God had shared His plans with Abraham because they were friends, Abraham "came near" to God and spoke openly and boldly about His plans—because they were friends. They had a relationship in which they could communicate freely; they could talk openly. The type of intimacy Abraham enjoyed with God comes from being secure in His love.

God wants to be your friend, too—to speak to you and to listen to what you have to say to Him. Begin today to accept in a whole new way the fact that you are God's friend and that you can approach Him as such.

GOD'S WORD FOR YOU TODAY: Develop a relationship with God in which you can speak freely to Him and you can easily hear what He speaks to you.

All Things Work Together for Good

We are assured and know that [God being a partner in their labor]
all things work together and are [fitting into a plan] for good to and
for those who love God and are called according to [His] design and
purpose. (ROMANS 8:28)

When God speaks to us and we obey, we do so by faith. We often
have no circumstance in the natural realm to let us know whether we
are doing the right thing or the wrong thing. This is how faith works.
We have to step out believing, not knowing in the natural sense, that
we are following God. We have to act, believing we have heard His
voice. Experience with God is a great teacher and often we will never
know if we were right or not unless we "step out and find out."

Sometimes we may be wrong. We might make a mistake. That
thought can be frightening, so we often think, *It is better to be safe than*
sorry. But if we do that, we will soon be miserable if God has truly told
us to move forward. Not only will we be miserable, but we will live boring, uneventful lives. We hunger for adventure, but fear will keep us
from ever knowing the joy of it.

I have discovered that if our hearts are right and we do the best we
know to do in our journey of learning to hear from God, He will honor
our efforts and steps of obedience. If we move in childlike trust to obey
what we believe in our hearts He has told us to do, then even if we don't
do everything exactly right, God will make even our mistakes work for
our good.

———————

GOD'S WORD FOR YOU TODAY: God is working everything out for your good.

Step Out and Find Out

*A wide door of opportunity for effectual [service] has opened to me
[there, a great and promising one], and [there are] many adversaries.*

(1 CORINTHIANS 16:9)

Sometimes the only way to discover God's will is to practice what I call "stepping out and finding out." If I have prayed about a situation and still don't seem to know what to do, I simply take a step of faith. God has shown me that trusting Him is like standing before an automatic door at a supermarket. We can stand and look at the door all day, but it won't open until we take a step forward and trigger the mechanism that opens it.

There are times in life when we must take a step forward in order to find out, one way or the other, what we should do. Some doors open as soon as we take a step of faith and others never open no matter what we do. When God opens the door, then go through it. If He does not open the door, then be satisfied to take another direction. But do not let fear trap you in total inactivity.

In the verse for today, Paul mentions the door of opportunity before him, but he also mentions "many adversaries," so we must be sure we don't mistake opposition for a closed door.

Paul and his coworkers, Silas and Barnabas, did not sit and wait for an angel to appear or a vision to come from heaven while they were seeking God's will. They took steps in the direction they felt was right. Many times God did open doors for them, but there were times when He closed doors. This did not discourage them, but they simply kept going forward in faith, searching for what God wanted them to do.

GOD'S WORD FOR YOU TODAY: Walk boldly through the doors God opens for you, and don't become discouraged when He closes one.

The Baptism in the Holy Spirit

If you then, evil as you are, know how to give good gifts [gifts that are to their advantage] to your children, how much more will your heavenly Father give the Holy Spirit to those who ask and continue to ask Him! (LUKE 11:13)

Today's verse promises that God will give the Holy Spirit to those who ask Him. You can ask God to fill you and baptize you in the Holy Spirit right now, right where you are. Here is a prayer you may want to use:

"Father, in Jesus' name, I ask You to baptize me in the Holy Spirit with all the evidence that accompanies being filled with the Spirit. Grant me boldness as You did those who were filled on the Day of Pentecost, and give me any other spiritual gifts You desire for me to have."

Now, you may want to confirm your faith by saying out loud, "I believe I have been filled with the Holy Spirit, and I will never be the same again."

If you have prayed the prayer above, or a similar one, wait on God quietly and believe that you have received what you have asked for. If you don't believe you have received, then even if you have received, it will be to you as though you have not. I want to stress again the importance of believing by faith that you have received, not making your decision based on how you feel. Throughout the day, meditate on the fact that God lives in you and through Him you can do anything you need to do.

Being filled with the Holy Spirit is one of the most wonderful things that can ever happen to a believer. His presence gives you courage, hope, peace, joy, wisdom, and many other wonderful things. Seek Him with your whole heart daily.

GOD'S WORD FOR YOU TODAY: Be sure that you seek God for Himself and the joy of His presence, and not merely for what He can do for you.

A Partner in Life

I know that [the determination of] the way of a man is not in himself;
it is not in man [even in a strong man or in a man at his best] to
direct his [own] steps. (JEREMIAH 10:23)

Jeremiah spoke the truth in the verse for today. It really is impossible for us human beings to properly run our own lives. You and I need help, and a lot of it. Admitting that is a sign of spiritual maturity, not a sign of weakness. We are weak unless we find our strength in God, and the sooner we face that fact, the better off we will be.

You may be like I once was—trying so hard to make things work out right and always failing. Your problem is not that you are a failure; your problem is simply that you have not gone to the right source for help.

God won't allow us to truly succeed without Him. Remember that true success is not just the ability to accumulate material wealth; it is the ability to truly enjoy life and everything God provides in it. Many people have position, finances, power, fame, and other similar things, but they may not have what really matters—good relationships, right standing with God, peace, joy, contentment, satisfaction, good health, and the ability to enjoy life.

According to Psalm 127:1, unless the Lord builds the house, those who build it labor in vain. We may be able to build, but what we build will not last if God is not involved in it. He is our Partner in life, and as such, He desires to be part of everything we do. God is interested in every facet of our lives and He wants to speak to us about everything that concerns us. Believing this truth is the beginning of an exciting journey with Him.

GOD'S WORD FOR YOU TODAY: Let God be your Partner in life.

Lean on Him

We have heard of your faith in Christ Jesus [the leaning of your entire human personality on Him in absolute trust and confidence in His power, wisdom, and goodness] and of the love which you [have and show] for all the saints. (COLOSSIANS 1:4)

God wants us to lean entirely on Him and to hear and obey His voice above all others; that is what faith really is. I love the definition of faith given in the verse for today and the fact that we lean everything about ourselves on the Lord.

We can lean on God to keep us in His will. I am glad about that because trying to stay in God's will through our own strength is too difficult! I don't know even one person who can honestly say he or she knows with 100 percent certainty what to do each day.

We can do everything we know to do to make right decisions. How can we know if we are right? We can't. We have to trust God to keep us in His will, straighten out any crooked paths in front of us, keep us on the narrow path that leads to life, and keep us off the broad path that leads to destruction (see Matthew 7:13).

We need to pray, "God, Your will be done in my life." I know some things about God's will for my life, but I don't know everything, so I have learned to stay at rest and peace by leaning on God and committing myself to Him and praying for His will to be done in and through me.

Sometimes we think only weak or frail people lean, but I have learned that leaning is a good thing if we are leaning on God.

GOD'S WORD FOR YOU TODAY: Lean on God completely today.

We Have to Ask

It must be in faith that he asks with no wavering (no hesitating, no doubting). (JAMES 1:6)

If we read the New Testament book of James, we will see that James opens by telling us how to handle life's problems and trials. There is a natural way of dealing with these things, but there is also a spiritual way to handle them.

In James 1:5–6, James basically says, "If you are having trouble, ask God what you should do." You may not hear His voice and receive an answer immediately, but if you ask in faith, you will find as you go about your business a wisdom operating through you that is divine and beyond your natural knowledge.

In Psalm 23:2, the psalmist says that God leads His people into green pastures and beside still and restful waters. In other words, God will always lead us to a place of peace and safety if we seek Him.

Look back at today's verse and notice that we have to ask in faith. All too often we do not receive help because we do not ask for it. The Holy Spirit is a gentleman; He waits until we invite Him into our situations. We cannot assume and presume; we have to ask!

———————————

GOD'S WORD FOR YOU TODAY: When you need something, ask God for it.

Be a True Worshipper

A time will come, however, indeed it is already here, when the true (genuine) worshippers will worship the Father in spirit and in truth (reality); for the Father is seeking just such people as these as His worshippers. (JOHN 4:23)

The world often thinks of worship as "religion," which could not be further from the biblical concept of worship. When people ask, "Where do you worship?" they often simply want to know where we go to church. When we read about worship in the Bible, we are reading about a personal relationship with a God we can speak to and Who speaks to us. We are reading about spiritual intimacy and passionate expressions of devotion from people who love and worship God with all of their hearts. This is true worship—the kind that bubbles up out of us when we have zeal and enthusiasm for God in our lives.

According to today's verse, God is seeking true, genuine worshippers who will really worship Him with all their hearts.

I have always been saddened by the fact that God has to seek true worshippers. I think there should be an abundance of us! But I find it interesting that He does not want just anybody to worship Him; He wants *true* and *genuine* worshippers. He is not looking for people who will worship Him out of fear or obligation, but out of a loving relationship.

True worship is much more than attending a church service and singing songs. We should worship God with our entire lives, doing all that we do for and through Him. Sincere worship comes out of intimacy with God and it makes us sensitive to hear His voice.

GOD'S WORD FOR YOU TODAY: Don't worship out of fear; worship out of love.

Make People a Priority

Far be it from me that I should sin against the Lord by ceasing to pray for you. (1 SAMUEL 12:23)

One key to effective prayer is to focus on others and not obsess about our own needs. We can certainly pray for ourselves and ask God to meet our needs, but we need to avoid praying for ourselves all the time. Prayers of self-indulgence—selfish, self-centered prayers—are not effective, so we really need to make sure that we spend time praying for other people also. I am constantly hearing of four or five people who need prayer, and just when some of those prayers are answered, I will become aware of other people to pray for. Your life is probably similar. You hear of someone who recently lost a loved one, someone who needs a job, somebody who needs a place to live, somebody who just received a bad report from the doctor, someone whose child is sick, or somebody whose spouse just walked out.

People have all kinds of needs, and they need our prayers. God wants us to pray for one another with sincere love and compassion. When we pray for other people we are sowing seeds that will bring a harvest in our own lives. I remember a woman who told me that she attended one of my conferences where I prayed for sick people to be healed. Even though she had leukemia, she began to pray for others to be healed and did not even think to pray for herself. The following week she had a doctor's appointment and after a checkup and blood tests she was told that although they did not understand what happened, she no longer had the disease.

GOD'S WORD FOR YOU TODAY: The more you reach out to others, the more God reaches out to you.

Hold Fast to Hope

Whatever was thus written in former days was written for our instruction, that by [our steadfast and patient] endurance and the encouragement [drawn] from the Scriptures we might hold fast to and cherish hope. (ROMANS 15:4)

We all need to be encouraged. Sometimes we need encouragement to lift us out of the pit of discouragement, but at all times we can use an affirming word, a ray of hope, or a message that says to us, "You can do it!"

God Himself is the best source of encouragement I know and we should seek encouragement and hope from Him. He encourages us through His Spirit, but He also speaks encouragement to us through His Word. Many times, when I need to be encouraged or strengthened in hope, I go to the Bible. I have several favorite passages I read or meditate on when I need strength, support, or encouragement.

God's Word is filled with encouragement and as long as we have a Bible we have a prescription for encouragement. One translation states that the Word of God is the medicine we need.

Go to God's Word when you need to be encouraged—when you are hurting, frustrated, disappointed, confused, or weary. Let His words sink into your heart and mind as you wait in His presence. God will never fail you and you can always depend on His Word, especially when you need hope and encouragement.

GOD'S WORD FOR YOU TODAY: No matter what you do today, keep holding on to hope.

You Have an Advocate

Who shall bring any charge against God's elect [when it is] God Who justifies [that is, Who puts us in right relation to Himself? Who shall come forward and accuse or impeach those whom God has chosen?].

(ROMANS 8:33)

The Holy Spirit is our Advocate. If we trace the word *advocate* back to its original meaning in biblical Greek, we find that He is called to come to our aid; He is appointed by God to assist us, come to our defense, or plead our cause.

The Holy Spirit is literally called to our side to give us aid in every way. When we need to be defended, He defends us, acting as a legal assistant would for a client. It is good to know that we don't have to defend ourselves when we are accused of some wrong action or motive. We can ask for help from the Holy One and expect to receive it because He is our Advocate. That thought alone should bring us comfort and encouragement.

Most of us spend a great deal of time and energy trying to defend ourselves, our reputations, our positions, our actions, our words, and our decisions. We are truly wasting our time. When others are judgmental toward us, we may finally after much effort convince them of our purity of heart. But the problem lies in the fact that if they are judgmental in nature or character, they will quickly find something else to judge us for. The best course of action is for us to pray and let the Holy Spirit do His job and be our Advocate and Defense.

GOD'S WORD FOR YOU TODAY: The Holy Spirit is your Advocate and Defense.

Think First

You ought to be quiet (keep yourselves in check) and to do nothing rashly. (ACTS 19:36)

Committing to do something without asking God about it and waiting for Him to speak to us is not wise; nor is it wise to jump into things without thinking first about what we are getting ready to do. We often obligate ourselves to too many things and end up weary and worn out. God certainly strengthens us through His Spirit, but He doesn't strengthen us to do things that are outside of His will for us. He won't strengthen us to be foolish! Once we commit to do something, God expects us to keep our word and be people of integrity, so His advice to us in the verse for today is to "think before we speak." In our thinking, we ought to ask God what He thinks about the matter we have under consideration.

This is certainly a lesson I have had to learn. I used to allow enthusiasm to get the best of me and say yes to things without asking for God's advice and then end up complaining about my schedule. God had to let me know that if I had sought Him first and followed His guidance, I could have avoided being frustrated and stressed.

I am sure you have many opportunities to get involved in things you would enjoy or consider important. I simply encourage you today not to commit to anything without giving it serious thought and without seeking God's guidance concerning whether or not He would have you do these things.

———————

GOD'S WORD FOR YOU TODAY: Think before you speak!

Look to Jesus

*Looking away [from all that will distract] to Jesus, Who is the Leader
and the Source of our faith [giving the first incentive for our belief]
and is also its Finisher [bringing it to maturity and perfection].*

(HEBREWS 12:1–2)

Many things we want and need to know about God's will are clear to
us in the pages of His Word. However, there are certain specific questions we may have that are not answered for us in Scripture. If I'm praying for something that's not clearly covered in the Word of God, if I'm
facing a decision that I can't find chapter and verse to lead me through,
then I pray this way:

"God, I want this, but I want Your will more than I want my own. So
if my request is not in Your timing, or if what I'm asking for is not what
You want for me, then please don't give it to me. Amen."

We can get emotionally driven to do something that seems like it
is from God, but after we start it, we may find that perhaps it is just a
good idea that doesn't have a hope without God's help to make it successful. But God is not obligated to finish anything He doesn't origi-
nate. We can pray about the projects we start, but there is no point in
getting mad at God if He won't finish them for us. He is not obligated to
finish anything He does not author! Be very careful about starting anything just because it seems like a good idea. Good things are often the
enemy of the best that God has for us. When an idea comes to you, take
the time to check with God to see if your spirit bears witness before you
actually take action.

GOD'S WORD FOR YOU TODAY: Make sure your good
ideas are God-ideas!

Little Things, Big Things

Cause me to hear Your loving-kindness in the morning, for on You do I lean and in You do I trust. Cause me to know the way wherein I should walk, for I lift up my inner self to You. (PSALM 143:8)

One of the ways I learned to trust God and hear His voice in the big events and decisions in my life was to hear Him in the little things. One time Dave and I got ready to watch a movie with some family members, but we couldn't find the remote control. We didn't know how to play the movie without it, so everyone searched diligently for it, but we still couldn't locate it.

I decided to pray. So I said silently in my heart, "Holy Spirit, please show me where the remote control is." Immediately, I thought of the bathroom—and that's where we found it.

The same thing happened to me with my car keys. I had looked everywhere, but to no avail. Then I prayed, and in my spirit I saw the keys on the front seat of my car, which is exactly where they were.

These two stories are examples of a gift of the Holy Spirit called "word of knowledge" (1 Corinthians 12:8). God gave me words of knowledge concerning the remote control and my misplaced keys. This gift and others are available to everyone who is filled with the Holy Spirit. The gifts are supernatural endowments of power given to believers to help us live our natural lives in supernatural ways.

God loves us. He cares enough to speak to us (in my case, His "speaking" was to give me a thought about the remote and show me a picture or a vision about my car keys) about the little things in our lives. Just think how eager He must be to talk to us about the bigger things also.

GOD'S WORD FOR YOU TODAY: Remember that God cares about you so much that He wants to speak to you about even the little things in your life.

Promises, Promises

No unbelief or distrust made him waver (doubtingly question) con-
cerning the promise of God, but he grew strong and was empowered
by faith as he gave praise and glory to God. (ROMANS 4:20)

In Genesis 17:16, God spoke to Abraham and promised him an heir.
But the problem was that Abraham and his wife, Sarah, were both
old—*really* old. He was one hundred years old and she was ninety, so
their childbearing years were long gone! But Abraham knew God had
spoken and was determined not to focus on the natural impossibility
that he and Sarah could have a child. Instead, he planted his faith in
God's promise and held on to that promise by praising God, as we read
in today's verse.

Let me say again that, naturally speaking, Abraham had absolutely
no reason to hope. In fact, if any situation has ever been beyond hope,
it would be the possibility of two people past ninety being able to have
a biological child. Nevertheless, Abraham kept hoping; he kept believing God's promise. He looked at his circumstances and was well aware
of the odds that were piled against him, but he still did not give up,
even though the Bible says that his body was "as good as dead" and
that Sarah's womb was barren and "deadened." In the face of a genuine
natural impossibility, Abraham did not give in to unbelief; he did not
waver in his faith or question God's promise. Instead, "he grew strong
and was empowered by faith" as he praised God.

If God has spoken promises to you and you are still waiting for them
to be fulfilled, be like Abraham: remember what God has said and keep
praising Him.

GOD'S WORD FOR YOU TODAY: Praise God while you're
waiting for His promises to be fulfilled.

God Helps Us Grow

Let us not become vainglorious and self-conceited, competitive and challenging and provoking and irritating to one another, envying and being jealous of one another. (GALATIANS 5:26)

Every person's relationship with God and ability to hear His voice is different, so feel free to pursue communication with Him in the way He leads you. A relationship with God is not about laboring or striving or trying to perform; it's simply about talking to Him and listening to His voice. We do not need to try to be where someone else is or hear God with the clarity and accuracy someone else has because that person may be enjoying a relationship with God that has taken years of practice and we may not be as far along in our walk with God as that person is. It's all right for us to be "younger" than others spiritually; God still hears and answers us, no matter the extent of our experience. Comparing ourselves with others only makes us miserable. God is happy simply because we are learning and growing.

Comparing yourself with others will hinder your spiritual growth. God knows you intimately and He has a personalized plan for your advancement. He knows your background, what you have experienced, your disappointments, and your pain. He also knows just what it will take to make you completely whole and you can be assured that He is working in you as long as you are seeking Him.

I have four children who are all very different and I don't expect them to be anything other than what they are. I have learned that God is the same way with us. Be yourself, enjoy yourself, and enjoy the level of spiritual growth you have attained so far.

GOD'S WORD FOR YOU TODAY: Enjoy where you are on the way to where you're going.

God Is Listening

Those who feared the Lord talked often one to another; and the Lord listened and heard it, and a book of remembrance was written before Him of those who reverenced and worshipfully feared the Lord and who thought on His name. (MALACHI 3:16)

Today's verse says God likes conversations in which we talk about how good He is. When He hears them, He gets out His book of remembrance and records them. He does not record our murmuring, grumbling, or complaining, but He records the words we speak when praise is on our lips.

Just think about how you would feel if you overheard your children saying, "Our mom is awesome. We have the greatest mother in the world. Don't we have the most incredible mom and dad? They're the best parents around!" I am sure that if you witnessed such a conversation between your children, you could hardly wait to bless them.

But, on the other hand, what if you walked into a room and your children were saying, "I'm so sick and tired of Mom and Dad. They never do anything for us. They've got all these rules. They don't want us to have any fun. Mom always nags us and makes us do our homework. If our parents really loved us, they would give us what we want, not what they think is best."

Our lives with God are no different than the two scenarios I have described above. We are God's children! He hears everything we say and He knows what is in our hearts even when we don't say it. What does He want to hear us talking about? How great He is! How awesome He is! The wonderful things He's done, can do, and will do! Speak well of God, from your heart, and you create an atmosphere for God to speak to you.

GOD'S WORD FOR YOU TODAY: Say things you will be glad for God to overhear today.

The Holy Spirit Intercedes for You

The Spirit also helps in our weaknesses. For we do not know what we should pray for as we ought, but the Spirit Himself makes intercession for us with groanings which cannot be uttered.

(ROMANS 8:26 NKJV)

God's Word teaches us that only the Spirit of God knows God's thoughts accurately and for that reason we need Him to intercede for us and lead us in our intercession and prayers.

If we are to pray according to God's will, which I believe you want to do, we need to know what God is thinking and what He wants. Many times, we can't perceive those things, but the Holy Spirit does, so He intercedes on our behalf. I do the best I can in prayer, but I am very grateful to know that the Holy Spirit is my prayer partner and He is praying for me. We also know by the Word of God that no matter what happens in our lives we can trust God to work it out for good as long as we keep praying, loving God, and desiring His will.

The verse for today, Romans 8:26, is quickly followed by Romans 8:28, which says: "We are assured and know that [God being a partner in their labor] all things work together and are [fitting into a plan] for good to and for those who love God and are called according to [His] design and purpose." What a comfort it is to know that God has sent His Holy Spirit to help us in everything, including prayer. There is no situation that He cannot work for good. As you pray today ask the Holy Spirit to help you. Even if you're hurting so deeply that all you can do is groan, the Holy Spirit can even articulate that accurately to God and bring your answer. You have a Divine Helper Who is with you all the time, so be sure to call on Him often.

GOD'S WORD FOR YOU TODAY: You can trust the Holy Spirit to intercede perfectly for you.

The Source of Your Strength

The Lord is my Strength and my Song, and He has become my Salvation; this is my God, and I will praise Him, my father's God, and I will exalt Him (EXODUS 15:2)

We need to be like Moses and the Israelites, whom we read about in the verse for today. I want to point out that God not only *gave* them strength (we see that throughout the Old Testament), but He Himself *was* their Strength. First Samuel 15:29 refers to God as "the Strength of Israel." You see, there was a time when Israel knew God was their Strength, but then they forgot. When they forgot this vitally important truth, they always began to falter and fail as a nation, and their lives began to be destroyed. When they turned back to God as their Strength, things turned around for them.

Even if you know that God is your Strength, you still must receive it by faith. I begin every day by telling God that I cannot do anything apart from Him and that I lean entirely on Him to enable and strengthen me. He will strengthen us by speaking a word that encourages us or gives us direction when we need it. He will strengthen us by speaking words of wisdom and insight. He also strengthens us physically by giving us supernatural energy when we are tired or weary, and He gives us strength to endure difficult people and situations.

Trust God to be your Strength rather than trying to do things yourself. You may have a lot of people leaning on you and you can only help them as you lean and rely on God. Receive Him today by faith as the Strength of your life and you will be amazed at what you can accomplish with ease.

GOD'S WORD FOR YOU TODAY: Let God *be* your Strength.

A Heart to Obey

This day the Lord your God has commanded you to do these statutes and ordinances. Therefore you shall keep and do them with all your [mind and] heart and with all your being. (DEUTERONOMY 26:16)

One of the best ways to ensure a deepening friendship with God is to have a heart that wants to obey Him. When our hearts are pure, tender toward His leading, and eager to respond obediently, we are in a terrific position to experience God's friendship and hear His voice. God knows that we will not arrive at a place of perfection while we are on this Earth, but we can and should have perfect hearts toward Him, hearts that seek and crave to do what is right to please and glorify God.

As you grow in your friendship with God, never forget that your relationship must be based on Who He is and not on what He can do for you. Keep seeking His presence, not His presents; keep seeking His face and not His hand, because one of the hindrances to a vibrant, maturing friendship with God is allowing ourselves to focus on the benefits of friendship with God instead of focusing on *Him* as our friend. As human beings, we do not appreciate finding out that certain people want to be our friends because we have an ability to get them something they want; we feel valued when we know people have a right heart attitude toward us and that they want to be friends with us simply because of who we are and just because they enjoy us. The same principle applies with God.

GOD'S WORD FOR YOU TODAY: Base your relationship with God on Who He is, not on what He can do for you.

Whose Voice Are You Listening To?

*I appeal to you therefore, brethren, and beg of you in view of [all]
the mercies of God, to make a decisive dedication of your bodies
[presenting all your members and faculties] as a living sacrifice, holy
(devoted, consecrated) and well pleasing to God.* (ROMANS 12:1)

In order to obey the verse for today, we have to choose to give the Lord
our "members and faculties." In other words, we offer Him our bodies, minds, abilities, and emotions. We must be careful not to let the
devil use our minds. The human mind is his favorite battleground and
he will fire thoughts at us all day long, thoughts that will drown out
the voice of God if we choose to listen to them. The thoughts the devil
sends us are usually sly, subtle, and deceptive so we will find them
easy to believe. He lies and accuses and tells us anything he can think
of to steal our joy, rob our peace, and make us feel ashamed, guilty,
and unworthy. He fills our minds with ungodly thoughts about other
people. We cannot stop him from sending thoughts our way, but we
can resist them in the power of Christ. Then we can deliberately turn
our thoughts toward God and the things He speaks to us.

To be honest, there are days when I have to cast down a dozen
thoughts just in the time it takes to put on my makeup! But, thank
God, I know how to do it. You can do it, too. Think of it this way: two
voices are competing for your attention. You can focus on one or the
other. Choose to hear the voice of God and to think about the things
He says, not the things the enemy says. When we fill our thoughts with
right things, the wrong ones have no room to enter.

GOD'S WORD FOR YOU TODAY: Give your mind to God
and focus on the thoughts He speaks to you.

Choose to Surrender

Those whom He foreknew … He also destined from the beginning [foreordaining them] to be molded into the image of His Son.

(ROMANS 8:29)

According to the verse for today, one of God's goals in our lives is to make us become like Jesus. He wants us to continue to become more like Jesus in our thoughts, in our words, in the way we treat other people, in our personal lives, and in our actions. Becoming like Jesus does not happen overnight; it's a process we have to choose to embrace.

Remember yesterday's verse, Romans 12:1: "I appeal to you therefore, brethren, and beg of you in view of [all] the mercies of God, to make a decisive dedication…" This means we have to make a deliberate decision to give ourselves to God. God has given us a free will, and the only way we will ever belong to Him completely is to give ourselves freely to Him. He will never force us to love Him or serve Him. He will speak to us, lead us, guide us, and prompt us, but He will always leave the decision to surrender up to us.

God created human beings, not robots, and He will not try to program us to behave a certain way because He has given us the freedom to make our own choices—and He wants us to choose Him. He wants us to willingly put our lives before Him every day and say, "God, Your will be done, not mine." That short, simple prayer is extremely powerful when we really mean it, and it represents the kind of full surrender God requires. If God has been speaking to you or dealing with you about anything, I encourage you not to put off surrendering it any longer. Choose to obey His voice and surrender today. Ask Him to be your Strength and remember that through Him you can do all things.

GOD'S WORD FOR YOU TODAY: Choose to surrender to God.

Pray in Agreement; Live in Agreement

Blessed (enjoying enviable happiness, spiritually prosperous—with life-joy and satisfaction in God's favor and salvation, regardless of their outward conditions) are the makers and maintainers of peace, for they shall be called the sons of God! (MATTHEW 5:9)

The prayer of agreement is effective only when those who agree in prayer are living in agreement in their natural, everyday lives. Living in agreement does not mean never having our own opinions, but it does mean that there is harmony, mutual respect, and honor in our relationships. It means an absence of the things that cause division and strife—like selfishness, anger, resentment, jealousy, bitterness, or comparison. Living in agreement is like being on the same ball team—everyone works together, supports and encourages each other, believes in and trusts each other as they all pursue the same goal and share the victory.

The prayer of agreement is very powerful, but it can be used effectively only by those who make the effort to live in agreement. For example, if Dave and I argued and had strife most of the time, but wanted to pray in agreement when we had a pressing need, then that would not work. There is no power in agreeing occasionally; we must live in agreement. Live with others respectfully and peacefully. Adapt and adjust yourself to people and things in order to be a maker and maintainer of peace (see Romans 12:16).

Maintaining unity and harmony does require effort, but the power released when people pray who live in agreement is worth it.

GOD'S WORD FOR YOU TODAY: It is easier not to get upset than it is to calm down after you have gotten upset.

Follow the Law of Love

You, brethren, were [indeed] called to freedom; only [do not let your] freedom be an incentive to your flesh and an opportunity or excuse [for selfishness], but through love you should serve one another.

(GALATIANS 5:13)

Sometimes as we go through life, we hurt people without even knowing we are doing it. I am a very straightforward individual and that is a good quality, but I have also had to learn to be sensitive to what others are going through as I approach them in conversation. What we say at one time may be totally inappropriate at another time. We are indeed set free by Christ and have the right to be ourselves, but the law of love demands that our freedoms not be used as an excuse to be selfish.

Just because we feel like saying or doing a thing does not mean it is the best thing for the situation we are in. If you were talking to a person who had been sick for quite a long time, that would not be the best time to tell them how good you always feel. Or, if you were talking to a person who just lost their job, that would not be the best time to tell them about the pay raise and promotion you just received. Jesus died so we might enjoy freedom, yet He also makes it clear in His Word that we should serve one another through love.

GOD'S WORD FOR YOU TODAY: If you make others happy, you will be happier yourself.

What Do You Want, God?

Who then is willing to consecrate himself this day to the LORD?
(1 CHRONICLES 29:5 NKJV)

Christians become dangerous to the enemy when they start living consecrated lives that are fully dedicated and sold out to God. This kind of devotion means we offer everything we are and have to God; we cannot hold anything back. When we consecrate ourselves, we invite God to speak to us and deal with us about any area He chooses to address in our lives.

If we really are serious about being set apart for God's use, we must ask ourselves if there are any areas of our lives in which we are holding out on God. What little, hidden secret places do we have in our hearts? What are the things about which we say, "Well, God, You can have everything but *that*," or "Oh, no, God! I'm not ready for *that!*" or "God, just don't touch *that* relationship yet," or "Lord, just don't ask me to quit doing *that*"? Full consecration is not saying, "Lord, I'll read my Bible every day; I'll memorize verses and hide Your Word in my heart and pray many hours a day, but please do not ask me to give up my one little favorite vice!" No, full consecration is saying and meaning with all of your heart: "I give myself—entirely—to You, Lord. Speak to me and tell me what You want."

I don't mean to sound as if we should expect God to take everything we enjoy away from us, because He won't do that. But, everything must be available to Him. He must make the choices about what is really good for us and what is not; our job is to trust Him completely.

GOD'S WORD FOR YOU TODAY: Be entirely available to God, holding nothing back from Him.

Want to Know God's Will?

In everything give thanks; for this is the will of God in Christ Jesus for you. (1 THESSALONIANS 5:18 NKJV)

One of the main reasons many people want to hear God's voice is that they want Him to tell them what His will is for their lives. Sometimes people treat God's will like the world's most complicated mystery and say things like, "Well, if I only knew God's will, I would obey," or "I really want to follow God; I'm just not sure what His will is."

I cannot say whether or not God's will is for you to move to Minneapolis, change jobs, or take the lead role in the Easter play at church, but I can give you one absolutely certain way to know and obey God's will for your life: be thankful. Be thankful—all the time, no matter what you go through. That's right; just keep a grateful heart in every circumstance and it will open the way for clearer direction in all other things. Sometimes thanksgiving comes easily and sometimes it is difficult, but if you will develop and maintain an *attitude* of thanksgiving, you'll be in God's will. Notice that the verse above does not instruct us to just be thankful *for* everything; it tells us to be thankful *in* everything. For example, let's say you open the refrigerator one day and see that the light is out and your food is not as cold as it should be. You don't have to start thanking God that the refrigerator is broken, but you can be thankful that you have a refrigerator and that you have food to put in it. It means being thankful that it can be repaired and keeping a grateful heart while you are waiting for it to be fixed. I encourage you to practice thanksgiving as you go through your day today and every day.

GOD'S WORD FOR YOU TODAY: Give thanks in everything.

We Need the Holy Spirit

*The grace (favor and spiritual blessing) of the Lord Jesus Christ and
the love of God and the presence and fellowship (the communion and
sharing together and participation) in the Holy Spirit be with you all.*

(2 CORINTHIANS 13:14)

Before Jesus' death on the cross, He spoke to His disciples and tried
to prepare them for life without Him. He told them that when He went
away, the Father would send another Comforter, the Holy Spirit who
would live in them—counseling, helping, strengthening, interceding,
being an advocate, convicting of sin, and convincing of righteousness.
The Holy Spirit would come into close fellowship with them, guide
them into all truth, and transmit to them everything that was theirs as
joint heirs with Jesus Christ (see John 16:7–15; Romans 8:17).

As you can see, God's intention in sending the Holy Spirit to us was
for us to develop intimate relationships with Him and be able to receive
everything He offers us. If we are going to allow Him to comfort us,
counsel us, teach us, and do the other things God has promised He
will do, we have to listen for His voice because part of the way He ministers to us, leads us, and helps us is to speak to us.

We need the Holy Spirit in our lives, and God has given Him to us.
Our fellowship with Him can be as close and deep as we want it to be.
All we have to do is take time to be with Him, ask Him to speak, and
open our hearts to His words.

GOD'S WORD FOR YOU TODAY: Your relationship with
God can be as deep and close as you want it to be.

Quiet, Please

Commit your works to the Lord, and your thoughts will be established. (PROVERBS 16:3 NKJV)

God intervenes in our lives when we ask Him to. When we stop trying to do our own thing in our own way, He takes over. When does God really begin to speak to us intimately and powerfully? When we stop talking and start listening. Instead of trying to solve our own problems, worrying and fretting over them, we should quietly listen to what God has to say.

The verse for today mentions our "works." Many times, our works are the things we "work" in our minds—our reasoning, our analyzing, and our attempts to figure out what is going on or what we should do. God says that if we will commit our works to Him, our thoughts will be established. In other words, if we can get our minds to calm down, we will be clearheaded and God can give us ideas and speak to us about innovative strategies and directions.

Once I was upset and fretting over what to do about a problem I had and I was getting no answer. I finally got quiet and asked God what I should do and He simply said, "Do what you would tell someone else to do if they came to you for advice in this same situation." I instantly knew what to do and my peace returned. God has answers for us if we will simply be quiet and listen.

GOD'S WORD FOR YOU TODAY: Keep your mind and your mouth quiet so God can speak to you and establish your thoughts.

The Comforter

I, even I, am He Who comforts you. (ISAIAH 51:12)

The various names of the Holy Spirit describe His character and His ministry in our lives. He is called our Teacher, our Helper, our Intercessor, our Advocate, our Strengthener, and our Standby. These names reveal what the Holy Spirit wants to do for believers. Today I want to focus on Him as our Comforter (see John 14:16).

For many years I regularly became angry with my husband because he wouldn't comfort me when I felt I needed comforting. I'm sure he tried, but I now realize that God would not allow Dave to comfort me because I needed to be seeking comfort from the Holy Spirit instead. He would have given me all the comfort I needed, had I simply asked for it.

God will allow people to do only a certain amount for us, and no more. Even those people who are extremely close to us cannot give us everything we need all the time. When we expect others to do for us what only God can do, our expectations are in the wrong place and we will always be disappointed.

God's comfort is much better than anyone else's. A person can never give us what we really need unless God assigns and anoints that person to minister to us, which He often does. Nevertheless, God is the only source of true comfort and when we need it, we should go to Him for it and receive it as He sees fit to send it to us. If you are hurting today, I encourage you to ask God for divine comfort.

GOD'S WORD FOR YOU TODAY: Seek and receive comfort from God.

Be Bold!

The wicked flee when no man pursues them, but the [uncompromis-ingly] righteous are bold as a lion. (PROVERBS 28:1)

One of the main reasons people do not pray and that they are reluc-tant to ask God for what they need and want is that they do not feel worthy. They do not feel good about themselves; they do not feel that they are spiritual enough, so they don't believe God would listen to them anyway. We all make mistakes and when we do we should receive God's forgiveness and mercy, which allows His blessings to flow even when we have made mistakes.

When we talk to God and make requests of Him, we must under-stand our position as sons and daughters of God who are made righ-teous through the blood of Jesus. Otherwise, we may not hear His voice clearly or perceive His answers accurately. You see, we so often think our righteousness is based on doing things "right"—saying the "right" words, behaving the "right" ways, or having the "right" attitude. The truth is that we cannot make ourselves righteous. We can make our-selves religious, but we cannot make ourselves righteous. True biblical righteousness is not based on what we do right, but it is based on what Jesus did for us. His righteousness becomes ours by faith, and once we believe that, then we progressively display more and more right behavior. But, we must always remember that God answers our prayers because He is good, not because we are. We can approach Him boldly in prayer and expect to hear from Him daily.

GOD'S WORD FOR YOU TODAY: God will turn your mis-takes into miracles if you trust Him and pray boldly.

No Limits

God may speak in one way, or in another. (JOB 33:14 NKJV)

We all need to hear from God each day about many different issues, but there are critical times in our lives when we especially need to know we are hearing clearly from Him. God wants to speak to us, but we have to be careful that we don't develop a closed mind-set about *how* He speaks to us. We don't need to say, "I will let God speak to me through His Word, but I will not let Him speak to me through a dream." We shouldn't say, "I will let God speak to me through my pastor, but not through my friends." As I have pointed out, God has many ways through which He may choose to speak to us, but no matter which way He chooses to speak, we can count on Him to direct our paths because He promises to do so.

It's not always easy to know if we are hearing from God or if we are hearing from our own mental or emotional reasoning. Some people say it took them years to learn how to hear from God, but I believe that's because there hasn't been enough clear teaching on how God communicates to His people. God wants us to know He is willing to lead us and guide us as a good shepherd leads his sheep.

God speaks in many ways, so ask Him to speak to you today and allow Him to lead you in any way He chooses. God once spoke to a prophet through a donkey, so we want to keep an open mind about how He may choose to speak to us.

GOD'S WORD FOR YOU TODAY: Keep an open mind about how God speaks to you.

God Speaks Through Doors of Opportunity

These are the words of the Holy One, the True One, He Who has the key of David, Who opens and no one shall shut, Who shuts and no one shall open. (REVELATION 3:7)

Sometimes God speaks by opening or closing a door to something we want to do. Paul and Silas tried to go into Bithynia to preach the gospel and minister to the people there, but the Spirit of Jesus prevented them from doing so (see Acts 16:6–7). We do not know exactly how that occurred; it is possible that they simply lost their peace. I sense that they actually tried to go into that province, and God somehow kept them from getting there.

Dave and I know from experience that God can open doors of opportunity that no one can close, and He can also close doors that we simply cannot open. I pray that God will open only the doors through which He wants me to pass. I may sincerely think something is right to do, when it may really be wrong; therefore, I depend on God to close doors I am trying to walk through if I am in fact making a mistake.

I spent years of my life trying to make things happen that I wanted to do. The result was frustration and disappointment. It is much more peaceful and enjoyable to do my part and then simply trust God to open the doors that agree with His plan for my life and close tightly the ones that do not. God loves you and you can be assured that at the right time, He will open the right door for you.

GOD'S WORD FOR YOU TODAY: Don't try to make anything happen for yourself. Trust God to open the right doors and close the wrong ones for you.

God's Righteous Friend

For our sake He made Christ [virtually] to be sin Who knew no sin,
so that in and through Him we might become [endued with, viewed as
being in, and examples of] the righteousness of God [what we ought
to be, approved and acceptable and in right relationship with Him,
by His goodness]. (2 CORINTHIANS 5:21)

I cannot think of anything more awesome than being a friend of God.
There is nothing I would rather hear God say than, "Joyce Meyer is My
friend." I do not want Him to say, "Joyce Meyer—knows all the prayer
principles; she can quote dozens of Bible verses; she sounds very eloquent
when she prays; but she really doesn't know Me at all and we are not really
friends." I want to know that God thinks of me as His friend, and I believe
you long for Him to think of you that way, too. Through Jesus Christ,
we have a right to be comfortable with God, to hear His voice, and to go
boldly to the throne of grace to get the help we need in plenty of time to
meet our needs and the needs of others (see Hebrews 4:16).

One of the best things you can ever do is to develop your friendship
with God. Jesus has made you righteous through the blood He shed at
the cross, so there is no reason you cannot approach God as boldly and
as naturally as you would your best friend on Earth. Remember, friendship with God takes an investment of time and energy to develop. But
also remember that as your friendship deepens, your ability to hear
God's voice increases. A growing, vibrant, increasingly intimate friendship with God will naturally lead to increasingly effective communication with Him.

GOD'S WORD FOR YOU TODAY: Make an effort to
develop an increasingly intimate friendship with God today.

Be a Fruit Inspector

You will fully know them by their fruits. (MATTHEW 7:20)

I encourage you to examine your own fruit and the fruit of others. Don't examine others to judge and criticize them, but simply to determine if they are who they claim to be. This is one way we try or "test the spirits" and stay out of trouble. Most of us have had the painful experience of being hurt by someone who deceived us. We thought we knew the person, but it turned out that he or she was not what they seemed to be. We can learn from these experiences to not be so impressed by what people say, but to watch for the kind of fruit they display. A person can appear to be religious and even quote entire chapters of the Bible, but if they are rude to people, greedy, and selfish, then they are not what they appear to be.

Being a genuine Christian is very important to me. I want to bear the fruit of what I claim to be and I am sure you feel the same way. I like to look daily at the fruit of my own life. There is no point in judging the fruit of other people if I am unwilling to look at my own. Am I being patient? Am I generous? Do I really care about other people and am I willing to sacrifice in order to help them? Am I promptly obedient to the leading of the Holy Spirit? We will deceive ourselves into thinking we are something we are not if we don't take the time to examine the fruit of our lives.

David asked God to examine him and Paul told the Corinthians to examine, test, and evaluate themselves to see whether they were holding to the faith and showing the proper fruit of it (see Psalm 26:2; 2 Corinthians 13:5–6). Let us test and examine our ways and ask God to prune off bad fruit so the entire tree does not become diseased.

GOD'S WORD FOR YOU TODAY: Take time daily to examine the fruit of your life!

Faith, Not Feelings

We walk by faith [we regulate our lives and conduct ourselves by our conviction or belief respecting man's relationship to God and divine things, with trust and holy fervor; thus we walk] not by sight or appearance. (2 CORINTHIANS 5:7)

The Bible teaches us to live by faith rather than by what we see and feel; however, there are times when God does use our circumstances to speak to us. For example, when Dave and I began to sense God speaking to us about going on television, the two of us certainly did not know how to produce a program and we could not air it without money. We had no way of getting enough money on our own, so God had to provide it. Had we written to our friends and partners and not received the finances, we could not have taken another step. No matter how much faith we had about going on television, we also had to have money. We believed God had spoken in our hearts, but we also needed Him to speak through our circumstance. We must know the difference between faith, foolishness, and presumption. It would have been foolish for us to go into debt to go on television.

Suppose a woman prays and feels she should go to work to help with the family expenses. She decides to get a job, but she has two small children. If she cannot find a dependable babysitter, she cannot go to work. That is a circumstance God must take care of in order for her to move forward. If God does not provide the babysitter then she will have to question her thoughts about going to work. Perhaps God is showing her that staying home with her family at this time in life is better than working.

We walk by faith, but we must also ask God to give us wisdom to know when to totally ignore circumstances and when to pay attention to circumstances because He is using them to speak to us and guide us.

GOD'S WORD FOR YOU TODAY: Live by faith, but don't be foolish.

Take Time for God

Those who wait for the Lord [who expect, look for, and hope in Him]
shall change and renew their strength and power; they shall lift their
wings and mount up [close to God] as eagles [mount up to the sun];
they shall run and not be weary, they shall walk and not faint or
become tired. (ISAIAH 40:31)

We live in a time-crunched world and just about everything we do seems to be urgent. The enemy has been extremely successful in his scheme to keep people from praying and spending time in the Word by keeping us so terribly busy. We live under incredible pressure and we run from one thing to the next to the next to the next—to the point that we often neglect the things that are really important in life: God, family and other relationships, our health, and building up our spiritual lives. Then we get more and more stressed out—and the only way to deal with that and get life back in order is to get with God and listen to what He says to us. It's true; we really cannot handle life apart from Him. We cannot handle the pressure, the confusion, and the stress without Him. Our marriages will suffer, our children will suffer, our finances will get messed up, our relationships won't thrive—if we do not spend time in the Word and in prayer. God will strengthen us and enable us to handle life peacefully and wisely if we start praying about things instead of merely *trying* to get through the day. When we take time with God and listen to His voice, He renews our strength and enables us to handle life and not be weary. But we have to start by using the time we have wisely by always putting God first.

———————

GOD'S WORD FOR YOU TODAY: Take time to hear God's voice every day.

God's Thoughts Aren't Man's Thoughts

My thoughts are not your thoughts, neither are your ways My ways, says the Lord. (ISAIAH 55:8)

One time our son David, who leads our world missions department, came to me wanting advice on whom to hire to fill a job opening. He felt God wanted him to offer the job to someone he would not have chosen naturally. He tried to fill the position with several seemingly qualified people, only to have each one turn down the job. He said, "It seems that God wants the person I would not have chosen."

God says in today's verse, "My thoughts are not your thoughts, neither are your ways My ways" (Isaiah 55:8). The individual God placed on David's heart was the only one genuinely interested in the job. We knew this was another example of God's helping us to hear from Him through open and closed doors. God does not always give a job or task to the most qualified person. Often, a person's heart attitude is more important than experience or credentials, especially in ministry positions.

I have discovered that what God chooses to do does not always make sense to us; it does not always fit into our reasoning. Our minds do not always understand the spiritual leadings that we have from God. His thoughts are indeed above ours! All His ways are right and sure.

———————

GOD'S WORD FOR YOU TODAY: Let your spirit take the lead and don't be led by your head.

Be Expectant

My soul, wait only upon God and silently submit to Him; for my hope and expectation are from Him. (PSALM 62:5)

God's power is released when we pray in faith, trusting and believing Him, because faith pleases Him. Expectancy is an attribute of faith that carries its own kind of power—the power of hope. Faith reaches out into the spiritual realm and expects God's supernatural power to show up and do what no person on Earth could do. Doubt, on the other hand, is afraid nothing good will happen; it does not please God and is not something He is able to bless. We are powerless when we live with doubt, disappointment, and a lack of confidence in God.

Just think about a time when you were not really sure God would come through for you. You were not able to pray very powerful prayers, were you? Now recall a time when your heart trusted completely in God and you really believed that He would come through for you. You were able to pray then with a certain sense of power, weren't you? That's the power of expectation in prayer. Even if things don't work out exactly the way you hoped they would, trust God to know what is best and keep expecting Him to do great things.

GOD'S WORD FOR YOU TODAY: Expect God to do great things in your life and pray boldly.

Please, Don't Be Religious

Woe to you, scribes and Pharisees, pretenders (hypocrites)! For you clean the outside of the cup and of the plate, but within they are full of extortion (prey, spoil, plunder) and grasping self-indulgence.

(MATTHEW 23:25)

Jesus frequently chastised the religious leaders of His day because although they did lots of good works, they did them with wrong motives. An abundance of religious works does not always mean the person doing them is close to God. I believe that religious activity can keep us from having an intimate relationship with God and hearing Him speak to us.

Jesus died to open the way for us to have intimacy with God, and that should always come before any good works. It is actually possible to do religious things while our hearts are far from God. We should frequently do "motive checks." God is more concerned with *why* we do things than He is with *what* we do when it comes to religious works. He said true religion is to visit, help, and care for widows and orphans in their affliction (see James 1:27). God wants us to genuinely love and care for hurting people much more than He wants us to try to impress one another with long, eloquent prayers.

Religious people do many things to enhance their reputation rather than to serve God. They may engage in all sorts of good works, but they rarely, if ever, engage in really sharing their hearts with God or allowing Him to share His with them. These people seldom truly hear God's voice or enjoy deep communion with Him.

GOD'S WORD FOR YOU TODAY: Focus on your relationship with God, not on being religious.

Seek God, Then Serve God

Know the God of your father [have personal knowledge of Him, be acquainted with, and understand Him; appreciate, heed, and cherish Him] and serve Him with a blameless heart and a willing mind.

(1 CHRONICLES 28:9)

Jesus has empathy for people who have been abused by religious law and oppressed by harsh religious leadership. He wants to see people healed and restored so they can know that God is good, that He is full of mercy and is long-suffering, slow to anger, and ready to forgive. God gives grace—His power to help us do what we cannot do on our own—freely. When He tells us to do something, He doesn't leave us powerless; He gives us what we need to do it.

When He said, "Come to Me, all you who labor and are heavy-laden" (Matthew 11:28), He was talking to people suffering from spiritual burnout. He wants to comfort those who are worn out from trying to serve and feeling like failures. There are thousands of people in the church today who are overworked and underfed spiritually. People want to have a powerful relationship with God and have done everything so-called religion has told them to do, and yet they still find themselves empty.

In their desire to please God, they have replaced *seeking* God and hearing His voice with *working* for God without always having specific direction from Him. He wants us to do Kingdom works, which are things He leads us to do; but He does not want us to be so busy in religious activity, thinking He is pleased with our sacrifices, which He did not ask us to make. How can people do the works of God if they have not taken time to hear from Him that they should do them?

GOD'S WORD FOR YOU TODAY: Ask God what He wants you to do, and then do it with all of your heart.

Come to Me

Come to Me, all you who labor and are heavy-laden and overburdened, and I will cause you to rest. [I will ease and relieve and refresh your souls.] (MATTHEW 11:28)

One of the greatest hindrances to hearing from God is trying to get to Him through works instead of through a personal relationship with Him by being born again and fellowshipping with Him regularly. God will give you the strength and power you need to serve Him in righteousness and holiness. Jesus is not a harsh taskmaster, as we see in the verse for today. In this verse, Jesus was saying, "I am good. My system is good—not harsh, hard, sharp, or pressing." You can easily become overburdened trying to do everything you feel is expected of you. But Jesus is saying to you today, "I will not load you down with burdens and demand things of you that wear you out. My plan for you is comfortable, gracious, and pleasant."

When God gives us something to do He always helps us do it. He gives us ability, strength, peace, and joy. When we are doing the will of God, He refreshes us while we work. If you feel overburdened, you may be doing things God has not asked you to do, or you may be trying to do them in your own strength. Ask Him what He wants you to do and not do, and be bold enough to eliminate anything He is not blessing.

GOD'S WORD FOR YOU TODAY: Eliminate from your schedule anything that is not bearing good fruit.

Sons and Daughters of God

*You must submit to and endure [correction] for discipline; God is
dealing with you as with sons. For what son is there whom his father
does not [thus] train and correct and discipline?* (HEBREWS 12:7)

If we want to be led by the Spirit of God, we must be willing to grow up
and become mature sons and daughters of God. We must not allow our
fleshly desires, our natural appetites, the devil, our friends, our emotions, or merely what we think to lead us; we look only to God's Spirit
for leadership and direction.

The more we know God's Word, the more we understand that He
will not lead us astray or direct us into anything that is not good for us.
Even things that may seem uncomfortable in the beginning will ultimately turn into great blessings in our lives if we will simply follow the
leading of the Holy Spirit. Learning to follow Him is part of spiritual
maturity.

The Bible sometimes refers to us as "children of God" and sometimes as "sons of God." There is a difference between children and
mature sons and daughters. Though all are equally loved, mature sons
and daughters enjoy liberties, privileges, and responsibilities that children are not yet old enough to have.

We come into God's Kingdom as babes; we go through a time of
being children; and then we learn how to behave as sons and daughters
of God and joint heirs with Christ. God wants to do wonderful things
for us, but we must grow up in Him in order to receive them. I encourage you to do everything you can to pursue spiritual maturity. Begin
today to ask Him to help you in this process.

GOD'S WORD FOR YOU TODAY: Be willing to grow up
into maturity in God.

Make the Sacrifice

Through Him, therefore, let us constantly and at all times offer up
to God a sacrifice of praise, which is the fruit of lips that thankfully
acknowledge and confess and glorify His name. (HEBREWS 13:15)

We often interpret the "sacrifice of praise," mentioned in the verse for today, to mean nothing more than praising God when we do not feel like praising Him, and that can certainly be a type of sacrifice. But, I believe the writer of Hebrews is actually making reference to the Old Testament sacrificial system that required the blood of animals to atone for people's sins.

We, however, live in New Testament times, when we no longer need to put slain sheep and goats and bulls on an altar. Instead, the sacrifice—the offering—God wants from us today is to hear right words coming out of our mouths. Just as the smoke and the aroma of the animal sacrifices went up before His throne under the Old Covenant, the praise from our hearts rises up as a sacrifice before Him today. In Hebrews 13:15, the Lord was really saying, "The sacrifice I want now is the fruit of your lips thankfully acknowledging Me."

We need to apply this Scripture to our everyday lives, making sure we speak God's praises every chance we get. We need to tell people about all the great things He's doing for us; we need to thank Him and tell Him we love Him. In our hearts and with our mouths, we should say continually, "Lord, I love You. Thank You so much for everything You're doing in my life. Lord, I praise You for taking care of everything that concerns me today." We need to be people of praise, acknowledging God "constantly and at all times," continually offering up to Him the sacrifice of praise.

GOD'S WORD FOR YOU TODAY: Praise God as often as you can today.

"In" but Not "Of"

I have given and delivered to them Your word (message) and the world has hated them, because they are not of the world [do not belong to the world], just as I am not of the world. (JOHN 17:14)

The verse for today teaches us that as believers we are in the world but not of the world, which means that we cannot take a worldly view of things. Not becoming like the world in our ways and attitudes requires constant vigilance. Watching too much graphic violence in the form of entertainment, as happens in the world, can sear or harden our consciences and reduce our sensitivity to God's voice. Many people in the world today are desensitized to the agonies real people suffer because they see tragedies portrayed so often on television.

The news media frequently deliver negative reports or tragic stories in unemotional, matter-of-fact ways and we often see and hear these things without feeling. We hear of so many terrible things that we no longer respond to tragedy with the appropriate emotions of compassion or outrage we should display.

I believe these things are part of Satan's overall plan for the world. He wants us to become hard-hearted and unengaged emotionally when we become aware of horrible events that take place around us. He does not want us to care about those affected by such things. But, as Christians, we should care, we should feel, and we should pray. Whenever we hear about what is happening in the world, we should ask God for His perspective and inquire as to how He wants us to respond. We then need to listen for His response and act accordingly. This is one way we can be in the world but not of the world.

GOD'S WORD FOR YOU TODAY: Take a stand for godly values and never compromise.

Open Your Heart

Jesus wept. (JOHN 11:35)

Many people do not feel godly emotions because they have endured so much pain in the past that they simply "turned off" their feelings. People who have refused to feel anything for a long period of time are afraid to begin to feel again because all they can remember about feelings is pain.

Eventually, emotional pain must be dealt with in order to let godly emotions flow in our lives again. Allowing ourselves to feel again will turn a hard heart into a tender one, but it requires patience and a willingness to work with God to get those feelings turned back on.

No matter what has caused your pain or how terrible it was, don't stay in the bondage of hard-heartedness. That will only treat symptoms, not roots, of your pain. It will not protect you from further pain, but it will hinder your ability to hear God's voice. Hard-heartedness is not from God; He created us to have feelings. According to today's verse, even Jesus wept.

Anytime you allow yourself to feel, you will be vulnerable to pain, but it will be different when you have Jesus the Healer living inside of you. Anytime you get hurt, He will be right there to take care of the wound.

If you have turned off your emotions, please realize that you have compromised your ability to hear God's voice. Open your heart to Him; ask Him to tenderize your heart and heal you so you can hear His voice and enjoy intimate fellowship with Him.

GOD'S WORD FOR YOU TODAY: If you build walls to keep people out of your life, you will live behind those walls in a self-made prison.

Bitterness Hinders Hearing

Let all bitterness and indignation and wrath (passion, rage, bad temper) and resentment (anger, animosity) and quarreling (brawling, clamor, contention) and slander (evil-speaking, abusive or blasphemous language) be banished from you, with all malice (spite, ill will, or baseness of any kind). (EPHESIANS 4:31)

Bitterness toward God is a sure hindrance to hearing His voice. Anytime bitterness tries to take hold of you, refuse it. Many times, the devil tries to make us think we are the only ones having a hard time. I don't mean to sound unsympathetic, but no matter how bad our problems are, someone else always has a worse problem.

A woman worked for me whose husband walked out on her after thirty-nine years of marriage. He simply left her a note, and was gone. It was a tragedy for her! I was so proud of her when she came to me after a few weeks and said, "Joyce, please pray for me that I will not get mad at God. Satan is tempting me so severely to get mad at Him. I can't get mad at God. He's the only friend I have. I need Him!"

Bitterness was trying to take root in my friend's heart because her life had not turned out the way she wanted it to. When we get hurt, we must realize that every person has a free will and we can't control that free will—even through prayer. We can pray that God will speak to people who may hurt us; we can ask Him to lead them to do right instead of wrong, but the bottom line is that He must leave them to make their own choices. If someone makes a choice that hurts us, we shouldn't blame it on God and become bitter toward Him.

GOD'S WORD FOR YOU TODAY: If you get hurt, don't ever blame God. He is the best friend you have.

Wherever He Leads

*Jesus said to Simon Peter, Simon, son of John, do you love Me
more than these [others do—with reasoning, intentional,
spiritual devotion, as one loves the Father]? He said to Him,
Yes, Lord, You know that I love You.* (JOHN 21:15)

In today's verse we see that Jesus asked Peter, "Do you love Me?" In
fact, Jesus asked Peter this same question twice more. By the third
time, Peter was grieved that Jesus kept asking the same question. He
said, "Yes, Lord, You know that I love You."

Then, in John 21:18, we discover the reason Jesus was asking Peter
if he loved Him: "I assure you, most solemnly I tell you, when you were
young you girded yourself and you walked about wherever you pleased
to go. But when you grow old you will stretch out your hands, and
someone else will put a girdle around you and carry you where you do
not wish to go."

God challenged me with this Scripture because I had my own plan
and was walking in my own way. If we really want God's perfect will, He
may ask us to do things we do not want to do. If we really love Him, we
will do what He tells us to do and let Him have His way in our lives.

When Jesus spoke the words from John 21:18, I believe He was
showing us that when we were young Christians, and less mature than
we are now, we went wherever we pleased. As baby Christians, we did
what we wanted to do. But as we mature, we are to stretch out our
hands and surrender ourselves to God. We must be willing to follow
Him to places we may not want to go.

Let's be quick to follow Him, wherever He leads us.

———————

GOD'S WORD FOR YOU TODAY: Will you say an eternal
"yes" to God today, even though you don't know where it may
lead you?

Spiritual Authority

Obey your spiritual leaders and submit to them [continually rec-
ognizing their authority over you], for they are constantly keeping
watch over your souls and guarding your spiritual welfare, as men
who will have to render an account [of their trust]. [Do your part to]
let them do this with gladness and not with sighing and groaning, for
that would not be profitable to you [either]. (HEBREWS 13:17)

Our modern society is absolutely filled with rebellion, and rebellion keeps us from hearing God. I have observed that many, many people have trouble relating to authority. This is true in marriages, families, schools, businesses, civic activities, and throughout our culture. Submission to spiritual authority is practically nonexistent.

Often when a pastor tries to bring some kind of correction, people tend to become upset and want to leave the church—and that is not right. Paul corrected people often; that was part of his job as a spiritual leader and it remains a responsibility for spiritual leaders today. Paul said: "Not that we have dominion [over you] . . . but [rather that we work with you as] fellow laborers [to promote] your joy" (2 Corinthians 1:24). If we will understand and believe that spiritual authority exists to promote our joy, we will embrace it and when we do, our joy will increase—and so will our ability to hear God's voice.

The spirit of rebellion that is at work in the world today is the spirit of the antichrist according to 2 Thessalonians 2:7–8, one that is willing to submit to no one. People today say they are demanding their *rights,* but in reality they are often only resisting any authority but their own.

———————

GOD'S WORD FOR YOU TODAY: Be submissive to authority as a service to the Lord, and He will bless and prosper you.

Legalism Is Finished

When Jesus had received the sour wine, He said, It is finished! And He bowed His head and gave up His spirit. (JOHN 19:30)

When Jesus spoke from the cross, saying, "It is finished!" He meant that the system of legalism was finished, that now, not only the religious high priests could enter God's presence, but that all people could enjoy His presence, speak to Him, and hear His voice.

Before Jesus died on our behalf, the only way to receive God's promises was to live a perfect, sinless life (by being very legalistic), or to offer a blood sacrifice for sin, the sacrifice of slain animals. When Jesus died and paid for the sins of humankind with His own blood, He opened up a way for every person to enjoy the presence of God. When Jesus said, "It is finished," He invited us to a life of freedom rather than fear. One in which we could be led by the Holy Spirit instead of rules and regulations. Ordinary people who don't do everything right all the time can now enter freely into the presence of God.

Freedom from legalism is not a call to lawlessness or laziness. It is a responsibility for each of us to learn God's Word and to hear from God for ourselves, which is what God has always wanted from the beginning of time.

GOD'S WORD FOR YOU TODAY: God loves you and wants you to enjoy your life.

The Power of the Holy Spirit

You shall receive power (ability, efficiency, and might) when the Holy Spirit has come upon you. (ACTS 1:8)

The Spirit of God gives power to those who want to hear His voice and serve Him. A person may desire to do something and not have the power to do it, but that power can come through receiving the baptism of the Holy Spirit.

You may remember that Jesus was baptized by immersion in water, but He was also baptized in the Holy Spirit. In other words, He was immersed in power, which enabled Him to do the task His Father sent Him to do. Acts 10:38 says, "God anointed Jesus of Nazareth with the Holy Spirit and with power," and that He "went about doing good and healing all who were oppressed by the devil, for God was with Him" (NKJV).

Before Jesus' public ministry began, He was anointed with the Holy Spirit and with power. When we are filled with the Holy Spirit, we are able to hear God's voice more clearly and we are equipped for service in the Kingdom of God because we are able to draw on the power (ability, efficiency, and might) of the Holy Spirit we received when He came upon us to be His witnesses. This power enables us to do what God wants us to do.

It is important to see that Jesus did not do any miracles or other mighty acts until after He was empowered by the Holy Spirit. If Jesus needed the power of the Spirit, we certainly do, too. Ask Him to fill you with the power of His Spirit today and every day.

GOD'S WORD FOR YOU TODAY: You have access to power—turn on the light!

Ask, Seek, Knock

Keep on asking and it will be given you; keep on seeking and you will find; keep on knocking [reverently] and [the door] will be opened to you. (MATTHEW 7:7)

Jesus said to ask, seek, and knock. If nobody knocks, no doors open. If nobody seeks, nobody finds. If nobody asks, nobody receives.

Because we need to ask in order to receive, our petitions are very important. As we make requests of God, though, we do want to make sure our petitions do not outweigh our praise and thanksgiving, because we do not need to be asking for more than we are thankful for. Remember that Philippians 4:6 instructs us to "be anxious for nothing, but in everything by prayer and supplication, with thanksgiving, let your requests be made known to God" (NKJV). When our requests are in balance with our praise and gratitude, petitioning God is awesome and exciting. It really is. It is awesome to ask God for something, believe Him for it, and then watch Him bring it to pass in our lives. We may know in our hearts that we have received the answer and never need to mention it to God again or we may feel we have to persevere in prayer; either way, we can be sure that God loves to give; He loves to answer our prayers, in His wisdom and His timing and His way. So don't hesitate to ask, seek, and knock!

GOD'S WORD FOR YOU TODAY: Don't ever let petition outweigh praise and thanksgiving.

Father Knows Best

Seek (aim at and strive after) first of all His kingdom and His righteousness (His way of doing and being right), and then all these things taken together will be given you besides. (MATTHEW 6:33)

God wants us to seek righteousness, peace, and joy, which is His Kingdom (see Romans 14:17). He wants us to deeply desire right behavior and do all that we can to pursue it, and when we do He promises to add the things we need and desire. He wants us to seek Him, and when we do He is pleased to bless us.

When we have a desire, we should simply ask God and trust Him completely; however, we should avoid lusting after things. I believe we are lusting when we want something so much that we feel we cannot be happy without it. I once heard a woman say that she just could not be happy if God did not give her children. I have also heard single ladies make the same comment regarding their desire to be married. Attitudes like this are wrong and offensive to God. Anything we feel that we must have in order to be happy besides God is something the enemy can use against us, so be sure to keep your desires balanced.

It is much better to pray and let God provide than to torment yourself trying to make things happen yourself. Always remember that God is good and He wants to be good to you, so keep your eyes on Him and His Kingdom and look forward to His providing the things that are right for you.

GOD'S WORD FOR YOU TODAY: Anything you have to have to be happy is something the devil can use against you.

Keep Your Desires Under Control

Lord, all my desire is before You; and my sighing is not hidden from You. (PSALM 38:9)

God says in His Word that if we delight ourselves in Him, He will give us the secret desires and petitions of our hearts (see Psalm 37:4). I like that plan because I certainly spent plenty of years frustrated trying to get the things I wanted for myself. In the process of seeking things, we often fail to pursue God and delight ourselves in getting to know Him. Many years ago, I even let that happen because of my strong desire to be in ministry. I thought the most important thing in the world was ministering for God, but I needed to learn that it was not as important as God Himself.

Are you keeping your desires in balance and delighting yourself in God above all else? If not, you can easily make an adjustment by reminding yourself of what is truly important. Place all of your desires before God, as our Scripture for today instructs us to do, trusting Him to remove any that are not His perfect will for you.

Every desire is not from God and therefore every desire we have will not be met, but we can trust God to meet the ones that will work out for our good. God wants you to know that if you ask for something and don't get it, it may be that He has something much better in mind for you. So relax; delight yourself in God, and let Him take care of the rest.

GOD'S WORD FOR YOU TODAY: God's plans for you are better than your plans for yourself.

Somebody's Praying for You

I am praying for them. (JOHN 17:9)

We know that Jesus prays for us. In Luke 22:32, He says to Peter, "I have prayed especially for you." In the verse for today, He says concerning His disciples, "I am praying for them." Also in John 17, He continues and says, "I do not pray for these alone, but also for those who will believe in Me," and that means you and me (v. 20 NKJV).

What does an intercessor do? An intercessor prays for others, standing in the gap that exists between God and an individual. We all have a gap between God and ourselves. In other words, we are not as holy as He is, but Jesus is right there, standing in that gap, bringing God and me—or God and you—together so we can have fellowship with Him and He can answer our prayers. Isn't it awesome to know that as long as our hearts are right and as long as we believe in Jesus, He will intercept, make right, and take care of every imperfect thing we do? I want you to imagine Jesus standing before the throne of God on your behalf praying for you. As you do, you will be able to trust that your imperfections are taken care of through His intercession for you.

GOD'S WORD FOR YOU TODAY: Jesus is praying for you.

It's Like Going to the Bank

Because of our faith in Him, we dare to have the boldness (courage and confidence) of free access (an unreserved approach to God with freedom and without fear). (EPHESIANS 3:12)

We should never feel insecure when we approach God in prayer. He knows all of our weaknesses and loves us anyway. God wants to give us more than enough, not barely enough, and we need to ask boldly.

Approaching God boldly in prayer can be likened to going to a bank to make a withdrawal. If I know I have fifty dollars in the bank because I deposited it there last week, I will not hesitate to pull up to the drive-through window and cash a fifty-dollar check. I know I have the money; it's mine, and I can get it out of the bank if I want to. When I present my check, I fully expect to get my fifty dollars. We need to approach God with that same kind of boldness, not because of our own righteousness, but because of the privilege of being joint heirs with Jesus. We need to understand what is available to us because of Jesus and we need to pray confidently, with full expectation that we will receive what belongs to us. God has made incredible provision available to us in Christ and we simply need to ask in Jesus' name for the blessings He has already purchased for us. When we struggle with feelings of unworthiness, we should go to God's Word and let it remind us of our privileges as children of God. Ask the Holy Spirit to help us enter boldly into God's presence and receive the help we need because, "the Spirit Himself bears witness with our spirit that we are children of God, and if children, then heirs—heirs of God and joint heirs with Christ" (Romans 8:16–17 NKJV). He will speak to us and remind us that we belong to God!

––––––––––––––––––––

GOD'S WORD FOR YOU TODAY: You are God's child and He is looking and longing to be good to you.

First Place

Little children, keep yourselves from idols (false gods)—[from any-
thing and everything that would occupy the place in your heart due to
God, from any sort of substitute for Him that would take first place in
your life]. (1 JOHN 5:21)

As a person who desires to hear from God, it is very important that
you give God first place in your life. Until our desires for more of God
are stronger than our desire for other things, the devil will have an
advantage over us. Once we see the truth, he will lose his advantage,
and we will be in position to make radical progress in our relationship
and fellowship with God. It takes most of us a long time before we
finally learn that what we need is not what God can give us, but God
Himself.

If you are diligent to seek God and keep yourself from all other idols,
you are honoring Him and He will honor you. He will reveal Himself
to you and bless you in ways you could never have imagined. Ask yourself sincerely if there is anything or anyone in your life whom you put
before God. If you find there is, then simply ask God to forgive you and
make an adjustment in your priorities. He is our number one priority
and nothing else will work properly until we give Him the place He
deserves.

GOD'S WORD FOR YOU TODAY: Keep God in first place
in your life.

Rest in the Gift

While the promise of entering His rest still holds and is offered
[today], let us be afraid [to distrust it], lest any of you should think he
has come too late and has come short of [reaching] it.

(HEBREWS 4:1)

When I teach on righteousness, I like to use the following illustration, and I ask you to give it a try. Sit in a chair, then *try* to sit in the chair. I know that sounds silly, because you are already sitting in the chair. Once you are in the chair, you cannot get into it any more than you already are. The same idea applies to righteousness. Jesus has made us right with God through His sacrifice and we cannot do anything to make ourselves more righteous than He has made us. Our behavior can improve, but not until we fully accept our righteousness through Jesus. Jesus puts us in the seat of righteousness and we need to learn to relax and stop trying to be what we already are. No amount of right actions can ever make us right with God apart from Christ. Affirming this, the apostle Paul prayed that he would be found and known as being in Christ, having no righteousness of his own, but only that right standing that comes through faith in Christ (see Philippians 3:9).

When we truly understand that we cannot do anything to make ourselves righteous and that we do not have to prove anything to God, we are able to rest in the gift of righteousness Jesus gives to us—and that will make us bold in our petitions and confident in God's desire to answer us. I know that God does not hear or answer my prayers because I am good; He hears and answers because He is good!

GOD'S WORD FOR YOU TODAY: Love who you are because God created you with His own hand.

You Have an Assignment

You, O Lord of hosts, God of Israel, have revealed this to Your servant: I will build you a house. So Your servant has found courage to pray this prayer to You. (2 SAMUEL 7:27)

God sometimes speaks to us and gives us "prayer assignments." King David believed that he was given the assignment to build God a house and he was committed to pray about it until it came to pass. There are many people or situations I pray for once, and that is all. But I also believe God speaks to us and assigns us people to pray for until what He wants to do in them or for them is accomplished. I have prayed for one person, literally, for twenty-five years and will continue to do so until I die or until God releases me, or the person dies or what needs to happen comes to pass. There are actually times when I get tired of praying for this person, but it doesn't matter how I feel, I still find myself praying. I know God has given me this assignment and I will not give up! I believe God is using my prayers to help shape this individual's destiny.

There are other times when I feel that I "should" be praying for someone more than I do, but no matter how I feel, they just don't come to mind when I pray. I may also try to pray, but have no desire, or cannot find much to say and even what I do say is dry and lifeless.

If God speaks to you and gives you an assignment to pray for someone or something, you will not have to "try" to work up a desire to pray; you will find them in your heart and mind and prayer will be easy. You may even find yourself praying for them without even consciously planning to do so. When someone is on your heart or mind, believe you are hearing from God and pray!

GOD'S WORD FOR YOU TODAY: You can't do everything and do anything well, so find your assignment and enter God's rest.

The Power of Persistence

He said, Let Me go, for day is breaking. But Jacob said, I will not let You go unless You declare a blessing upon me. (GENESIS 32:26)

Sometimes, you pray a few words or a few sentences one time and never think about it again. At other times, though, a person or a situation keeps coming back to your heart and you just know you are not finished praying about it. When the Holy Spirit impresses something on you over and over again, He is probably drawing you to continue to pray persistently, to pray prayers that refuse to give up.

In my life, there have been things that I know are God's will because He has spoken clearly about them in His Word. When I pray about them and do not have a breakthrough, I go right back to God and say, "I'm here again. And God, I don't mean to sound disrespectful, but I'm not going to be quiet until I get a breakthrough." Sometimes I say, "I'm asking You again, Lord, and I am going to keep on asking until I see victory in this area." At other times, I just thank God that He is working and remind Him that I am expecting victory. We must be like Jacob and say, "I will not let You go until You bless me." God did indeed bless Jacob and said He did so because Jacob was a man who knew how to prevail with men and with God. In other words, Jacob was persistent and would not give up (see Genesis 32:24–28)!

When I know God's will, I can pray accordingly and refuse to give up. God delights in a determined person and encourages us in His Word not to faint or grow weary. Perseverance pays off, so stick with your goals in all of life, including your prayer assignments. Because of determination, Jacob prevailed with God and man and was rewarded with a new name and a new start in life.

GOD'S WORD FOR YOU TODAY: God delights in respectful persistence.

Like a Child

Truly I say to you, unless you repent (change, turn about) and become like little children [trusting, lowly, loving, forgiving], you can never enter the kingdom of heaven [at all]. (MATTHEW 18:3)

Today's verse describes children as trusting, lowly, loving, and forgiving. Just think about how much more we would enjoy our lives and our relationships with God and other people if we would simply operate in these four virtues. Obviously, Jesus thinks these qualities are extremely important because He says we cannot enter the kingdom of heaven without them. We cannot enjoy the benefits of God's Kingdom and maintain bad attitudes at the same time.

When I think about hearing God's voice, I see that being like a child is so important because children believe what they are told. Some people say children are gullible, meaning they believe anything, no matter how ridiculous it sounds. But I don't think children are gullible; I think they are trusting. God certainly doesn't want us to be gullible or naive; He wants us to be trusting. Sometimes we are betrayed by people we love and trust and are tempted to then distrust everyone, but we cannot make everyone pay for what one person did to us.

There are people in the world who cannot be trusted, but there are also a lot of good people and we must refuse to live with a spirit of suspicion.

God is completely trustworthy. All human beings, regrettably, cannot be trusted unconditionally, but God can.

God wants you to come to Him like a child, trusting Him completely and believing everything He says to you—because He is totally trustworthy.

GOD'S WORD FOR YOU TODAY: Don't let one or two bad experiences rule your entire life.

What Are You Expecting?

The Lord is good to those who wait hopefully and expectantly for Him, to those who seek Him. (LAMENTATIONS 3:25)

After we pray and ask God for what we want, need, or desire, we should wait expectantly. We must be full of hope, which is joyful and confident expectation of something good happening. After years of being disappointed in my childhood and early adult years, I developed what the Bible calls evil forebodings (see Proverbs 15:15). That means I was expecting bad news most of the time. I believe many people are caught in the trap of being afraid to expect something good because they do not want to be disappointed again. God wants everyone to aggressively expect good things from Him because He is good.

Don't be passive either. A passive person is someone who wants good things to happen and they are going to do nothing but wait to see what happens. Although the verse for today does tell us to wait, it says to *wait expectantly*. I like to confess Scriptures aloud while I am waiting on God to work in my behalf. They remind me of His promises, and they keep me encouraged. God's Word is filled with creative power and, when spoken in faith, it is equal to sowing seed that will bring a harvest.

If you have prayed and find yourself waiting longer than you had planned for an answer, thank God that He is working when you are tempted to be impatient. Tell God what you are expecting and look forward to your breakthrough. Don't fall into the trap of complaining and murmuring while you wait either. Be joyfully confident that your answer is on the way.

GOD'S WORD FOR YOU TODAY: Don't get discouraged. God is working and you will see the results soon.

Keep Your Receiver Deceiver-Free

The Lord God has given Me the tongue of a disciple … He wakens Me morning by morning, He wakens My ear to hear as a disciple [as one who is taught]. The Lord God has opened My ear, and I have not been rebellious or turned backward. (ISAIAH 50:4–5)

The first step in hearing from God is to believe we *can* hear from Him. Many people want to hear from God, but they don't really expect to hear from Him. They say, "I just can't hear from God; He never talks to me."

These people have too much static in their "receivers" to hear Him clearly. Their ears are jammed with too many messages coming from ungodly sources. Consequently, they have a hard time discerning what God is really saying to them.

It doesn't do any good for God to speak to us if we do not believe we are hearing from Him. The deceiver, the devil, doesn't want us to think we can hear from God. He doesn't want us to believe, so he sends little demons to stand around and lie to us day and night, telling us we can't hear from God. But we can answer, "It is written, God has given me the capacity to hear and obey Him" (see Psalm 40:6). God's Word declares that all believers have the capacity to hear and obey God and to be led by the Holy Spirit.

Jesus heard clearly from the Father all the time. Many people who were standing around Jesus when God spoke to Him heard only what they thought was thunder (see John 12:29). If you are having trouble hearing from God, I encourage you to take a few moments every day and confess your faith in hearing from Him. As you confess what you believe in your heart, your mind will be renewed and you will begin to expect to hear from God.

GOD'S WORD FOR YOU TODAY: Instead of feeling pressured to hear from God, just trust Him to speak to you.

Take Time, Make Time

Stand still and consider the wondrous works of God. (JOB 37:14)

I have heard numerous people say, "God never talks to me." But I am convinced it is more likely that they never listen to Him, don't know how to hear from Him, or have become desensitized to His voice. God makes many attempts to speak to us through His Word, natural signs, supernatural revelation, and internal confirmation, all of which I have written about in this devotional.

Sometimes we think we cannot hear God's voice because there are certain obstacles in our hearts or in our lives that prevent us from hearing Him clearly. One of these things is simply being too busy. We get so busy that we have no time to wait on God or listen to His voice. We can even become so busy with spiritual activities, such as church or ministering to others, that we don't have a place in our schedules for God. I can remember a time when I was working so hard *for* God that I had no time to spend *with* Him; this happens to a lot of people.

What we do for God should always be secondary to our personal relationship with Him. Time is ours to do with as we please so we should choose what we do with it wisely. Every person has the same amount of it daily and once it is used we cannot get it back. Work your schedule around God instead of trying to work Him into it.

GOD'S WORD FOR YOU TODAY: Use your time wisely because once you spend it, you can never get it back.

We Need What Jesus Has

The Spirit of the Lord shall rest upon Him—the Spirit of wisdom and understanding, the Spirit of counsel and might, the Spirit of knowledge and of the reverential and obedient fear of the Lord.

(ISAIAH 11:2)

God is looking for people who will demonstrate the glory of His presence in their lives. They will be people who obey Him in every little thing. Obedience keeps us from defiling our conscience and keeps us living for God's glory.

We know that the verse for today is a prophecy about Jesus, but if the Spirit of Jesus is dwelling in us and living through us, then we will enjoy all that is upon Him. We will have wisdom, understanding, counsel, might, and knowledge.

Problems dissolve in the presence of these virtues. We don't have to live in confusion if we are obedient to the leading of the Spirit. The Lord will give us quick counsel, wisdom, understanding, and might if we are reverential and submissive toward Him.

People who want to have understanding, who want to hear from God, who want to have wisdom and knowledge imparted to them must have reverential fear and awe of God. Reverential fear is to know that God is God and that He means business. He has called us His friends, even His sons and daughters, but we're to respect Him and honor Him with reverential obedience.

GOD'S WORD FOR YOU TODAY: Anything God asks you to do is for your own good, so be quick to obey today and every day.

God Speaks Specifically

*If they obey and serve Him, they shall spend their days in prosperity
and their years in pleasantness and joy.* (JOB 36:11)

Dave and I regularly need to hear from God about many things. We
need to hear from Him about how to handle people, circumstances,
and numerous events and specific situations. Our constant prayer is,
"What should we do about this? What should we do about that?"

It seems a hundred things happen every week in which Dave and
I have to be of quick understanding and make God-driven decisions. If we
don't obey God on Monday, our week can be in chaos on Friday. Therefore, we are determined that we are not going to live in disobedience.

Many people are concerned about the specific will of God for their
lives, wondering what He wants them to do. For example: "Lord, should
I take this job, or do You want me to take another job? Do You want me
to do this, or do You want me to do that?" I believe God wants to give
us the specific direction we long for, but He is even more concerned
about our obedience to His general will for our lives, which we find in
His Word—things like being thankful at all times in every situation,
never complaining, always being content, displaying the fruit of the
Spirit, and forgiving those who hurt or disappoint us.

If we are not obeying the guidelines He has already given us in Scripture, we will have difficulty hearing what He has to say about His specific will for us. As you endeavor to hear God more and more clearly and
to follow His will for your life, remember to make a priority of knowing
and obeying His general will by staying rooted in His Word. Then, you
can hear Him more easily when He speaks to you specifically.

GOD'S WORD FOR YOU TODAY: Keep doing what you
know to do and when you don't know what to do, God will
show you.

How to Gain Wisdom

If you will turn (repent) and give heed to my reproof, behold, I [Wisdom] will pour out my spirit upon you, I will make my words known to you. (PROVERBS 1:23)

We need to pray and obey God's leading when He speaks to us. Obedience is not to be an occasional event for us; it is to be our way of life. There's a big difference between people who are willing to obey God daily and those who are willing to obey only to get out of trouble. God certainly shows people how to get out of trouble, but He bestows abundant blessings on those who decide to live wholeheartedly for Him and who make obedience to Him their lifestyle. The only pathway to true peace is obedience to God.

Many people obey God in the big issues, but they aren't aware that obedience in the little things makes a difference in His plan for their lives. The Bible says plainly that if we are not faithful in the little things, we will never be made rulers over much (see Luke 19:17). There is no reason for God to trust us with a major responsibility if we are not going to be faithful to do the little things He has asked us to do.

I strongly urge you to be obedient to God even in the smallest of things. A sixteenth-century monk called Brother Lawrence was well known for walking continually in the presence of God. He said that he was pleased to pick up a piece of straw from the ground in obedience to God and because he loved Him.

In the verse for today, God says He will make known His words to us if we listen to Him when He corrects us. If we follow His guidance and are pleased to do each little thing He asks of us, then He will open His wisdom to us, and we will have more revelation than we could ever imagine.

GOD'S WORD FOR YOU TODAY: If you are faithful in little things, God will make you ruler over greater things.

God Has a Lot to Say

There are also many other things which Jesus did. If they should be all recorded one by one [in detail], I suppose that even the world itself could not contain (have room for) the books that would be written.

(JOHN 21:25)

God has a great deal that He wants to reveal to us as His children. If we want to make hearing from God a way of life, we must be obedient to Him when He speaks to us. Each time we hear and obey, it increases our sensitivity to the voice and heart of God.

We have the opportunity to be what I like to call *lifetime learners*. I want to learn something every day of my life. Our walk with God is a continual journey. It is a tedious one in which we need to hear from God and be led by His Spirit. The Holy Spirit has something to teach you today and every day. Don't just read the Bible in order to feel that you have done your duty for the day, but approach it with a desire to learn something you did not know. The Holy Spirit is our Teacher, and I believe He has something special for us each day if we will open our hearts and listen. Let the cry of your heart be, "God, I want to learn more and more about You and Your ways, and I want to obey You promptly."

———————

GOD'S WORD FOR YOU TODAY: You are learning and growing in Christ all the time. Look at how far you have come, not just how far you still have to go.

Love Him? Obey Him

If you [really] love Me, you will keep (obey) My commands.
(JOHN 14:15)

In the verse for today, Jesus says we demonstrate our love for Him by obedience to what He says. Whenever I think about hearing from God, I keep coming back to the fact that we won't hear Him clearly if we are not obeying Him in what we already know to do. Without obedience we have a guilty conscience. As long as we have that guilty conscience, we cannot have faith and confidence (see 1 John 3:20–24).

The goals of a Christian should be quite different from the goals of a nonbeliever. Those who are not serving God want money, position, power, and things, but as Christians our primary goal should be to obey and glorify God. I went to church for many years without giving a great deal of thought to obeying God. I was following a religious formula hoping that would make me acceptable to God, but I had not made a full commitment to be guided daily by His principles. Open your entire life to God and invite the Holy Spirit as your Teacher in life. Do your best to obey His directions, and when you fail, ask for forgiveness and begin again. Don't waste time and energy feeling guilty, because in Christ we can always have a new beginning. Pray about obedience, study it, and actively pursue it every day. In this way, we demonstrate our love for God.

GOD'S WORD FOR YOU TODAY: No matter how hard we try not to, we all make mistakes, but as long as we refuse to give up we will reach our goals.

God Sees Your Heart

Thank God, though you were once slaves of sin, you have become obedient with all your heart to the standard of teaching in which you were instructed and to which you were committed. (ROMANS 6:17)

When we receive Christ as our Savior, God gives us a new heart—one that wants to do what is right. However, it takes awhile for our behavior to catch up with our new heart and that is often very frustrating. One part of us wants to do right, yet another part of us fights against it. That is the war between the flesh and the spirit that Paul discusses in Galatians 5:17.

At the new birth, God equips us inwardly with all we need to live holy, obedient lives. We are made new creatures in Christ; old things pass away and all things are made new (see 2 Corinthians 5:17). I like to say we are made new spiritual clay and we spend our lives letting the Holy Spirit mold us into the image of Christ (see Romans 8:29). We need to thank God that we have a new heart, one that wants to be obedient.

Celebrate your progress and don't be discouraged because God sees your heart. If we let go of what lies behind and keep pressing toward the place of total obedience, God is pleased. We are learning to walk with God and walking is the slowest mode of travel that exists. You may not be where you want to be, but thank God you have an obedient heart.

GOD'S WORD FOR YOU TODAY: Focus on Jesus today, not on your failures.

Don't Quench the Spirit

Do not quench (suppress or subdue) the [Holy] Spirit.
(1 THESSALONIANS 5:19)

The verse for today tells us not to quench the Holy Spirit. I believe one way we quench the Spirit is through complaining. We need the Holy Spirit to work in our lives, and the more we choose to stop complaining and be thankful (the opposite of complaining), the more freedom the Holy Spirit has to work in our situations. It's natural to complain; it's supernatural to give thanks when we are tested and tried in the midst of life's circumstances.

People who grumble and complain do not hear God because to hear Him, they have to stop complaining! It took me years to discover this truth! I grumbled and complained and murmured and found fault with everything and everyone, and then was jealous because everyone around me was hearing from God and I wasn't!

"Why isn't anything good happening to me?" I groaned.

Dave kept telling me, "Joyce, good things aren't going to happen in our lives until you stop getting upset every time things don't go your way."

Then I would be angry with him for telling me that and I would snap back: "You just don't know or care how I feel!"

The problem was that I cared too much about how I felt and not enough about God's promise to help me. God offers to help us in our trouble and show us what to do if we remain patient (keep a good attitude) during our trials. Complaining is not a sign of patience, but gratitude and thanksgiving are. As I learned to live by the Word of God rather than my feelings I heard God's voice more clearly. Complaining opens a door for the enemy, but thanksgiving and gratitude open a door for God.

GOD'S WORD FOR YOU TODAY: Do not quench the Holy Spirit by complaining.

Roll Them Over

Roll your works upon the Lord [commit and trust them wholly to Him; He will cause your thoughts to become agreeable to His will, and] so shall your plans be established and succeed. (PROVERBS 16:3)

If we want to be in intimate relationship with God and live lives that are truly committed to Him, we have to take everything about ourselves and say to Him: "God, I give this to You. I give You this problem. I give You this situation. I give You this relationship. I completely release it and let it go. It is too much for me. I am going to stop worrying and trying to figure everything out—and I am going to let You take care of it. God, I also give myself to You because I can't do anything about myself either. I give it *all* to You. I give You my strengths and weaknesses. I want to change, but You have to change me." It was a great day for me when I finally learned that it was God's job to change me and my job to believe!

Psalm 37:5 says, "Commit your way to the LORD, trust also in Him, and He shall bring it to pass" (NKJV). What does it mean to commit our ways to God? It means to "roll" them off of ourselves and onto Him. When we roll our problems and human reasonings onto God, which means to trust them *completely* to Him, then He changes our thoughts and makes them agree with His will. In other words, His thoughts become our thoughts so that we want what He wants. When that happens, our plans will succeed because they are in complete agreement with God's plans. Release yourself and all your cares today and relax so you can hear God speak to you.

GOD'S WORD FOR YOU TODAY: Roll all your problems onto God.

Follow in Faith

I will make of you a great nation, and I will bless you [with abundant increase of favors] and make your name famous and distinguished, and you will be a blessing [dispensing good to others].

(GENESIS 12:2)

Obedience to God's voice was not easy for me when He first called me to leave the security of my job and start my own ministry. But, the verse for today is one that God used to speak to me and encourage me in the plans He had for me. It's easy to read this verse and think, *Yes! I want to be blessed. That sounds terrific!* But, we must remember that God required a sacrifice of obedience from Abraham before that great promise was fulfilled.

Abraham had to leave everything comfortable and familiar to him and move toward an unknown destination. Many people would find that unnerving—but Abraham didn't. Hebrews 11:8 says, "[Urged on] by faith Abraham, when he was called, obeyed and went forth to a place which he was destined to receive as an inheritance; and he went, although he did not know or trouble his mind about where he was to go."

When we obey God, we need to be like Abraham and not allow our minds to be troubled. When God speaks to us and leads us, we need to follow in faith, trusting and believing that He will bless our obedience and fulfill His promises to us.

GOD'S WORD FOR YOU TODAY: God is fulfilling His promises to you.

The Pure in Heart Will See God

Blessed (happy, enviably fortunate, and spiritually prosperous—possessing the happiness produced by the experience of God's favor and especially conditioned by the revelation of His grace, regardless of their outward conditions) are the pure in heart, for they shall see God! (MATTHEW 5:8)

If we have a pure heart, we will be able to hear God clearly. We will see with clarity His plan for our lives. We won't feel aimless or confused. The condition of our heart is one of the most important things to God. If the hidden man of the heart is kept in a right condition, it pleases God tremendously (see 1 Peter 3:3–4). The Bible says that we should guard our heart with all diligence, for out of it flow all the issues of life (see Proverbs 4:23).

Examine your heart, your inner attitudes, and your thoughts to see if there is anything there that God would not approve of. Do you have bitterness or resentment? Have you allowed a critical or judgmental attitude to take root? Is your heart tender or hard? Are you open to the opinions and ideas of others or have you closed your heart? The Bible says that we have the responsibility of keeping and guarding our heart in the right condition.

The physical organ of the heart is the most important organ in the body. If it is diseased or working improperly it could mean the difference between life and death. I believe our heart attitude is also one of the most important things we should pay attention to. If we let it get filled with disease or anything that is improper, it will definitely affect the quality of our lives.

GOD'S WORD FOR YOU TODAY: Ask God today and every day to show any heart conditions (attitudes of heart) that you need to change.

Listen Carefully

Be careful what you are hearing. The measure [of thought and study]
you give [to the truth you hear] will be the measure [of virtue and
knowledge] that comes back to you—and more [besides] will be given
to you who hear. (MARK 4:24)

The Bible says that in the latter days many false prophets will rise up
and tell people what their itching ears want to hear. People will search
for anyone who will tell them something pleasing and gratifying. To
suit their own desires, they will turn away from hearing the truth and
will wander off into listening to myths and man-made fiction (see 2
Timothy 4:3–4). They will turn to methods that may be called "spiritual," but are not safe in God's Kingdom. They are "spiritual," but they
come from the wrong spirit!

Never before have we seen such an influx of psychics vying for a
ready ear. Television shows feature mediums who claim to communicate with people who have died. These people are actually communicating with familiar spirits who tell half-truths about the past and lies
about the future. This is strictly forbidden in Scripture (see Leviticus
19:31). God says He will set His face against anyone who turns to mediums and spiritists (see Leviticus 20:6–7), yet Christians still read
horoscopes and consult psychics—then wonder why they live in confusion and don't have peace.

We must realize that it is wrong to seek guidance for our lives
through anything other than God Himself. If you have been involved in
activity of this kind, I urge you to thoroughly repent; ask God to forgive
you; and turn away completely from such practices. God alone has all
the answers you need.

GOD'S WORD FOR YOU TODAY: Don't play with matches;
they only lead to fire.

Listen More Than You Talk

He who has knowledge spares his words, and a man of understanding has a cool spirit. (PROVERBS 17:27)

We have said in this devotional that in our quest to hear from God we must train ourselves to listen. Sometimes we are talking so much that we simply cannot hear what God wants to say. We can also miss the important things people say to us because we are not listening.

If we learn the discipline of keeping ourselves calm and quiet, we will hear the things that God wants to say to us. My daughter, Sandra, said that recently, after she prayed, she just sat for a minute and asked God if He had anything He wanted to say to her before she began her day. She felt in her heart that He simply said, "Go; I am with you!" She was comforted by that thought, but it especially comforted her over the next few days when she found herself needing to deal with some unexpected bad news. The word God had given her increased her faith and kept her stable and calm as she faced her trials.

If we don't listen, we won't hear. Give God an opportunity on a regular basis to speak to you. When you pray, you don't have to do all the talking. You can spare your words and be considered a wise man or woman of God.

GOD'S WORD FOR YOU TODAY: You have one mouth and two ears, so that means God wants you to listen twice as much as you talk.

The Good Shepherd

I am the Good Shepherd; and I know and recognize My own, and My own know and recognize Me. (JOHN 10:14)

Hearing God speak to us is our right and privilege as believers. God gives us discernment to know His voice over the voices of deception. He parallels this discernment with the instinctive nature of sheep that recognize the voice of their shepherd, as we read in the verse for today.

If we truly belong to God, we will be able to discern His voice from voices that would seek to lead us astray. We should learn to examine the nature of a thing, and know God's character.

I am grieved when I hear people say, "God told me to do this," yet it is obvious that a good shepherd would never tell them to do what they are doing. I once knew a woman who was told by a spiritual leader that the two of them were destined by God to be married. The problem was that he was already married. The sad thing was that she believed him and encouraged him to divorce his wife so they could be together. This was ungodly, foolish, and could never have been God's will because it goes against His Word.

People often want to know, "How can I be sure I am hearing from God?" We will know the difference between His voice and the voice of deception if we truly know His character, nature, and the history of how He has led others before us. Jesus said of His sheep, "They will never [on any account] follow a stranger, but will run away from him because they do not know the voice of strangers or recognize their call" (John 10:5).

GOD'S WORD FOR YOU TODAY: Never let emotions rule you, especially if what they are leading you to do is against God's Word or character.

The Key to Fulfillment

Thus says the Lord of hosts: Consider your ways and set your mind on what has come to you. (HAGGAI 1:5)

God has a great big, wonderful, fulfilling life planned for you and me, but if we are stubborn (see Exodus 33:3) or hard-hearted, then we will miss what He has for us. Stubbornness and refusal to hear and obey God's voice keep us set in our ways and unable to make progress. When we find ourselves in this condition, we often fail to stop and ask ourselves what the problem is.

Today's verse recounts a time when God's people were dissatisfied and experiencing many problems, so God told them to consider their ways. Many times when people are not fulfilled in life, they look everywhere except within themselves to find the reason. If you are unfulfilled in your life, do as God told the Old Testament people to do and "consider your ways." Ask God to speak to you about "your ways," and pay attention to what He says. I have had to do this many times, and I have had to make changes in my thinking, my motives, or my behavior as a result.

As I considered my ways over time, I found I was stubborn, hard-headed, opinionated, proud, and many other things that kept me from making progress. But, thank God, He has changed me! I pray He keeps on changing me and never stops.

I want everything God wants me to have and nothing He doesn't. I belong to Him and so do you. He wants you to have a happy, blessed, wonderful life, full of satisfaction and fulfillment. If you aren't living that kind of life, take time to consider your ways; ask God to show you what needs to change, and then do what He tells you to do.

GOD'S WORD FOR YOU TODAY: Don't be afraid to face truth about yourself, because it sets you free.

Treat People Well

Whoever stops his ears at the cry of the poor will cry out himself and not be heard. (PROVERBS 21:13)

Today's verse means that when I do not pay attention to people in need and do not do anything to help them, then God may not be inclined to answer my call for help when I have a need.

Being good to people extends beyond our friends and family to our communities. I remember reading a statistic one time that said the average age of a homeless person in St. Louis was seven years old. In my city! My response to that twenty years ago might have been, "That is really pathetic." But now, I become aware of realities such as that one and say, "I'm going to do something about that!" People might say, "It's easy for *you* to say that, Joyce; you've got a big ministry and access to lots of people who can help." You may not have some of the resources we have in the ministry, but you have the same ability to pray that I do. You can give an offering to ministries that are trying to help and meet needs. You can go and volunteer a little bit of time. All of us can do something if we really want to.

I believe a lot of our prayers go unanswered and that we sometimes fail to hear God's voice because we do not extend mercy or compassion to the difficult situations around us. The truth is, we can receive a tremendous harvest just by being nice! It is very important to God that we treat people well. If you have ever been forgotten or mistreated, then you know how painful that is. If you want to pray effective prayers—if you want God's ears to perk up at the sound of your voice—you will have to treat people well and be good to them.

GOD'S WORD FOR YOU TODAY: One of the greatest things you can do is help someone less fortunate than you are.

Go Through

Yes, though I walk through the [deep, sunless] valley of the shadow of death, I will fear or dread no evil, for You are with me; Your rod [to protect] and Your staff [to guide], they comfort me. (PSALM 23:4)

We often speak of "what we are going through," but the good news is that we are *going through;* we are not stuck in our troubles with no way out. God never promises us trouble-free lives, but He does promise to be with us and to never leave or forsake us. When God takes us through something, He will always teach us valuable lessons that we can use in the future.

One of the most important times to hear from God is when we need direction as we go through difficulties. What should we do? How long will the problem last? Today's psalm says that God will guide us as we go through. Trusting God to help us will keep us from giving up in the midst of our difficulties.

The book of Hebrews says that God wants us to go all the way through so we can realize the fulfillment of our hope in the end (see Hebrews 6:11). Satan wants us to get discouraged and give up, but God gives us power to go through! Don't be someone who begins things but does not finish when times get tough. When we begin a thing, we should count the cost and be sure we have what it takes to finish it so we don't look foolish. Determination is what it takes to finish—being able to keep going even after all the good feelings are gone and others have given up. If you go through to the very end, you will receive the reward of your faith.

GOD'S WORD FOR YOU TODAY: As you go through the valleys of life, God will always guide and comfort you. *and help you make the right decisions*

Sanctified, Circumcised Ears

To whom shall I [Jeremiah] speak and give warning, that they may hear? Behold, their ears are uncircumcised [never brought into covenant with God or consecrated to His service], and they cannot hear or obey. (JEREMIAH 6:10)

Every time God speaks to us and we act as though we don't hear Him, our hearts become a little more calloused until we reach the point where it is extremely difficult to hear Him. Eventually, our stubbornness dulls our ability to hear Him at all. Each time we turn our backs on what we know to be the right thing to do, we become a little more obstinate until we are totally deaf to His leading.

In the verse for today, we see that God wanted Jeremiah to warn His people of imminent destruction, but they were not able to hear his voice because their ears were uncircumcised (not in covenant with God). How tragic!

In contrast, we see in John 5:30 that Jesus had a sanctified (set apart), circumcised ear. I believe this is one of the most important verses on the subject of hearing God in the Bible: "I am able to do nothing from Myself [independently, of My own accord—but only as I am taught by God and as I get His orders]. Even as I hear, I judge [I decide as I am bidden to decide. As the voice comes to Me, so I give a decision], and My judgment is right (just, righteous), because I do not seek or consult My own will [I have no desire to do what is pleasing to Myself, My own aim, My own purpose] but only the will and pleasure of the Father Who sent Me."

Jesus didn't do *anything* unless He heard the Father's voice concerning it. Imagine how different our lives would be if we asked for God's advice before we stepped into messes that we create and then need Him to rescue us from because we didn't seek His counsel.

GOD'S WORD FOR YOU TODAY: Listen to your heart before making decisions.

God Wants You

*I appeal to you therefore, brethren, and beg of you in view of [all] the
mercies of God, to make a decisive dedication of your bodies [pre-
senting all your members and faculties] as a living sacrifice.*

(ROMANS 12:1)

God wants you! He wants full custody of your heart, not just visitation
rights. People often complain that they pray in Jesus' name and nothing happens—but considering the amount of time they spend with
Him, it's obvious they're only "dating" Him. I didn't get my husband's
name until I married him. Jesus wants a marriage relationship with His
church.

Intimacy with God encourages His power to work in our lives. We
cannot view intimacy as all smiles and warm, fuzzy feelings. When a
relationship is intimate, one person can speak correction to the other
and complete honesty can flow between the two of them. In an intimate relationship with God, we have wonderful moments, but we also
have moments when He calls us to honestly face things that need to
change in our lives.

Some people haven't learned that their own breakthrough to peace
happens when they submit to God and obey Him promptly. They
are like unbroken colts resistant to a bridle and bit in their mouths,
which could be used by God to guide them to a place of security and
provision.

Some people are not willing to let God have the reins of their
lives, but they will never feel the security or peace they long for until
they surrender themselves completely to the Holy Spirit. He wants you;
let Him have all of you.

GOD'S WORD FOR YOU TODAY: Give God full custody of
your life.

Don't Forget God's Promise

[Abraham], having waited long and endured patiently, realized and obtained [in the birth of Isaac as a pledge of what was to come] what God had promised him. (HEBREWS 6:15)

God gave Abraham the promise of an heir, but he had to wait much longer than he could have ever imagined. Today's Scripture says that Abraham "waited long and endured patiently." During those times, I am sure he had to remind himself of God's original promise over and over again. Extended periods of waiting can tend to cause us to doubt that we ever heard from God at all. Perhaps you are waiting on something right now and need to remind yourself of what God originally spoke to your heart.

Doubt and unbelief did attack Abraham and when they did he offered thanksgiving and praise. When Satan attacks, we must not be passive, taking no action at all. We should war against him and his lies by reminding him of God's Word and promises to us. Speak them out loud, meditate on them, and write them down. When Habakkuk was waiting on God he was instructed to write the vision on tablets plainly so that everyone passing by might read it (see Habakkuk 2:2). Perhaps this was an Old Testament version of a billboard!

Fight the good fight of faith and hold fast your confession. No matter how you might feel right now, don't give up because God is faithful, and just as He fulfilled His promise to Abraham at the appointed time, He will also fulfill His word to you.

GOD'S WORD FOR YOU TODAY: When you talk to friends, don't talk excessively about how you feel; tell them what God's Word says.

Believe God Is Leading You

When you walk, your steps shall not be hampered [your path will be clear and open]; and when you run, you shall not stumble.

(PROVERBS 4:12)

In my journey of learning how to hear from God, I realized that eventually we must simply believe He is leading and guiding us. We ask Him to guide our steps and believe by faith that He is doing what we ask of Him. There are times when I hear a very clear word from God, but much of the time I pray about my day and then go about it in faith. I may have nothing occur that day that seems supernatural or mystical. There are no visions, no voices, nothing out of the ordinary, but I know in my heart that God kept me safe and following the right path.

God keeps us from many things that we never even know of. I wonder how often I could have been in an accident had I not prayed for God's guidance that morning? How many terrible traffic jams have I missed because I simply *felt* that I was to take a different route than the one I usually took? I want to strongly encourage you to pray, ask for God's guidance and leadership, and then say throughout the day, "I believe I am being guided by God today and every day."

Psalm 139:2 says that God knows our downsitting and our uprising. If He knows each time we sit down or stand up, and took the time to tell us about that in His Word, then surely He sees and cares about everything else.

***

GOD'S WORD FOR YOU TODAY: You can rest in the knowledge that God is busy with your every step.

Growing into Maturity

We consider and look not to the things that are seen but to the things that are unseen; for the things that are visible are temporal (brief and fleeting), but the things that are invisible are deathless and everlasting. (2 CORINTHIANS 4:18)

Even though Paul went through tremendous trials and tribulations, he did not become discouraged because he looked not to what was seen, but to what was unseen. We need to follow his example. Instead of looking at what we see around us, we need to look at what the Holy Spirit is doing. He will lead us to focus on God's answers instead of our problems.

Two people can read the Word and the person with carnal, fleshly ears will hear it differently than a person with spiritual ears. For example, 3 John 2 says, "Beloved, I pray that you may prosper in every way and [that your body] may keep well, even as [I know] your soul keeps well and prospers."

Less mature, carnal Christians (still lured by physical pleasures and appetites) may get excited about the promise of prosperity and healing, because that is all they hear in this verse. They think, *Wow! Praise God! He wants us to prosper and be in health!*

But mature believers who are sensitive to God's holy intent for their lives will also hear the part of the verse that says, "even as … your soul keeps well and prospers." They hear with understanding that God is going to give them prosperity and healing *in correlation with* how their souls are prospering.

Pray that you will have ears to truly hear what God is saying and that you will grow progressively into maturity as you continue to walk with God.

GOD'S WORD FOR YOU TODAY: Ask God to open your spiritual ears so you will hear the full meaning of what He wants to say to you in His Word.

Pray, Then Plan

Many plans are in a man's mind, but it is the Lord's purpose for him that will stand. (PROVERBS 19:21)

God's Word shows us clearly that we need to listen for His voice and commit our ears to a covenant with Him, letting Him sanctify and circumcise our ears so we can hear Him. Many times God clearly shows us what to do, but we don't do it because we don't like His plan. We can even pretend spiritual deafness when we don't like what we clearly hear Him say. Our fleshly appetites and desires can hinder our acceptance of God's truth.

We can come face-to-face with truth and still not accept it. I admit that truth is often much easier to accept when it concerns other people and their lives than it is when it concerns me and my life. We have a plan for how we want our lives to go, and we have a way that we want to work out that plan. Most of the time we want God to listen to our plan and make it work instead of listening for His plan and asking Him to do what He needs to do to fulfill it through us. We always need to pray first and then make plans instead of making plans and praying for God to make them work. Listen for God's plan; follow it, and you will always succeed.

GOD'S WORD FOR YOU TODAY: Get God's plan before making your own plans.

When God Speaks…

The Word that God speaks is alive and full of power [making it active, operative, energizing, and effective]; it is sharper than any two-edged sword, penetrating to the dividing line of the breath of life (soul) and [the immortal] spirit, and of joints and marrow [of the deepest parts of our nature], exposing and sifting and analyzing and judging the very thoughts and purposes of the heart. (HEBREWS 4:12)

We can accurately say that God's Word operates on us. It cuts out of our lives the things that are hindering God's plan for our lives. It locates and isolates the things that are fleshly and carnal, and removes them through the Holy Spirit.

In the early years of being a student of God's Word, I did not have enough experience to discern the difference between hearing from my own soul (mind, will, emotions), and actually being led by the Holy Spirit. If I wanted something, I tried to make it happen and if it didn't, then I became angry. I was selfish, carnal, and fleshly, but over the years, God used His Word to operate on me and cut off my wrong behavior.

Operations of any kind are never pleasant, but they are necessary at times to maintain good health. Is God trying to cut something out of your life? Is it painful? Most operations are, but they help us in the long run. If you want God's best for your life, then you must let Him get rid of the things that are interfering with your spiritual growth. There are no shortcuts to spiritual maturity.

GOD'S WORD FOR YOU TODAY: The long road to success is the one on which we learn valuable lessons that teach us wisdom.

God Hears You When You Pray

Depart from me, all you workers of iniquity, for the Lord has heard the voice of my weeping. The Lord has heard my supplication; the Lord receives my prayer. (PSALM 6:8–9)

When we pray, God hears us and He answers. It is important that we are as confident of that as David was when he wrote the verses for today. You can live with confidence as long as you know that God is on your side and that He will help you win your battles in life. You are not alone, God is with you!

Reading the Psalms is a great way to hear from God. He speaks to us through His Word and the Psalms are especially encouraging in times of trouble. As you read them, take them personally. Don't meditate on them as if they are for someone else, but remember that they are God's personal letter to you. He wants you to know that He has good plans for you and no matter who comes against you, He is for you. God delivered David from his enemies and He will do the same thing for you if you remain confident in Him.

Stay in peace and continue thanking God that He is working in your life. I can assure you that God has not forgotten you. He will not be late in delivering the answer to your prayer. He may not be early, but He won't be late! Keep your vision in front of you and don't give up.

GOD'S WORD FOR YOU TODAY: God will send you help; He will support, refresh, and strengthen you.

Don't Offend God

*Work out (cultivate, carry out to the goal, and fully complete) your
own salvation with reverence and awe and trembling (self-distrust,
with serious caution, tenderness of conscience, watchfulness against
temptation, timidly shrinking from whatever might offend God and
discredit the name of Christ).* (PHILIPPIANS 2:12)

We can allow the Holy Spirit to invade our lives. We can be so filled
with His presence and power that we allow Him into every aspect of
who we are and into everything we do. He can get into our thoughts,
emotions, and even our wills and bring healing and wholeness to our
entire being, but He wants an invitation.

Tell the Holy Spirit you are ready to work with Him to bring what
He has done in you by the grace of God to the forefront of your life.
"Work it out," which is the theme of our Scripture for today, means that
we must learn to live from the Spirit. We need to learn to live inside
out. Be cautious not to offend God by giving in to temptation and sin.
Learn to live in such a manner that your conscience is entirely clean at
all times.

You might be thinking, *Joyce, all of this sounds hard and I am not sure
I have what it takes.* But, I want to assure you that you do have what it
takes, because you have the power of the Holy Spirit in your life. You
cannot do it in your own strength, but as you partner with God you
can do whatever you need to do in life. Don't settle for a "barely get by"
kind of life when there is a life of abundance waiting for you.

GOD'S WORD FOR YOU TODAY: Turn away from anything that offends God.

237 In Spirit and Truth

In Spirit and Truth

God is a Spirit (a spiritual Being) and those who worship Him must worship Him in spirit and in truth (reality). (JOHN 4:24)

We communicate with God through our spirit. Jesus said in our verse for today that we must worship God in spirit and in truth. Being totally and completely truthful with God is one of the ways we can develop intimacy with Him. He knows everything about us anyway, so there is no reason to not be totally honest with Him. Tell Him how you feel, what you have done wrong, and what your desires are. Talk to God honestly as you would a good, trusted friend.

There are times when I know God wants me to do a thing and I tell Him honestly that I don't want to do it, but that I will do it in obedience to Him and because I love Him. Pretense and a close relationship with God will not work. A friend of mine once told me that although she knew she should give financially into the Kingdom of God that truthfully she did not want to. She was honest with God and told Him, "I will do it, but I don't really want to, so I am asking You to give me a desire to give." This woman eventually became very generous and did it with joy.

Only the truth will make us free (see John 8:32). God's Word is truth. He says what He means and means what He says. When we do something wrong we must be totally honest with God about it. Call sin what it is. If you were greedy, call it greed. If you were jealous, call it jealousy. If you lied, call it a lie. Ask God for forgiveness and receive it by faith.

When we worship God, we must do so from the spirit and do it with all truth, sincerity, and honesty. If we feel a friend is being untruthful, we often say, "Get real," meaning that we are asking them to stop pretending and just be honest. I think God wants the same thing from us.

GOD'S WORD FOR YOU TODAY: Get real!

The Inner Life

The Holy Spirit points out that the way into the [true Holy of] Holies is not yet thrown open as long as the former [the outer portion of the] tabernacle remains a recognized institution and is still standing.

(HEBREWS 9:8)

The Old Testament tabernacle had three compartments. It consisted of an outer court, a second compartment called the Holy Place, and the Holy of Holies, which was the interior chamber. Only the high priest could go into the Holy of Holies, for it contained the presence of God.

As humans we are tri-part beings with three compartments. We have a body, we have a soul, and we have a spirit. The verse for today states that as long as we continue recognizing the outer portion, which is an analogy of our body and soul, then the way into the Holy of Holies, an analogy of our spirit, is not opened. In simple terms, this means that if we obey and cater to our flesh we will never enjoy and dwell in the presence of God. For example, if I am angry I will not enjoy the presence of God.

Our fleshly parts will always make demands because the flesh is selfish and wants its own way, but we do not have to give in to those demands. We can simply say, "I do not recognize you any longer; you have no authority over me." As we take this stand against giving in to the demands of the fleshly life, we are honoring God and made able to enjoy His presence. The message for today is easy: "Say no to self and yes to God." The Bible says that we are dead to sin. Sin is not dead; it will always try to draw us in, but we can say no!

GOD'S WORD FOR YOU TODAY: Don't live the life of the flesh by catering to the appetites and impulses of your carnal nature.

Be Excellent

Everything is permissible (allowable and lawful) for me; but not all things are helpful (good for me to do, expedient and profitable when considered with other things). Everything is lawful for me, but I will not become the slave of anything or be brought under its power.

(1 CORINTHIANS 6:12)

God has an awesome plan to radically and outrageously bless us, but to fully enjoy His plan we must radically and outrageously obey Him. We need God's help to stay on the pathway to His blessings. Ask Him to deal with you firmly if there are any areas in your life that are displeasing to Him, and when He does, respond with prompt and complete obedience.

God puts His Holy Spirit in us to lead us to perfect peace. If we are listening to Him, we will make wise decisions and enjoy His peace. In the verse for today, we see that many things are permissible, but not good for us, and that it is unwise for us to allow anything to become a controlling factor in our lives.

There are many things we can do, but they would not be the best choice nor would they produce the best result. Paul said that we should choose and prize the most excellent things (see Philippians 1:10). God isn't going to give us a divine word about every single move we make, but He gives us His Word and wisdom and He expects us to live by it. Don't be mediocre and hope you get by with it, but instead choose to be excellent and know that you are pleasing God.

GOD'S WORD FOR YOU TODAY: Excellent choices produce excellent rewards.

Delight in God's Will

I delight to do your will, O my God; yes, Your law is within my heart.
(PSALM 40:8)

If we want to hear God's voice and obey His will, I believe our prayer every morning should be something like this:

"God, I want to walk in Your perfect will all my life. I don't want Your permissive will; I don't want to do anything without Your approval and blessing. If I try to do something that's not Your best for me, please let me feel hesitation in my heart, a check in my spirit, to keep me on the path of Your plan.

Help me to submit myself to You.

Help me not to be stiff-necked.

Help me not to be stubborn.

Help me not to be hard-hearted.

God, I want Your will to operate fully in my life. I've experienced the fruit of my own will enough to know that if I get my way, and it's not what You want, it's going to turn out badly. I'm willing to obey You, but please help me to hear clearly what You are telling me to do. Amen."

GOD'S WORD FOR YOU TODAY: Several times each day, whisper to God, "Your will be done."

Prayers of Petition and Perseverance

You do not have, because you do not ask. (JAMES 4:2)

God has provided a simple way for us to have the things we desire without struggling to get them. The verse for today says that we don't have certain things because we do not ask God for them. A prayer cannot be answered if it is not prayed; therefore, we need to pray and ask. The type of prayer we pray when we make requests is called a prayer of petition—and this kind of prayer is important because God does not do anything in the earth unless somebody prays and asks. You see, we partner with Him through prayer. Prayer is simply the means by which we cooperate with Him and work with Him in the spiritual realm in order to get things done in the natural realm. Prayer brings the power of heaven to Earth.

If our prayers are not answered quickly, we may be asking for something that is not God's will for us, or God may be waiting to answer because He is developing our faith and helping us build our spiritual muscles as we learn endurance and patience.

We need to petition God and make our requests known to Him instead of trying to make things happen ourselves. We also need to trust His wisdom in how and when He answers. Prayer opens the door for God to work, but our trying to get things in our own effort only frustrates us and hinders God. He is waiting for us to ask and trust His ways and timing. When we do, He will work mightily on our behalf.

GOD'S WORD FOR YOU TODAY: God wants to do more for you than you can imagine, so start asking boldly.

Wisdom and Common Sense

*Happy (blessed, fortunate, enviable) is the man who finds skillful
and godly Wisdom, and the man who gets understanding [drawing it
forth from God's Word and life's experiences] … Skillful and godly
Wisdom is more precious than rubies … Her ways are highways of
pleasantness, and all her paths are peace.* (PROVERBS 3:13–17)

When we listen to God's direction, we make wise decisions that lead
to honor, prosperity, pleasantness, and peace. Once Dave and I pray for
God to speak to us and guide us, we use wisdom and common sense
for both major and minor issues.

Wisdom will always lead you to God's best. For example, wisdom teaches that you won't keep friends if you try to control and domi-
nate everything that goes on in your life and theirs. You won't keep
friends if you talk about them behind their backs.

Common sense will guide you in money matters. You won't get into
debt if you don't spend more money than you make. The Holy Spirit
doesn't need to speak audibly to tell us that we can't have more money
going out than we have coming in. Common sense tells us that we'll get
in trouble if we do that.

Wisdom will not let us get overcommitted in our time. No matter
how anxious we may be to accomplish things, we need to take time and
wait on God to give us peace about what we are and are not to do. The
woman mentioned in Proverbs 31 considered buying new fields, but
would not do so if it meant she would have to neglect her present duties
by taking on new responsibility.

Wisdom is our friend. It helps us not live in regret, and it helps us
make choices now that we will be happy with later on.

***

GOD'S WORD FOR YOU TODAY: Practice wisdom and
common sense in all your decisions.

Catching Anything?

Jesus said to them, Boys (children), You do not have any meat (fish),
do you? [Have you caught anything to eat along with your bread?]

(JOHN 21:5)

John 21 tells the story of the disciples who fished all night long, but caught nothing. Have you ever felt like you were doing all you knew to do and still not getting a good result? If so, then you know how they must have felt.

Jesus showed up and called to them from the beach and asked if they had caught anything. They said no. He told them to cast their nets on the right side of the boat and they would find fish. They cast, and they had so many fish they could not even haul in the net. This story is an example of what happens when we follow God's will, compared to what happens when we follow our own will.

When Jesus questioned them, He was basically saying, "Are you doing any good at what you are trying to do?" That is a question we might ask ourselves when we have no fruit to show for all the effort we put into the projects we are working on.

When we "fish" outside the will of God, it's equivalent to fishing on the wrong side of the boat. Sometimes we struggle, strive, work, and strain, trying to make something great happen. We try to change things, people, or ourselves. We try to get more money or a higher position at work. We can work and work in all these ways and still have nothing to show for our efforts except being worn out.

Have you caught anything lately? Have you accomplished anything besides being worn out? If not, maybe you've been fishing on the wrong side of the boat.

GOD'S WORD FOR YOU TODAY: If you ask for God's help and listen for His voice, He will tell you where to throw your net.

Pray for Others

I admonish and urge that petitions, prayers, intercessions, and thanksgivings be offered on behalf of all men. (1 TIMOTHY 2:1)

When we pray, we both speak to God and listen to Him speak to us. One type of prayer is intercession, which is simply praying for someone besides yourself. It is crying out to God on someone else's behalf, taking their needs to Him in prayer, and at times hearing something from Him about their situation. Intercession is one of the most important kinds of prayer because many people do not pray for themselves or do not know how. Why? Because they have no relationship with God. There are also times when circumstances are so difficult, stress is so high, the hurt is too great, or things are so confusing that people do not know how to pray for their own situations. And, there are times when people have prayed and prayed and prayed for themselves and they simply have no strength left to pray.

For example, I once visited a friend who was in the hospital suffering with cancer. She had fought a valiant fight and prayed like a warrior, but she reached a point where she was not strong enough to pray the way she wanted to and she said, "Joyce, I just *cannot* pray anymore." She needed her friends to pray for her—not just to *pray* for her, but to really pray *for* her—to pray in her place because she could not.

I am sure there are people in your life who need prayer, people who need you to speak to God and hear from Him on their behalf. I encourage you to ask Him to show you who they are and to be faithful to pray for them.

GOD'S WORD FOR YOU TODAY: Be faithful to pray for people as God leads you.

Stand in the Gap

I sought a man among them who should build up the wall and stand in the gap before Me for the land, that I should not destroy it, but I found none. (EZEKIEL 22:30)

A gap is a space between two things; it keeps two objects, two spaces, two entities, or two people from being connected to each other. When I preach in foreign countries, there is a gap between the audience and me. There may be a physical gap if I am on a platform; there may be a cultural gap, but I am most concerned about the language gap. If I want the people to understand me, I need a translator, someone to stand in the language gap for me so that I can communicate the message effectively. The translator has to work on my behalf so that the gap can be eliminated and the people can comprehend what I am saying.

Ezekiel 22:29–31 talks about standing in the gap. Today's verse is found in that passage and it is one of the saddest statements in the Bible. In it, God was basically saying, "I needed somebody to pray, and I couldn't find anybody who would, so I had to destroy the land." All He needed was *one* person to pray, and the whole land could have been spared. Do you see how important intercession is? Just one person could have made a major difference in an entire country and saved the entire place through prayer! We need to be willing to pray; we need to be sensitive to those times when the Holy Spirit is leading us to intercede and we need to obey. We never know when our prayer might be the very one needed to fill a gap and result in connecting God's power with a desperate situation.

GOD'S WORD FOR YOU TODAY: Tell God you are available to pray for others and do so as He places various people on your heart.

We Can Make a Difference

The Lord turned from the evil which He had thought to do to His people. (EXODUS 32:14)

Do you know that prayer can change God's mind? As a result of someone who will simply take time to talk to Him and listen to Him, God can actually reconsider something He had planned to do.

When Moses went up Mount Sinai to get the Ten Commandments, he was gone longer than the people wanted him to be. In the absence of their leader, they forgot the Lord, gave in to their fleshly desires and decided to melt all their jewelry, make a golden calf, and worship it. God spoke to Moses on the mountain and said, essentially, "You better get back down there, because the people have really gotten themselves in a mess. And I'm angry about it." (Thank God, Psalm 30:5 says that His anger lasts only a moment, but His mercy is forever!)

Moses began to intercede for the people because he cared so much about them. God had already said to him, "Leave Me alone, for these people are stiff-necked and stubborn" (see Exodus 32:9–10). But Moses refused to give up because the issue was not settled in his heart. He loved the people, he knew the nature of God, and he knew the character of God. On top of that, he knew that God really loved the people and did not really want to leave them stranded.

Moses asked God to change His mind (see Exodus 32:12) and according to today's verse, God did. We *can* make a difference when we pray!

GOD'S WORD FOR YOU TODAY: When you pray, God hears and answers!

Listen with Your Spirit

*It is the Spirit Who gives life [He is the Life-giver]; the flesh conveys
no benefit whatever [there is no profit in it]. The words (truths) that I
have been speaking to you are spirit and life.* (JOHN 6:63)

Sometimes our own minds, wills, or emotions interfere with our ability to hear God's voice. When we try to hear and obey God, negative
thoughts can bombard us to the point that we feel like giving up. But
if we quiet our minds and see what is in our hearts, God will give us
confirmation of what He is speaking. We will sense His answer rising with peace and confidence from deep within our hearts, where the
Holy Spirit dwells.

One time I had finished a meeting, one I had worked very hard to
ensure would be helpful to the people who came. Although everyone
seemed to enjoy it, I kept hearing in my head, "No one was blessed and
most wished they hadn't even come."

I felt like a miserable failure, which I knew was not God's will
for me, so I got still and quiet and listened to see what the Holy
Spirit would say to me. I instantly heard the still, small voice, the knowing deep inside, say, "If the people did not want to be here, they would
not have come. If they were not enjoying it, many would have left.
I gave you the message, and I never give anyone bad things to preach,
so don't allow Satan to steal the joy of your labor." Had I not listened,
I would have continued to be miserable, but God's word brought life
to me.

We hear from God through our spirit, not through our mind.
Remember that, and always take time to stop and ask God what He is
truly saying to you.

GOD'S WORD FOR YOU TODAY: God's Word always
brings life.

Learn to Discern

Yes, if you cry out for discernment, and lift up your voice for understanding ... then you will understand the fear of the LORD, and find the knowledge of God. (PROVERBS 2:3–5 NKJV)

Discernment is something we can expect as we grow closer to God. It allows us to penetrate the surface of a thing and see into the deep areas of it. Things are not always the way they appear to be, so discernment is a valuable thing to have. If we possess a discerning mind and heart, we will avoid a lot of trouble. I encourage you to pray for discernment on a regular basis.

If we make our decisions according to the way things look, what we think, or how we feel, we will make a lot of unwise decisions. Something may appear to be good, yet deep down inside you have a feeling that you need to be cautious and not go forward with it. If that is the case, then you need to wait and pray some more, asking God to lead you by His Spirit by giving you discernment in your spirit. Never do anything if you don't have peace about it or it just doesn't fit right in your spirit.

Our verse for today encourages us to understand the fear of the Lord. Being careful not to go against what you sense in your heart is you practicing the fear of the Lord. It is displaying reverence for what you believe He is showing you even though your mind may not understand it at all. Learning to be led by the Spirit is learning to develop and respect the way God often speaks, which is through discernment, so continue praying and practicing in this area.

GOD'S WORD FOR YOU TODAY: Don't make decisions according to mental knowledge alone. Do an internal check and see what discernment wants to say to you.

Just Do Your Part

The Lord has heard my supplication; the Lord receives my prayer.
(PSALM 6:9)

Every believer is called to talk to God and listen to His voice through prayer, but not everyone is called into the spiritual office of an intercessor. For example, I believe God has called Dave as an intercessor for America. He seems to have an "official" assignment from the Lord to pray for our country, a true burden for national issues and affairs, a longing to see revival in our land, and a deep, sustained interest in the things that concern the United States. He diligently studies American history and stays informed about what is going on in the government of our country. There is also an unusual fervor that accompanies his prayers. That's what I mean by a person who functions in the office of an intercessor.

Since 1997, I have watched Dave pray and cry and bombard heaven on behalf of the United States. I do not weep over our nation the way he does, but that does not mean I do not care or that I do not pray for our leaders. It simply means that I cannot force myself to have Dave's passion, because that passion is God-given. It also means that God is using Dave and me as a team; He has Dave playing one position and me playing another one. If I start to wonder what is wrong with me because I do not intercede the way Dave does, I end up under condemnation— and that will keep me from fulfilling what God has called me to do. But, if I stay confident in my position and focus on being excellent in it, our team wins every time. God does not assign everything to everyone. The Holy Spirit divides things up the way He sees fit and all we need to do is our part.

GOD'S WORD FOR YOU TODAY: Relax and pray the way God leads you.

Yes and No

What man is there of you, if his son asks him for a loaf of bread, will hand him a stone? Of if he asks for a fish, will hand him a serpent?

(MATTHEW 7:9–10)

We are not always smart enough to know the right things to ask for, but today's verse promises that if we ask for bread, God will not give us a stone, and if we ask for fish, He will not give us a serpent. There are times when we think we are asking for bread, when in reality, we are asking for a stone. In other words, we may be asking for something we truly believe is right, but God knows that granting such a request would be the worst thing He could ever give us.

We have the ability, in all innocence, to ask for something that is potentially dangerous or bad for us without even realizing it. In that case, we need to be glad God does not give it to us! In such cases, little do we know that God's saying "yes" to that request would be like letting a serpent into a house. We have to trust Him enough to say, "God, I have the confidence to ask You for anything. But I don't want anything that is not Your will for me. And I trust You, God. If I don't get it, I will know that the timing is not right or that You have something better for me and I simply have not thought to ask for it yet." Don't ever let yourself get a bad attitude because God does not give you everything you want.

God wants us to be blessed. He wants us to have not only what we want, but what is best for us. If we truly trust God, we must trust Him when He says "no" to our requests as much as we do when He says "yes" to them.

GOD'S WORD FOR YOU TODAY: Trust God when He says "no" and when He says "yes."

A Very Powerful Prayer

Love your enemies, bless them that curse you, do good to them that hate you, and pray for them which despitefully use you, and persecute you. (MATTHEW 5:44 KJV)

One of the most powerful prayers you can pray is a prayer for your enemies. If you want to see someone who is mighty in prayer, look for the person who will intercede for an enemy. I believe that God blesses us tremendously when we intercede for those who have offended or betrayed us.

Remember Job? He had to pray for his friends after they had really hurt and disappointed him. But immediately after he prayed, God began to restore his life. In fact, God gave him back twice as much as he had lost (see Job 42:10)! Praying for someone who has hurt us is so powerful because, when we do, we are walking in love toward that person and we are obeying the Word of God.

We can hear God's voice in the verse for today. What does Jesus tell us to do in this verse? He instructs us to pray for our enemies. When you think about the people who have used you, abused you, harassed you, and spoken evil of you, bless them; do not curse them. Pray for them. God knows that blessing your enemies is not easy and that you may not feel like doing it. But you don't do it because you feel like it; you do it as unto the Lord. Choosing to pray and bless instead of curse is very powerful in the spiritual realm, and God will do great things in your life as a result.

————————

GOD'S WORD FOR YOU TODAY: Don't let mean-spirited people bring you down to their level by tempting you to act like they act.

Unity Brings Blessings

Behold, how good and how pleasant it is for brethren to dwell together in unity!... It is like the dew of [lofty] Mount Hermon and the dew that comes on the hills of Zion; for there the Lord has commanded the blessing, even life forevermore. (PSALM 133:1, 3)

When you have been praying about something and do not seem to be hearing from God, you may need to get someone to pray in agreement with you. That kind of unity is a powerful spiritual dynamic, and according to today's verses, it is good and it commands God's blessing.

When two or more people come in agreement, Jesus promises to be with them, and His presence exerts more power than we can even imagine in our lives and in our circumstances. He says in Matthew 18:19–20: "If two of you on earth agree (harmonize together, make a symphony together) about whatever [anything and everything] they may ask, it will come to pass and be done for them by My Father in heaven. For wherever two or three are gathered (drawn together as My followers) in (into) My name, there I AM in the midst of them." God is also with us as individuals, but our power increases as we come together in unity and agreement. The Bible says that one can put one thousand to flight and two can run off ten thousand (see Deuteronomy 32:30). I like that kind of math!

Because God's blessing rests on unity and His presence is with those who agree in His name, the enemy works diligently to divide people, to bring strife into relationships, and to keep people at odds with each other. We need to understand the power of unity and agreement, and we need to exercise that power by talking to God and listening for His voice with others.

GOD'S WORD FOR YOU TODAY: Don't forsake praying with others.

God Has Your Answers

May the Lord answer you in the day of trouble! May the name of the God of Jacob set you up on high [and defend you]. (PSALM 20:1)

If you have ever been in a relationship, tried to manage your money, held a job, tried to discover and fulfill God's purpose for your life, or tried to grow spiritually—then you have probably encountered some problems. Problems are a part of life and when you get rid of one problem, you will most likely have another one right behind it! That is true for all of us and even though we can develop and mature in our abilities to confront, endure, be steadfast, and live in victory, we will always be contending with one problem or another.

Only God has the solutions to life's problems, and the best thing we can do with our problems is to give them to Him. We need to quit rehearsing them in our minds, quit talking about them, quit fretting over them, and simply release the pressures and the problems of life to God and let Him work everything out. If we will learn to commit our stresses and situations to God, we will enjoy our lives more, we will be more fun to be around, and we will be happier and more relaxed.

God can do more in one moment than we can do in a lifetime of striving and struggle. He can speak to you in an instant and turn a situation around completely; one word from Him can solve everything. Nothing is too big for God to accomplish, and nothing is too small for Him to be concerned about. He cares about *everything* that concerns you, so give your problems to Him and let Him give you the solutions you need.

GOD'S WORD FOR YOU TODAY: Give God your problems and allow Him to give you solutions.

A Good Kind of Burden

Graciously consider the prayer and supplication of Your servant, O Lord my God, to hearken to the [loud] cry and prayer which he prays before You today. (1 KINGS 8:28)

Sometimes, as you are praying for others, you will get what some call a prayer burden, or an intercessory burden. A burden is something that comes to your heart and feels weighty and important; it is something God is asking you to carry in prayer; it is something you cannot shake. Sometimes God may speak to you and explain the burden to you. At other times you do not even know what the burden is or you do not fully understand it; you only know that you *have* to pray.

Some people are called to pray a lot for certain things. My husband prays a lot for America. I know people who pray for Israel all the time. One woman told me she prayed for veterans returning from war. I believe God has every need in the world covered. We don't all need to pray for the same thing because, if we did, all the needs would not be taken care of. Pay attention to what God is placing on your heart and pray for that.

One of the ways God speaks to us is through giving us burdens for others. He does this often without words, but by a sense of weightiness and concern for people in our hearts. When this happens, He is asking us to pray for them. Pay attention to the burdens He gives you and be faithful to pray when He is asking you to do so.

GOD'S WORD FOR YOU TODAY: As you pray for others, remember that God also has someone praying for you.

Put God in Remembrance of His Word

I have set watchmen upon your walls, O Jerusalem, who will never hold their peace day or night; you who [are His servants and by your prayers] put the Lord in remembrance [of His promises], keep not silence. (ISAIAH 62:6)

Today's verse instructs us to remind God of the promises He has made to us and one of the best ways to do that is to pray His Word back to Him.

God's Word is extremely valuable to Him and should be to us as well. After all, He speaks to us clearly through His Word and it is a trustworthy way to hear His voice. In fact, the Amplified Bible renders Psalm 138:2 as follows: "I will worship toward Your holy temple and praise Your name for Your loving-kindness and for Your truth and faithfulness; for You have exalted above all else Your name and Your word and You have magnified Your word above all Your name!" This verse indicates that God magnifies His Word even above His name. If He honors it to that extent, we need to make a priority out of knowing the Word, studying the Word, loving the Word, getting the Word deeply rooted in our hearts, esteeming the Word more highly than anything else, and incorporating the Word into our prayers.

When we honor the Word and commit ourselves to it as I have just described, we are "abiding" in it (see John 15:7). Abiding in the Word and allowing the Word to abide in us is directly related to confidence in prayer and to having our prayers answered. When we pray the Word of God, we are less likely to pray for things that are not God's will for us.

Jesus Christ is the living Word (see John 1:1–4), and as we abide in the Word, we abide in Him—and that brings unspeakable power to our prayers.

GOD'S WORD FOR YOU TODAY: The Word of God is renewing your mind and teaching you to think like God thinks.

A Spiritual Force

How could one have chased a thousand, and two put ten thousand to flight, except their Rock had sold them, and the Lord had delivered them up? (DEUTERONOMY 32:30)

As I have already shared, God answers prayers of agreement when the people who are praying are already expressing agreement in their everyday lives. He so appreciates those who pay the price to live in agreement, unity, and harmony, that He says to them, essentially, "When you get together like that, My power is released among you. The power of your agreement is so dynamic that you're going to break through—no doubt about it. I'll do it."

You see, agreement is so powerful that it is a principle of multiplication, not addition. That is why the verse for today says that one person can put a thousand to flight and two, ten thousand. If agreement were based on addition, one would put a thousand to flight and two would put two thousand. But unity commands God's blessing—and God's blessing brings multiplication. For that reason, the prayer of true agreement is a strong and mighty force in the spiritual realm.

When we are divided we become weak and when we are united we are strong. Surely the power that is available to us is worth the effort it takes to maintain unity and harmony. No matter what anyone else does or doesn't do, you do your part and God will bless you.

GOD'S WORD FOR YOU TODAY: You cannot make everyone be agreeable, but you can refuse to let them upset you.

Receive Strength from Prayer

Being in an agony [of mind], He prayed [all the] more earnestly and intently, and His sweat became like great clots of blood dropping down upon the ground. (LUKE 22:44)

When the time was close for Jesus to go to the cross, He endured a great struggle in His mind and emotions. He needed God's strength to go through with God's will just like we do at times. He prayed and received that strength. The Bible states that as He prayed angels came and ministered to Him.

Never just assume that what God is asking you to do is too difficult. If you are willing to do the will of God and you ask God to strengthen you, He will. Don't waste words telling God and others how impossible your task is. Use that same energy asking God to give you courage, determination, and strength. I think it is a beautiful thing to witness when God joins in partnership with an individual and enables him or her to do impossible things.

Many things are impossible with man by himself, but with God all things are possible. Perhaps you are facing a crisis or a difficulty right now; if you are, then I ask you to remember the struggle that Jesus went through in the garden. He felt such pressure that His sweat became blood. Surely if He could do what He did through God's strength, then you can gain a victory also through prayer.

GOD'S WORD FOR YOU TODAY: God never gives you anything to do that is beyond your ability with Him by your side.

Confess the Word

My tongue shall speak of Your word, for all Your commandments are righteousness. (PSALM 119:172 NKJV)

God's Word is such a treasure. It is filled with wisdom, direction, truth, and everything else we need in order to live purposeful, powerful, and successful lives. We need to incorporate the Word into our prayers, confessing it over every circumstance and situation. The word *confess* means "to say the same thing as," so when we confess the Word, we are saying the same things God says; we are putting ourselves in agreement with Him. If we really want a deep and vibrant relationship with God, we need to agree with Him and nothing will help us do that like confessing the Word. Our confession strengthens our knowledge of the Word and our faith in God, which increases the accuracy and effectiveness of our prayers.

In order to confess the Word, we need to know the Word, because we can agree with God only when we know what He has done and what He has said. I often encounter people who are asking God to give them something they already have or to make them something they already are, and I want to say, "Stop praying that way! God has already finished the work you are asking Him to do." There is no need to ask God to bless you because He already has. It would be better to say, "God, thank You that according to Your Word I am blessed." Prayers that ask God for something that He has already given us are totally unnecessary. When we pray God's Word back to Him or put Him in remembrance of it, we are honoring His Word and reminding ourselves of what it says. Each time we speak His Word, power is released from heaven to make a change in the earth!

GOD'S WORD FOR YOU TODAY: God's Word coming out of your mouth in faith is one of the most powerful forces in heaven and Earth.

Learn from Jesus' Prayers

Father, forgive them, for they know not what they do. (LUKE 23:34)

I believe that the way people pray and the things they pray about reveal a lot about their character and spiritual maturity. There was a time when my prayer life did not indicate much spiritual maturity. Even though I was a born-again, filled with the Holy Spirit and teaching God's Word, my prayers were pathetically carnal. When I prayed, I had a list of requests I thought God had to say yes to before I could be happy—and all of them were natural things: "Lord, make my ministry grow. Give us a new car; do this; do that. Make Dave change. Make the kids behave," and so on.

In response, God simply said to me, "I want you to examine the prayers of Jesus and the prayers of Paul. Then we'll talk about your prayer life." Of course, there are many prayers throughout the Bible, especially in Psalms, but God told me to pray the prayers of Jesus, which are found in the Gospels, and the prayers of Paul, which are found in the Epistles.

When I began to pray the way Jesus prayed, I discovered that there really is no more powerful way to pray than to pray the Word of God because it shows us what is important to Him. He prayed prayers such as we read in today's verse and many others, including His prayer to "sanctify them [purify, consecrate, separate them for Yourself, make them holy] by Truth; Your Word is Truth" (John 17:17); His prayer for unity among His people (see John 17:23); and His prayer for Peter: "I have prayed especially for you [Peter], that your [own] faith may not fail" (Luke 22:32).

I encourage you to read the Gospels and see how Jesus prayed, then pray similarly as you talk and listen to God.

GOD'S WORD FOR YOU TODAY: Pray that God would reveal His love to you, and that you would become conscious and aware of it.

Learn from Paul's Prayers

[I always pray to] the God of our Lord Jesus Christ, the Father of
glory, that He may grant you a spirit of wisdom and revelation.
(EPHESIANS 1:17)

I want to focus today on some of Paul's prayers. When I read his prayers
in Ephesians, Philippians, and Colossians, I felt bad about the carnality
of my prayer life, and Paul's prayers affected me so powerfully that my
own prayer life has not been the same since. I saw that Paul never prayed
for people to have easy lives or to be delivered from difficulties. Instead,
he prayed that they would be able to bear whatever came their way with
good temper, that they would be patient, steadfast, and living examples of
God's grace to other people. He prayed about the things that are important to God, and I can assure you from experience, He releases incredible
power to us when we pray that way. We should care more about our spiritual condition than we do about getting all the things that we want.

Today's verse is one of Paul's prayers. This verse teaches us to pray for a
spirit of wisdom and revelation—and that needs to be one of our primary
requests. In fact, I believe that asking God for revelation—spiritual insight
and understanding—is one of the most important prayers we can pray.
Revelation means "to uncover," and we need to ask God to uncover for us
everything that belongs to us in Christ. We need Him to reveal and uncover
the truths of the Word to us so that we will understand how to pray for
ourselves and for others. When someone tells you about a biblical principle
or a spiritual truth, that is a piece of *information*. But when God helps you
understand it, it becomes a *revelation*—and revelation is something that
makes a truth so real to you that nothing can ever take it away.

GOD'S WORD FOR YOU TODAY: Take a break from asking God for things and instead ask Him for more of His presence in your life.

God Is with Us Always

This God is our God forever and ever; He will be our guide [even] until death. (PSALM 48:14)

It is comforting to believe that God has promised to guide us as long as we are on this Earth. We are never alone for He is always with us. He is always watching over us.

As you develop your ability to "hear" from God, you must remember that divine guidance is one of the major ways that He speaks. Form a spiritual habit of acknowledging God in all that you do, asking for His guidance and then believing by faith that you have it.

I am going shopping later today and I will ask God to guide me. He may lead me to a sale I was not expecting, or while I am out He may guide my path in such a way that I meet someone who needs encouragement. I trust that my steps are ordered by the Lord (see Psalm 37:23). I trust God to lead me to what I need to purchase and to help me not to buy things I don't need. I want Him involved in everything I do and I hope you do also.

In my teaching ministry, I often experience divine guidance. I study and prepare what I believe I will be saying, but often when I begin talking I find myself being led by God in a different direction than I had planned. He knows what the people in attendance need to hear and it is my job to let Him take the lead.

I encourage you to remember that hearing from God can often seem quite natural. Don't seek supernatural experiences, but instead seek God's divine guidance. His Spirit is in you and He delights to be involved in all of your activities. Whatever you do today or wherever you go, expect Him to guide you.

GOD'S WORD FOR YOU TODAY: God is always with you and will guide you in everything you do today.

Spirit-Led Persistence

What am I to do? I will pray with my spirit [by the Holy Spirit that is within me], but I will also pray [intelligently] with my mind and understanding. (1 CORINTHIANS 14:15)

I really want to encourage you to pray persistent, persevering prayers by the leading of the Holy Spirit—not mere repetitious prayers that do not come from your heart, but prayers that refuse to give up. It is possible to use your mouth to speak words of prayer that have no meaning behind them at all, and those prayers are nothing but dead works. I could quote the entire Lord's Prayer while I am thinking about something else, and that would not bless God or do me any good, but if I am sincere and pray from my heart, God hears and works in my behalf.

Lip service doesn't do anything for God or accomplish anything in our lives, so even when we pray about the same thing over and over again, we need to be careful not to fall into meaningless repetition. Instead, we need to allow the Holy Spirit to lead us in a fresh way, even when we are addressing a subject about which we have prayed for a long time. Sometimes He will lead us to be diligent and persistent about a matter, but there is a difference between repetition and Spirit-led persistence.

Words spoken in prayer that are not connected to our hearts are words without power. When we pray we should focus and concentrate on what we are saying. We should never merely verbalize things we have memorized while our hearts are far from God. The earnest (heartfelt, continued) prayer of a righteous man makes tremendous power available (see James 5:16).

GOD'S WORD FOR YOU TODAY: Your heartfelt prayers to God have power and He hears them.

Pray Before It's Too Late

When He came to the place, He said to them, Pray that you may not
[at all] enter into temptation. (LUKE 22:40)

The disciples were being tempted in many ways as they waited with Jesus in the Garden of Gethsemane. They may have wanted to run away, to hide, or do as Peter did when he denied knowing Christ. Jesus did not tell them to pray that they would not be tempted, but He told them to pray that they would not enter into the temptation.

We would love it if we never felt tempted to do wrong things, but that will never happen. The Bible says that temptation must come. One reason we have faith in God is so we can resist the temptation to do wrong things. Jesus wanted them to pray ahead of time so when the pressure got really bad they would already be strong enough to resist.

If a person has a problem with appetite it is best to pray for strength to say no to wrong choices before they ever sit down to the table. Why wait until the pressure is staring them in the face and they are being tempted by all the good smells from the food? I truly believe that if we would recognize our weak areas and pray for strength regularly, we would see a lot more victory. I know that I am tempted to display impatience if I have to do a lot of waiting, so I pray before I even get into those types of situations and it helps me. God has promised us His strength, but we must ask Him for it.

GOD'S WORD FOR YOU TODAY: You can do all things through Christ Who strengthens you.

Forgiveness Is Essential

Whenever you stand praying, if you have anything against anyone,
forgive him and let it drop (leave it, let it go), in order that your
Father Who is in heaven may also forgive you your [own] failings and
shortcomings and let them drop. (MARK 11:25)

If we want to hear from God, we simply must have clean hearts when we approach Him—and one sure way to be clean before Him is to make sure that we have forgiven everyone who has hurt or offended us. Forgiveness is not easy, but it is a prerequisite for effective prayer, as we read in today's verse.

Although Jesus' disciples were familiar with His teachings on forgiveness, they still found it a challenge. Peter asked Him one day, "Lord, how many times may my brother sin against me and I forgive him and let it go? [As many as] up to seven times?" (Matthew 18:21). Jesus essentially said: "No. How about seventy times seven?" The number "seven" represents completion or perfection, so all Jesus was really saying was: "Don't place any limits on forgiveness; just keep on doing it."

When we forgive, we are being Christlike; we are acting as God acts—because He is a forgiving God. Forgiveness is manifested mercy; it is love in action—not love based on a feeling, but love based on a decision, an intentional choice to obey God. In fact, I believe forgiveness is the highest form of love. Forgiveness and love go hand in hand and expressing them honors and glorifies God, puts us in agreement with Him, and causes us to obey His Word—which helps us hear His voice.

GOD'S WORD FOR YOU TODAY: Be sure you forgive
quickly, frequently, and completely.

Free to Follow the Spirit

The Lord is the Spirit, and where the Spirit of the Lord is, there is liberty (emancipation from bondage, freedom).

(2 CORINTHIANS 3:17)

Although I have already mentioned the subject of legalism as a deterrent to a Spirit-led life in this book, I want to elaborate on it more because I believe it is a tremendous hindrance to hearing from God.

I don't believe we can experience joy unless we are led by God's Spirit, and we cannot be led by the Spirit and live under the law simultaneously. A legalistic mentality says that everyone has to do everything the same way, all the time. But God's Spirit leads us individually and often in unique, creative ways.

God's written Word says the same thing to everyone and it is not a matter of private interpretation (see 2 Peter 1:20). This means God's Word does not say one thing to one person and something else to others. However, the direct leadership of the Holy Spirit *is* a personal issue.

God may lead one person not to eat sugar because of a health issue in that person's life. That doesn't mean no can eat sugar. People who are legalistic try to take God's Word to others and make it a law for them.

I once heard that by the time Jesus was born, the scribes and Pharisees had turned the Ten Commandments into two thousand rules for people to follow. Imagine trying to live under that kind of law. That's bondage!

Jesus came to set captives free. We are not free to do whatever we feel like doing, but we have been set free from legalism and are now free to follow the Holy Spirit in all the creative, personal ways in which He leads us.

———

GOD'S WORD FOR YOU TODAY: Trust the Holy Spirit to speak to you and lead you as you go through life.

An Attitude of Submission

He who turns away his ear from hearing the law [of God and man],
even his prayer is an abomination, hateful and revolting [to God].

(PROVERBS 28:9)

Today's verse says a startling thing about our prayers when we are not properly related to authority or if we are rebellious—that they are revolting to God.

We simply cannot grow up or mature without correction. If we are rebellious toward company rules, traffic laws, or toward any other form of authority, then we have more serious attitude problems than we might think. Being rebellious is something we need to be diligent to eliminate from our attitudes and behaviors! Why? Because if we refuse to submit to earthly authority, then we will not submit to God's authority. That is disobedience and it will keep us from effective prayer.

God placed me in someone else's ministry for several years before He allowed me to start my own. I had to learn how to come under authority. That was not easy for me. I did not always agree with the decisions that were made and I did not always feel I was treated fairly, but one of the lessons God taught me is that we are not ready to be in authority until we know how to come under authority.

You might want a pay raise or a promotion at work, yet you regularly gossip and say critical things about your boss. This is a form of rebellion and it can hinder your progress. Have a submissive attitude and you will see more answers to prayer and hear God's voice more clearly.

GOD'S WORD FOR YOU TODAY: Everything you are asked to do in life may not be fair, but in the end God always brings justice.

God Gives Authority

Let every person be loyally subject to the governing (civil) authorities.
For there is no authority except from God [by His permission, His
sanction], and those that exist do so by God's appointment.

(ROMANS 13:1)

An attitude of honor and submission toward authority needs to per-meate our everyday lives—because God puts authority in place in order to keep us safe and to promote our joy. He gives us both spiritual authority and natural authority, and it is important to obey both. Even signs placed by people in authority should be respected. If there is a "No Parking" zone, do not park there. If the only parking space available is a handicapped space and you are not handicapped, don't park there even if it means having to walk a long way! If a red light flashes, "Do Not Walk," then don't walk. Don't cross the street anyway simply because you are in a hurry. If you are in a "No Passing" zone on the highway, then don't pass.

You may be thinking, *Well, those things can't make any difference. That's all little stuff. I've got big problems that I need answers to.* We'll all keep our big problems until we learn that our seemingly little, everyday choices to respect authority or not to have a huge impact on our life.

Behaviors similar to the ones I have just described reflect a disrespectful attitude toward authority, and that hinders our ability to hear God's voice because God Himself places authority in our lives and wants us to honor it. We honor Him when we honor the authority around us.

GOD'S WORD FOR YOU TODAY: Be very careful to obey God in little things and they will make a big difference in your life.

Hear God Through His Word

Establish Your word and confirm Your promise to Your servant,
which is for those who reverently fear and devotedly worship You.
(PSALM 119:38)

God speaks to us through His Word and His Word is designed to help us, direct us, and encourage us in our everyday lives. We can hear His voice in every situation because we can find Bible verses or passages to pray in various circumstances. At times, verses or passages will give us remarkably specific, detailed direction. At other times we need to take a nugget of wisdom or a general spiritual principle and apply it to the matter with which we are dealing. For example, listed below are several common, specific circumstances and emotions with which the enemy threatens us and corresponding verses to pray in each case:

- When you are going through a season of difficulty or something that is wearing you out, you can pray Isaiah 40:29: "He gives power to the weak, and to those who have no might He increases strength" (NKJV).
- When you are concerned about the future, you can pray Jeremiah 31:17, which says, "There is hope for your future."
- When you are struggling financially, you can pray Psalm 34:9–10, which says, "Oh, fear the LORD, you His saints! There is no want to those who fear Him. The young lions lack and suffer hunger; but those who seek the LORD shall not lack any good thing" (NKJV).

I truly believe that God's Word holds the answer to every question we have and the wisdom to meet every need.

GOD'S WORD FOR YOU TODAY: Emotions can lead you astray, but God's Word leads you to safety.

God Hears the Consistently Righteous

The Lord...hears the prayer of the [consistently] righteous (the upright, in right standing with Him). (PROVERBS 15:29)

God promises in today's verse that He will hear our prayers if we seek to be faithful in our walk with Him. What does it mean to be "consistently righteous"? Simply put, I think the best way to be consistently righteous is to refuse to compromise.

A person who compromises is someone who tends to go along with what everybody else wants to do, even though it may not be totally right. A compromiser knows when something is not right, but does it anyway and hopes to get away with it. We compromise when we know in our hearts—and even have the conviction of the Holy Spirit—that we should not say or do a certain thing and then do it anyway. We are saying, "God is showing me what to do, but I'm going to do what I want to." In that case, we can blame only ourselves if we do not see the results we would like. When we refuse to compromise and devote ourselves to being consistently righteous to the best of our ability, God sees our hearts, hears our prayers, and answers us.

GOD'S WORD FOR YOU TODAY: If you refuse to compromise, you will put a smile on God's face.

A Good Attitude Is Effective

Hear my prayer, O God; give ear to the words of my mouth.
(PSALM 54:2 NKJV)

We all want our prayers to be effective and we want to be able to talk to God in ways that successfully bring His heart and His plans into our lives and the lives of other people. The Bible says, "The effective, fervent prayer of a righteous man avails much" (James 5:16 NKJV). If we want to pray effective prayers that avail much, then we need to know what can make them ineffective. All of our prayers are not successful. For example, sometimes we want something so desperately that we fail to pray according to God's will—and those prayers are not effective. Sometimes we are so angry or hurt that we pray prayers that are based on our emotions instead of on God's Word or His heart—and those prayers are not effective either.

Through His Word, God tells us what to do in order to pray effective prayers. Effective prayer does not result from following formulas or abiding by certain principles. Effective prayer is based on God's Word; it is simple, sincere, and filled with faith; it has nothing to do with rules or guidelines, but it does need to issue from a heart with a right attitude.

GOD'S WORD FOR YOU TODAY: A bad attitude can be changed by simply making a decision to change it.

A Delay Is Not a Denial

My times are in Your hands; deliver me from the hands of my foes and those who pursue me and persecute me. (PSALM 31:15)

When we pray, we don't always get answers right away. Sometimes we have to wait a long time, but that does not necessarily mean that God is saying no to our request. It is very important to trust God's timing in all matters concerning ourselves and our lives. Perhaps you have been waiting a long time for a breakthrough in something you have prayed about and the silence of God has brought confusion into your life. Please remember that God is not the author of confusion. He wants you to trust Him, not be confused.

Many delays are "divine delays." They are designed by God to do a work in us that needs to be done. If we continue serving God faithfully even during times of darkness we develop strong godly character. Think of Joseph, who waited thirteen years to see the answer to his prayers; or Abraham, who waited twenty years. If they had given up they would never have enjoyed the reward of their trust in God. God may not be early, but He won't be late. Most things worth having usually take longer than we thought they would, and are more difficult than we think we can endure. But, God does know exactly what He is doing and He wants you to trust His timing.

God promises to deliver us from our enemies, but while we are waiting we need to pray for them and be a blessing to as many people as we possibly can be. God is working while you are waiting!

GOD'S WORD FOR YOU TODAY: Learn to wait peacefully or a lot of your life may be miserable.

Keep God's Secrets

When you pray, go into your [most] private room, and, closing the door, pray to your Father, Who is in secret; and your Father, Who sees in secret, will reward you in the open. (MATTHEW 6:6)

I have come to realize over the years in my experience with God that we are not very good at keeping things secret that should be kept secret. The verse for today indicates that what we pray about is between us and God and does not need to be done as a display for others. We want to hear from God, yet the moment we feel that He does tell us anything, we cannot wait to tell others what He has said. Perhaps that is all right at times, but there are also times when things between us and God need to be kept secret.

When Joseph had a dream that his father and brothers would someday bow down to him, perhaps it was childish foolishness that prompted him to tell them about it. Perhaps it was that very foolishness that God had to work out of Joseph before He could trust him with the responsibility He had in mind. Very often our unwillingness to keep secrets is a symptom of immaturity. I think we might well see more of God's rewards manifested in our lives, as the verse for today says, if we could learn to discern the difference between what to tell and what to keep secret.

God will reveal more to us if He can trust us. Let us learn to hold things in our heart until God gives us permission to release them.

GOD'S WORD FOR YOU TODAY: Be careful what you say when your emotions are stirred up.

Never Give Up

Let us not lose heart and grow weary and faint in acting nobly and doing right, for in due time and at the appointed season we shall reap, if we do not loosen and relax our courage and faint.

(GALATIANS 6:9)

One reason people do not hear God's voice is simply that they give up too soon. Paul and Silas were found still worshipping and praising God in their jail cell at midnight (see Acts 16:25). Many people would have given up and gone to sleep much earlier. Our motto should be: "Never give up."

I encourage you not to give up talking to God and waiting for Him to speak to you, no matter what. Spend time with God daily. A person who refuses to quit is one whom Satan cannot defeat. He wants you to give up right now and to say things like:

- "I'll never get a better job."
- "I'll never get married."
- "I'll never get out of debt."
- "I'll never lose weight."

Attitudes like these may guarantee that we will not receive anything! But we can also choose the attitude that says, "God is faithful to His Word and I will never give up." One of the biggest reasons that people never see the results of their prayers is that they give up. We will reap in due time, but what time is that? It is when God knows that we are ready to receive what we are asking for. Until that time our one job is to remain faithful. Keep praying and keep obeying.

GOD'S WORD FOR YOU TODAY: God offers us second chances, so if you need a new beginning, today is the day!

Trust in God's Power

My language and my message were not set forth in persuasive (entic-
ing and plausible) words of wisdom, but they were in demonstration
of the [Holy] Spirit and power... so that your faith might not rest in
the wisdom of men (human philosophy), but in the power of God.

(1 CORINTHIANS 2:4–5)

Education is important, but we must always keep in mind that the wisdom of God is better and more valuable than worldly education and human philosophy. The apostle Paul was a highly educated man, but he firmly stated that it was God's power that made his preaching valuable, not his education.

I know lots of people who graduate from college with honors and degrees and have difficulty getting jobs. I also know people who have not had the opportunity to go to college who depend on God to give them favor and they end up with great jobs. Where is your trust? Is it in God or in what you know? No matter what we know, or whom we know, our trust should be in Christ alone and in His power.

Paul mentioned in 1 Corinthians 1:21 that the world with all of its human wisdom and philosophy failed to know God, but He chose to reveal Himself, and save humankind through the foolishness of preaching. Sadly, we often find that the more highly educated some people are, the more difficult it is for them to have simple, childlike faith. Too much head knowledge and reasoning can actually work against us if we are not careful, because we can know God only by the Spirit and the heart, not by the brain. Be sure to let your faith rest in the power of God and not in human philosophy to help in all areas of life.

GOD'S WORD FOR YOU TODAY: God's power can over-come any obstacle you may face in life.

The Spirit of Grace

Anyone who has rejected Moses' law dies without mercy on the testimony of two or three witnesses. Of how much worse punishment, do you suppose, will he be thought worthy who has trampled the Son of God underfoot . . . and insulted the Spirit of grace?

(HEBREWS 10:28–29 NKJV)

The Holy Spirit is the Spirit of Grace. Grace is the power of the Holy Spirit to do with ease what we cannot do by working at it. But first, it is the power that enables us to be right with God so He can live in us and we can become His home. With the Holy Spirit inside us, we can reach inside our hearts to draw on the power of the Spirit of Grace to do what we cannot do by striving in our own power.

For example, I spent years trying to change myself because I saw so many defects in my character. Most of the time I felt frustrated because all my effort and hard work were not producing change. If I realized I was saying unkind things I shouldn't be saying, I would determine to stop. But no matter what I did, I couldn't change, and sometimes I seemed to get worse.

Finally, I cried out to God, admitting that I couldn't even try to change anymore. At that point, I heard God speak to my heart, "Good. Now I can do something in your life."

When God makes the changes in our lives, God gets the glory; therefore, He won't let us change ourselves. When we try to change without leaning on God, we leave Him "out of the loop." Instead of trying to change ourselves, we simply need to ask Him to change us and then let His Spirit of Grace do the work in us.

GOD'S WORD FOR YOU TODAY: Never try to do anything without asking God to help you.

The Spirit of Truth

When He, the Spirit of Truth (the Truth-giving Spirit) comes, He will guide you into all the Truth (the whole, full Truth). (JOHN 16:13)

I was very unhappy and had many difficulties in my life, but for years I blamed them on other people and my circumstances. I had a hard time developing and maintaining good relationships, and I was convinced that all the people in my life needed to change so we could get along. It really never occurred to me that I might be the one causing the problems.

One day in 1976, as I prayed for my husband to change, the Holy Spirit began speaking in my heart. I was shocked as He gently unveiled to me the deception into which I had led myself by believing everyone except me was the problem. For three days, the Holy Spirit revealed to me that I was hard to get along with, impossible to keep happy, critical, selfish, dominating, controlling—and that was just the beginning of the list.

Facing this truth was extremely difficult for me, but as the Holy Spirit gave me the grace, I began a journey of much healing and freedom in my life. Many of the truths I teach today came out of that time. Satan is the great deceiver and the father of lies; if he can keep us in darkness, then he can keep us in bondage and misery. Even though facing truth can be painful, it is vitally necessary for progress and freedom.

As Jesus said in the verse for today, the Holy Spirit is the Spirit of Truth, and He will speak to us and guide us into all truth.

GOD'S WORD FOR YOU TODAY: Ask the Holy Spirit to reveal any areas of deception in your life.

Are You Hard of Hearing?

I have learned how to be content (satisfied to the point where I am not disturbed or disquieted) in whatever state I am. I know how to be abased and live humbly in straitened circumstances, and I know also how to enjoy plenty and live in abundance. (PHILIPPIANS 4:11–12)

We are always willing to follow the Holy Spirit into blessings, but we can get "hard of hearing" if His leading means we are not going to get what we want.

After his conversion and baptism in the Holy Spirit, Paul heard from the Spirit about some of the difficulties he would be required to endure (see Acts 9:15–16). Paul went through many difficult situations, but he was also to be blessed in his lifetime. He wrote a large portion of the New Testament under divine inspiration. He saw visions, received angelic visitations, and many other wonderful things. He also had to follow the leading of the Holy Spirit when things weren't so full of blessing. He heard and obeyed the voice of God whether it was convenient or inconvenient, comfortable or uncomfortable, to his advantage or not to his advantage.

In today's verses, Paul wrote of being content whether he was enjoying blessings or facing struggles. In the following verse, he declared that he could do all things through Christ, Who gave him strength. He was strengthened for good times, to enjoy them and keep a right attitude, and also for hard times, to endure them and keep the proper attitude in the midst of them, too.

The Holy Spirit leads us during good times and during difficult times. We can count on Him no matter what is going on in our lives.

GOD'S WORD FOR YOU TODAY: God is the same no matter what our circumstances are, and He is always worthy of praise and gratitude.

The Spirit of Supplication

*I will pour out upon the house of David and upon the inhabitants of
Jerusalem the Spirit of grace or unmerited favor and supplication.*
(ZECHARIAH 12:10)

According to today's verse, the Holy Spirit is the Spirit of Supplication, which means He is the Spirit of Prayer. The Holy Spirit gives us the desire to pray; that is one of the ways He speaks to us. We may not realize how often He leads us to pray and may think we simply have a certain person or situation on our minds. Learning to recognize when God is asking us to pray often takes time and is a lesson I certainly had to learn by practice.

One Monday I began thinking of a pastor I know. Over the next three days, he came to my mind repeatedly. On Wednesday, I saw his secretary when I went to an appointment at a place of business and I immediately asked her how he was doing. I discovered that the pastor had been sick that week and, in addition, he had learned his father had been diagnosed with cancer that was spreading throughout his body.

I quickly realized why the pastor had been on my heart so much that week. I must admit I had not prayed for him; I had simply thought about him. Of course, I was sorry I missed the leading of the Holy Spirit, but am sure God used others to pray for and minister to him while I was learning this important lesson about hearing His voice.

When such things happen to us, we are not to feel condemned; we are simply to learn. The Spirit of Supplication lives within us, guides us, and speaks to us. We need to continue to grow in our sensitivity to His leading so we can pray for others when He is asking us to do so and see God do great things in their lives.

GOD'S WORD FOR YOU TODAY: It is better to pray for
someone than it is to merely think about them.

Your Father Wants to Talk to You

[The Spirit which] you have received [is] not a spirit of slavery to put you once more in bondage to fear, but you have received the Spirit of adoption [the Spirit producing sonship] in [the bliss of] which we cry, Abba (Father)! Father! (ROMANS 8:15)

The Holy Spirit is the Spirit of Adoption. This means that by the power of the Holy Spirit we are actually part of God's family. We were once sinners serving the devil, but God redeemed us, purchased us with the blood of His Son, and calls us His own beloved sons and daughters.

Adoption is amazing! Someone who wants a child purposely chooses one and takes them as their own to love and care for. In some instances, this can be even better than being born into a family because when children are born into a family, they are not always wanted. Sometimes their birth results from choices their parents regret. But when children are adopted, they are wanted, specifically picked out, and chosen on purpose.

When we choose to put our faith in Jesus Christ, the new birth brings us into the family of God. He becomes our Father; we become heirs of God and joint heirs with Christ (see Romans 8:16–17). He treats us as a loving, perfect Father. A good father is not silent toward his children. He does many things for them, just as God does for us, including speaking to them to tell them how much he loves them, instructing them, guiding them, warning them, affirming them, and encouraging them. You belong to God; He has adopted you and is now your Father; and He wants to speak to you today. If you have had the painful experience of being rejected or abandoned by your natural parents, let me remind you that God adopts you and takes you as His own child (see Psalm 27:10).

GOD'S WORD FOR YOU TODAY: God thinks you are special. He has chosen you to be His own child.

Good Words

Speak out to one another in psalms and hymns and spiritual songs, offering praise with voices [and instruments] and making melody with all your heart to the Lord. (EPHESIANS 5:19)

The King James Version translates today's verse: "Speaking to yourselves in psalms and hymns and spiritual songs, singing and making melody in your heart to the Lord." I like to apply this Scripture both ways. The way I speak to myself is important, and the way I speak to others is important, too.

It is easy to fall into the trap of talking about negative things, problems, disappointments, and struggles. But none of that helps us stay filled with the Sprit and none of that reflects what the Holy Spirit wants to speak to us because He is not negative in any way. Even when He speaks to us about a problem, He speaks to bring a solution; and when He speaks to us about difficult situations, He does so to bring us comfort and strength. The more we think and talk about our problems, the weaker we become, but we are strengthened as we talk and think about Jesus and His promises to us.

Life is not always easy; we all face difficulties at times. God has filled us with His Spirit to enable us to do difficult things with ease. When you are going through a hard time, keep your ear tuned in to the voice of God. Speak the positive things God says to you through His Word and through the voice of His Spirit in your heart. We all feed on our own words so it is very important to speak good words that are full of life.

GOD'S WORD FOR YOU TODAY: Choose your words wisely today, for they have the power of life or death.

Pray the Word

Forever, O Lord, Your word is settled in heaven [stands firm as the heavens]. (PSALM 119:89)

You know that God speaks to us through His Word. We can speak His Word back to Him when we pray by "praying the Word." Perhaps you have never heard the phrase "pray the Word" and are wondering how to do it. I think praying the Word, or "praying the Scriptures," as some people say, is the simplest form of prayer available to any believer. All it takes is reading or memorizing words in the Bible and praying them in a way that makes them personal or applies them to someone else. I believe the best way to do this is to preface the Scripture with, "God, Your Word says (insert Scripture) and I believe it."

If you were praying Jeremiah 31:3 for yourself, you would say something like this: "God, Your Word says that You have loved me with an everlasting love and that You have drawn me with loving-kindness. I thank You for loving me so much and for continuing to draw me closer to You with such kindness. Help me, Lord, to be conscious and aware of Your love for me." If you were praying that same Scripture for your friend Susie, who had been struggling to believe God really loved her, you would say something like, "God, Your Word says that You have loved Susie with an everlasting love and that You have drawn her with loving-kindness. God, You know that Susie hasn't felt very secure in Your love lately, so I am asking You to override her emotions with the truth of this promise."

God's promises are for you; they are for every believer—and He loves it when we know His Word and pray it back to Him.

GOD'S WORD FOR YOU TODAY: God loves you just the way you are and He will help you become what He wants you to be.

The "Holy Thing"

The angel said to her, The Holy Spirit will come upon you, and the
power of the Most High will overshadow you [like a shining cloud];
and so the holy (pure, sinless) Thing (Offspring) which shall be born
of you will be called the Son of God. (LUKE 1:35)

The Virgin Mary became pregnant by the working of the Holy Spirit, Who came upon her and, according to today's verse, planted in her womb a "holy Thing." The Spirit of Holiness was planted in her as a Seed. In her womb the Seed grew into the Son of God and the Son of Man, Who was necessary to deliver people from their sins.

When we are born again, a similar dynamic takes place in us. The "holy Thing," the Spirit of Holiness, is planted in us as a Seed. As we water that Seed with God's Word and keep the "weeds of worldliness" from choking it out, it will grow into a giant tree of righteousness, "the planting of the Lord, that He may be glorified" (Isaiah 61:3).

God's Word teaches us to pursue holiness (see Hebrews 12:14). When we set our hearts on this pursuit, the Spirit of Holiness helps us. If we want to be holy, we need to be filled with the Holy Spirit and permit Him to speak to us, correct us, guide us, and help us in every area of our lives.

Never forget that a "holy Thing" lives inside of you. Water that seed with God's Word and let the Holy Spirit speak to you and teach you how to help it grow.

***

GOD'S WORD FOR YOU TODAY: The Holy Spirit desires to be your close companion as He teaches and instructs you in holiness.

God Uses All Kinds

His gifts were [varied; He Himself appointed and gave men to us]
some to be apostles, … some prophets, … some evangelists, … some
pastors … and teachers. His intention was the perfecting and the full
equipping of the saints. (EPHESIANS 4:11–12)

One of the ways God speaks to us is through people. Sometimes these people are friends or family members and sometimes they are the pastors, teachers, evangelists, apostles, and prophets He places in our lives. God gifts these people specifically to help and build up believers, as today's verse says, for "the full equipping of the saints."

One of the gifts God has given me is the gift of teaching His Word. Although my gift of teaching has been a great blessing to my life, God actually put it in me for the benefit of others. Some people decide for whatever reason that they don't like me, don't like the way I teach, or don't believe God has called me to minister. When they do this, they quench the work the Holy Spirit could do in their lives, not through me, but through the gift He Himself has chosen to flow through me.

What's true of me is true for other ministers, too. God has placed valuable gifts in them and there will always be some people who will open their hearts to these gifts and others who will not. We should learn to receive God's Word from a variety of people. We make a mistake when we focus too much on the vessel God chooses to use and not enough on what He wants to give us through that vessel.

I encourage you to allow God to speak to you through whomever He chooses and to not resist a message from Him by rejecting someone He sends to speak His word to you.

——————————

GOD'S WORD FOR YOU TODAY: Learn to enjoy a variety of people and the gifts God has placed in them for your benefit.

Get Excited!

I was glad when they said to me, Let us go to the house of the Lord!
(PSALM 122:1)

As Christians, we have so many blessings! We can know God, hear His voice, receive His love, trust Him to do what's best for us, and rest in the fact that He has every aspect of our lives under control. We have lots of reasons to be excited! We get excited about all kinds of other things, so why shouldn't we be excited about our relationship with God?

People often say that any visible display of enthusiasm in a spiritual setting is "emotionalism." I finally realized that it was God Who gave us emotions and that although He does not want us to let them lead our lives, He does give them to us for a purpose, part of which is enjoyment. If we are truly enjoying God, how can we not show some emotion about it? Why must our spiritual experience be dry and boring, dull and lifeless? Is Christianity supposed to be expressed by long faces, sad music, and somber rituals? Certainly not!

In today's verse, David said he was glad to go to God's house. In 2 Samuel 6:14, he danced before God "with all his might." He also played his harp, sang to God, and rejoiced greatly. But David lived under the Old Covenant. Today we live under the New Covenant and under it, we who believe in Christ are full of hope, joy, and peace (see Romans 15:13). We no longer have to strive or struggle to be acceptable to God, but we rest in the grace that Jesus has made us acceptable. We no longer have to try to justify ourselves by our works, but we are justified by faith. We can hear His voice and enjoy His presence. We have been set free from every kind of bondage! These are great reasons to be excited!

GOD'S WORD FOR YOU TODAY: Write down ten reasons to be enthusiastic about your relationship with God.

Open the Door

Behold, I stand at the door and knock; if anyone hears and listens to and heeds My voice and opens the door, I will come in to him and will eat with him, and he [will eat] with Me. (REVELATION 3:20)

As I opened the door of my heart to the fullness of the Holy Spirit's ministry in my life, He began to speak to me and deal with me about every area of my life; there was nothing He was not involved in. I liked it, but I didn't like it, if you know what I mean.

God spoke to me about how I talked to people and about them. He spoke about how I spent my money, how I dressed, who my friends were, and what I did for entertainment. He talked to me about my thoughts and my attitudes. I realized He knew my deepest secrets and that nothing was hidden from Him. He was no longer in the "Sunday morning room" of my life, but it seemed as though He was running the entire house! I never knew when He might begin to speak to me about something in my life. As I mentioned, it was exciting, but it was also challenging because I knew His speaking to me would lead to many changes in my life.

We all want change in certain areas, but when it comes, it can be frightening. We often want our lives to change, but not our lifestyles. We may not like what we have in life, but we wonder if it may be better than the alternatives. We can become anxious or even afraid of losing control over our lives and allowing Someone we cannot see to take over.

To hear and obey the voice of God as He works in our lives means living for His pleasure and glory, not our own. We may be nervous or apprehensive about opening the doors of every area of our lives to Him, but I guarantee that it is worth it.

GOD'S WORD FOR YOU TODAY: Invite God into every area of your life.

Faith and Favor

Man's steps are ordered by the Lord. How then can a man understand his way? (PROVERBS 20:24)

When Dave and I sensed God calling us to begin a television ministry, we began to take steps in that direction by faith. We could not do it without money, so the first thing we did was write to the people on our mailing list, asking friends and ministry partners to give financially toward helping us start a television ministry. We felt God had spoken to our hearts concerning a certain amount of money we would need to begin, and that amount is exactly what we received.

We then took another step. We needed a producer and God provided. A man had applied for a job as a television producer three months before God spoke to us about being on television. Since we were not on television we told him we would not need his services. When the time came, we remembered that man and realized that God had met our need before we even knew we had one.

The next step we took was to buy time on a few stations once a week. As the programs paid for themselves and we saw good fruit from them, we bought more time. Eventually we went on daily television and now have a daily program that airs around the world and, prayerfully, is helping millions of people.

God led Dave and me one step at a time and that is how He will lead you. Every time we took a step of faith, God gave us favor, and I encourage you to expect favor also. God already knows your needs and He has your answer, so when fear knocks on your door, answer with faith and you will do great things.

GOD'S WORD FOR YOU TODAY: Be confident that God is leading you and giving you favor.

He'll Change You

The Spirit of the Lord will come upon you mightily, and you will show yourself to be a prophet with them; and you will be turned into another man. (1 SAMUEL 10:6)

Being able to hear God's voice is an important result of knowing Him and being filled with His Spirit, but it is not the only evidence of a Spirit-filled life. Another simple but powerful proof of the Holy Spirit's power within a person is a changed life.

At Jesus' trial, Peter denied Him three times because he was afraid of the Jews (see Luke 22:56–62); but after being filled with the Holy Spirit on the Day of Pentecost, he was no longer afraid, but stood and preached an extremely bold message. The result of Peter's preaching was that three thousand souls were added to God's Kingdom that day (see Acts 2:14–41). The fullness of the Holy Spirit changed Peter; it turned him into another man—one who was very courageous, not fearful at all.

Peter was not the only one who took a bold stand that day. All eleven of the remaining disciples did the same. They were all hiding behind closed doors for fear of the Jews when Jesus came to them after His resurrection (see John 20:19–22). Suddenly, after being filled with the Holy Spirit, they all became fearless and brave.

The power of the Holy Spirit has changed countless people over the years. It changed Saul, as recorded in today's verse. It changed Peter and the other disciples. It has changed me; and it continues to change earnests seekers the world over. Do you need to be changed? Ask the Holy Spirit to fill you today.

GOD'S WORD FOR YOU TODAY: You need the power of the Holy Spirit in order to change.

The Working of Miracles

To one is given in and through the [Holy] Spirit [the power to speak]
a message of wisdom, and to another . . . the working of miracles.

(1 CORINTHIANS 12:8–10)

Jesus worked many miracles. For example, He turned water into wine (see John 2:1–10) and fed a multitude with a little boy's lunch so that there were baskets full of fragments left over (see John 6:1–13). There are many kinds of miracles—miracles of provision and supply, miracles of healing, and miracles of deliverance, just to name a few.

Dave and I have seen many miracles over the years. We have certainly seen miracles such as physical healings and deliverances from longtime bondages. We have also experienced miracles of supply— times when God has provided for us and for our ministry so supernaturally that we know God Himself intervened in our situation and provided what we needed.

Miracles are things that cannot be explained, things that do not occur through ordinary means. We all can and should believe God for miracles in our lives. Don't be satisfied to live an ordinary life when the gift of miracles is available. Ask for and expect God to work miraculously in your life and the lives of other people. The same God Who parted the Red Sea wants to help you today.

———————

GOD'S WORD FOR YOU TODAY: Don't settle for the ordinary, but expect the extraordinary.

The Answer Is *Not* in the Stars

Turn not to those [mediums] who have familiar spirits or to wizards;
do not seek them out to be defiled by them. I am the Lord your God.
(LEVITICUS 19:31)

As believers, we have access to God and to the spiritual realm. We can hear God's voice and receive direction from Him. Many people want spiritual guidance, but not everyone seeks it from God.

Many people worldwide seek advice and direction from the stars, psychics, fortune-tellers, and other such things and people. This is wrong and offensive to God. Satan deceives a lot of people through this avenue. People are searching for direction and solutions for their lives, but sadly they have not been taught that God will provide it. My purpose in writing today's devotional is to let you know that God wants to be your source of information. He wants to give you daily guidance for your life through His Word and His Spirit.

I once worked with a woman who was deeply involved in astrology. She consulted the stars before making any decisions. She even checked with the alignment of the stars to see what day she should get her hair cut. Why should we consult the stars when we can consult God, Who made the stars?

If you are involved in seeking guidance or direction from any source besides God, I urge you to repent, turn to Him, and ask the Holy Spirit to be your only guide in life from now on.

———————————

GOD'S WORD FOR YOU TODAY: Seek information and guidance from God alone.

Face the Truth

Let our lives lovingly express truth [in all things, speaking truly, dealing truly, living truly]. (EPHESIANS 4:15)

You and I live in a world filled with people who are living false lives, wearing masks of pretense, and hiding things they don't want others to know. That is wrong. But the reason it happens is that people have not been taught to walk in truth. As believers, we have the Holy Spirit living inside of us; He is the Spirit of Truth, and He speaks the truth to us.

Sometimes Satan deceives us, but at other times we deceive ourselves. In other words, we fabricate lives we are comfortable with instead of facing life as it really is and dealing with issues with the help of the Holy Spirit.

The Holy Spirit speaks to me and confronts me with issues in my life frequently, and He has also taught me to be a confronter, not a coward. Cowards hide from the truth; they are afraid of it. You don't have to be afraid of the truth. Jesus told His disciples that the Holy Spirit would lead them into truth, but He also told them they were not ready to hear certain things (see John 16:12), so He did not reveal those things at that time. The Holy Spirit will always speak truth to you, but He won't speak certain truths to you until He knows you are ready to hear them.

If you are brave enough to welcome the Spirit of Truth into every area of your life and let Him speak to you about issues in your life, you are in for an unforgettable journey of freedom and power.

GOD'S WORD FOR YOU TODAY: Never be afraid of the truth.

Never Alone

Jesus, full of and controlled by the Holy Spirit, returned from the Jordan and was led in [by] the [Holy] Spirit for (during) forty days in the wilderness (desert), where He was tempted (tried, tested exceedingly) by the devil. (LUKE 4:1–2)

We learn from today's verses that immediately after Jesus was baptized in the Holy Spirit, He was led into the wilderness by the Holy Spirit, to be tempted by the devil for forty days and nights. That was probably a very difficult experience, but Jesus promptly obeyed the Spirit's leading. He trusted the Holy Spirit, knowing even the difficulties He would face would work out for His good in the end.

At the end of the forty days in the wilderness, Jesus began His public ministry, as we see in Luke 4:14: "Jesus went back full of and under the power of the [Holy] Spirit into Galilee, and the fame of Him spread through the whole region round about." Jesus not only had to be willing to follow the leading of the Holy Spirit into power and fame; He also had to be willing to follow Him into difficult times, times of trial and testing.

Obeying God in difficult times helps develop godly character. Jesus set an example for us that we should follow. Following the leadership of the Holy Spirit during seasons of hardship develops faithfulness, determination, and strength in us—qualities God wants us to have.

God has given us the Holy Spirit to help us fulfill His plans for our lives. Sometimes, we must encounter difficulties in order to develop the character we need in order to do what God has planned. We must always remember we never face anything— difficulties or good times— alone. The Holy Spirit is always with us to help us and His ways are always the best.

GOD'S WORD FOR YOU TODAY: Don't be afraid of hard times, because they ultimately make you stronger.

The Holy Spirit Is a Gentleman

To the end that through [their receiving] Christ Jesus, the blessing
[promised] to Abraham might come upon the Gentiles, so that we
through faith might [all] receive [the realization of] the promise of the
[Holy] Spirit. (GALATIANS 3:14)

In this book, I have written a great deal about the Holy Spirit and about being filled with the Spirit, and I want to make sure you have an opportunity to know the Holy Spirit in this way as you journey through these pages.

The Holy Spirit is a gentleman. He will not force Himself into your life in His fullness uninvited. He will fill you, but only if you ask Him to do so. In Luke 11:13, Jesus promises that God will give the Holy Spirit to those who ask Him. And James 4:2 tells us that the reason we do not have certain things is that we do not ask for them.

I encourage you to go boldly before God and daily ask Him to fill you with the Holy Spirit. Ask expecting to receive. Don't be double-minded or allow doubt to fill your heart, but ask in faith. Believe you receive, and thank God that He lives in you. God is not a man, that He should lie (see Numbers 23:19). He is faithful to fulfill His Word whenever anyone steps out on it in faith, so ask and receive that your joy might be full (see John 16:24).

Today's verse says that we receive the promise of the Spirit through faith. Gifts cannot be forced on anyone; they must be offered by the giver and then received by those to whom they are offered. God makes the offer of His Spirit, so all you need to do is relax and receive by faith.

GOD'S WORD FOR YOU TODAY: Never be shy about asking and continuing to ask God to meet all of your needs.

Are You Hungry for More of God?

He satisfies the longing soul and fills the hungry soul with good.
(PSALM 107:9)

When we are hungry we make a great effort to get food. We think about food, talk about it, go to the store to purchase it, and carefully prepare it. I believe that if we are hungry for more of God in our lives, we should behave the same way. God said that we should seek Him with our whole heart, diligently, with enthusiasm, zeal, and all seriousness.

We spend a lot of time each week on natural food, but how much do we spend on spiritual food? I estimate that most of us spend a minimum of fourteen hours a week seeking, preparing, and eating natural food. We must honestly ask ourselves how much time we spend seeking God and learning about Him. How close we are to God depends on how much time we are willing to put into developing our relationship with Him. Time is valuable to all of us and we should use it on the things that are most important to us. You can waste your time or invest your time; it is your choice. What we waste we lose, but what we invest we get back with dividends.

I strongly recommend that you spend at least as much time seeking God as you spend seeking natural food, and you will soon be filled with His wisdom and presence. You will find a satisfaction like you have never known as He fills your soul with Himself.

———————

GOD'S WORD FOR YOU TODAY: Only God fills the hungry soul, so give Him priority in your schedule.

The Fruit of the Spirit

The fruit of the [Holy] Spirit … is love, joy (gladness), peace, patience (an even temper, forbearance), kindness, goodness (benevolence), faithfulness, gentleness, (meekness, humility), self-control (self-restraint, continence). (GALATIANS 5:22–23)

When we are filled to overflowing with the Holy Spirit, we see His fruit manifested through us. We have peace and joy and we are good to people. Jesus has commanded us to love one another as He loved us. It is important for the world to see this love manifested. The people of the world are hungry for truth and need to see that God can change people. They need to see God's love in action in order to make them hungry and thirsty for Him.

The Bible teaches us that we are to be light and salt (see Matthew 5:13–14). The world is in darkness, but Christians filled with the Holy Spirit bring light everywhere they go. The world is tasteless, but Christians bring salt (flavor) to life when they are present.

We have a big job to do as Christians and we should always be sensitive to the Holy Spirit concerning how we treat people. God is in us making His appeal to the world through us; we are His personal representatives (see 2 Corinthians 5:20). In view of that fact, Paul said we should lay hold of the divine favor offered to us. We must work with the Holy Spirit to develop the fruit of the Spirit to a full measure so we can behave in a way that glorifies God and draws people to Him.

The fruit of the Spirit is developed as we go through difficulties in life and continue, with God's help, to treat people the way He would. Stay strong in the Lord and remember that the world is watching you and they need you to be salt and light.

GOD'S WORD FOR YOU TODAY: No matter what challenges you might face today, continue to be kind to everyone you encounter.

The Spirit of Holiness

[As to His divine nature] according to the Spirit of holiness was openly designated the Son of God in power [in a striking, triumphant and miraculous manner] by His resurrection from the dead, even Jesus Christ our Lord (the Messiah, the Anointed One). (ROMANS 1:4)

Today's verse refers to the Holy Spirit as the "Spirit of holiness." He is called by this name because He is the holiness of God and because it is His job to work that holiness into everyone who believes in Jesus Christ as Savior.

God wants and instructs us to be holy (see 1 Peter 1:15–16). He would never tell us to be holy without giving us the help we need to make us that way. An unholy spirit could never make us holy. So God sends His Spirit into our hearts to do a complete and thorough work in us.

In Philippians 1:6, Paul teaches us that God, Who began a good work in us, is well able to complete that work and bring it to its finish. The Holy Spirit will continue to work in us as long as we are alive on this Earth. God hates sin, and anytime He finds it in us, He quickly works to cleanse us of it.

This fact alone explains why we need the Holy Spirit living inside of us. He is there not only to lead and guide us through this life, but also to immediately work in cooperation with the Father to remove from us anything that is displeasing to Him. He will both speak to us about the things that need to change so we can grow in holiness and empower us to make the changes we need to make.

GOD'S WORD FOR YOU TODAY: You are growing in holiness because the Spirit of Holiness lives in you.

We All Work Together

*As in one physical body we have many parts…and all of these parts
do not have the same function or use, so we, numerous as we are, are
one body in Christ (the Messiah) and individually we are parts one of
another [mutually dependent on one another].* (ROMANS 12:4–5)

Today's verses teach us about the diversity of gifts given to individuals. We are all parts of one body in Christ, and He is the Head. In the physical realm, all body parts must relate to the head if everything is to be in good working order. The various parts of the physical body work together; they are not jealous or competitive. The hands help the feet put their shoes on. The feet take the body wherever it needs to go. The mouth does the talking for the rest of the body. There are many parts to the body; they don't all have the same function, but they all work together for one combined purpose. The spiritual body of Christ should work the same way. That is why the Holy Spirit used the example of the physical body when He inspired Paul to write the book of Romans.

When we attempt to function in any way other than the way God has created and assigned us to function, we end up with pressure in our lives. But when we do what God has designed us to do, we experience joy, satisfaction, and great reward. We need to work with the Holy Spirit to discover what our unique, customized destiny is, and then do everything we can do to fulfill it. When God has gifted or enabled you to do something, you will be good at it, so find something you are good at and start doing it.

GOD'S WORD FOR YOU TODAY: If you want to be used
by God, then find a need and meet it.

Keep Moving Forward

God did not give us a spirit of timidity (of cowardice, of craven and cringing and fawning fear), but [He has given us a spirit] of power and of love and of calm and well-balanced mind and discipline and self-control. (2 TIMOTHY 1:7)

In spiritual things, either we are moving forward or we are starting to slip backward. We are either growing or dying. There is no such thing as dormant or neutral Christianity. We cannot put our Christian walk on hold or in storage until later. It is vital to keep pressing on. That's why Paul instructed Timothy to stir up the gift of God within him and to rekindle the fire for God in his heart (see 2 Timothy 1:6).

Evidently, Timothy needed this encouragement. Judging from the verse for today, he must have been struggling with fear. Anytime we allow fear to get a grip on us, we become immobile instead of active. Fear freezes us in place; it prevents progress.

Perhaps Timothy was afraid because Christians in his day were suffering extreme persecution. After all, his mentor Paul had been thrown into prison and he may have wondered if the same thing would happen to him.

Yet Paul urged him to stir himself up, get back on track, be faithful to the call on his life, and to remember that God had not given him "the spirit of fear; but of power, and of love, and of a sound mind" (KJV).

This is exactly what we get when we receive the fullness of the Holy Spirit—power, love, and a sound mind. When you are tempted to fear, remember this truth. Get alone with God and let the Holy Spirit fill you with courage and confidence so you can move forward.

GOD'S WORD FOR YOU TODAY: Be sure you fellowship with Jesus today and not with your problems; think about Him and not about them.

Say Less; Show More

Dwell in Me, and I will dwell in you. [Live in Me, and I will live in you.] Just as no branch can bear fruit of itself without abiding in (being vitally united to) the vine, neither can you bear fruit unless you abide in Me. (JOHN 15:4)

The more we develop our relationship with God, the more excited and enthusiastic we become and that is good. However, we must show people something more than excitement; they need to see evidence of real change and good fruit.

Paul said that our lives should be letters that people can read (see 2 Corinthians 3:3). In other words, our behavior speaks louder than words or emotions. I have found over the years that enthusiasm and zeal must be mixed with patience, goodness, kindness, good manners, and a willingness to help people. Our actions really do speak louder than our words. Of course, we should tell people about Jesus because words spoken at the right time can be very helpful, but true Christians are known by their fruit.

The more time you spend with God, the more fruit you will have resulting from that relationship. It is good fruit that glorifies God and it is good fruit that speaks most loudly to people. I know people that I tried to convince with words that I had changed and they were never convinced, but in later years they needed help and when I helped them, they realized God had definitely worked in my life. It is very difficult to argue with good fruit, because it is the proof that we are what we say we are. I encourage you to be careful how you treat people at all times.

GOD'S WORD FOR YOU TODAY: Before this day is over you will more than likely encounter many people. Leave them smiling!

The Spirit of Love

*No man has at any time [yet] seen God. But if we love one another,
God abides (lives and remains) in us and His love (that love which is
essentially His) is brought to completion (to its full maturity, runs its
full course, is perfected) in us!* (1 JOHN 4:12)

We cannot give away what we don't have. Trying to love others is useless if we have never received God's love for ourselves. We should love
ourselves in a balanced way, not a selfish, self-centered way. I teach
that we should love ourselves, not be in love with ourselves.

To love yourself, you simply need to believe in the love God has for
you; know that it is everlasting, unchangeable, and unconditional. Let
His love affirm you and make you feel secure, but don't begin to think
of yourself more highly than you should (see Romans 12:3). Loving
ourselves does not mean we love all of our behavior; it means that we
love and accept the unique person God has created us to be.

I believe loving ourselves in a balanced way is what prepares us to
let love flow through us to others. Without receiving God's love for ourselves in a healthy, appropriate way, we may have feelings of affection
or respect for others, a humanistic type of love; but we certainly cannot
love people unconditionally unless God Himself inspires and provokes
that love.

The Holy Spirit purifies our hearts so we can allow the sincere love
of God to flow through us (see 1 Peter 1:22) to others. This is part of
being filled with the Spirit.

God wants us to express love to others. When we think of others
and how we can bless them, we keep ourselves filled with the Holy
Spirit, Who is the Spirit of Love.

GOD'S WORD FOR YOU TODAY: You have something wonderful to give to the world today— the love of God that is in you.

Where Is God?

Seek, inquire for, and require the Lord while He may be found [claiming Him by necessity and by right]; call upon Him while He is near.

(ISAIAH 55:6)

Throughout my years in ministry, I have frequently been asked, "Why can't I sense God's presence?" At times, I have asked myself the same question.

We know from Scripture that the Holy Spirit does not run away and leave us every time we do something that displeases Him (see Hebrews 13:5). Actually, He is committed to stick with us and help us work through our problems, not leave us abandoned in them with no help.

No, the Holy Spirit never leaves us, but He does sometimes "hide." I like to say that sometimes God plays hide-and-seek with His children. Sometimes He hides from us until eventually, when we miss Him enough, we begin to seek Him. And when we seek Him, He promises that we will find Him (see 1 Chronicles 28:9; Jeremiah 29:13).

In His Word, God repeatedly tells us to seek Him—to seek His face, His will, His purpose for our lives. To seek means to crave, pursue, and go after with all of your might. We are also told to seek Him early, earnestly, and diligently. If we don't seek God, we will live disappointed lives. Seeking God is something He wants us to do and instructs us to do; it is central to our walk with Him and vital for spiritual progress. Tell God how important He is to you and that you cannot do anything without Him.

GOD'S WORD FOR YOU TODAY: Honor God today and every day by asking Him to be involved in every aspect and detail of your life.

Self-Control, Not Self-Indulgence

She who lives in pleasure and self-gratification [giving herself up to luxury and self-indulgence] is dead even while she [still] lives.

(1 TIMOTHY 5:6)

I once saw a ring I wanted and could afford because I had saved some money. I took time to pray about it, tested my impulses by not buying it immediately, and then asked, "God, is it all right for me to get this ring? You know I'll do whatever You want me to do with this money, but I'd like to have it if it's okay."

I felt no conviction that I shouldn't buy it, so I did.

That would have been a good ending to the story, but there was more—a bracelet. The salesman told me, "It's on sale, but only until tomorrow. And it looks great on you."

I was hesitant, but went to find Dave, thinking, *Maybe he will buy it for me.*

Dave looked at it. He thought it was nice and said, "Well, sure, you can get it if you want to."

I knew in my heart I should not buy that bracelet. Buying it certainly wouldn't have been a sin, but I knew the greater benefit for me at that time would be to develop the character needed to walk away from something I really liked but didn't need.

At that time, I sensed that maybe God would release me to get it later if I still wanted it. I simply did not have peace about buying it the same day I bought the ring. Looking back now, I see that the self-control I exercised was more satisfying than self-indulgence.

If we want to be truly happy, we need to listen to God. He will let us know whether something is right for us or not.

———————

GOD'S WORD FOR YOU TODAY: Let God lead you in the small areas of life as well as the big ones.

How to Be Happy

Having gifts (faculties, talents, qualities) that differ according to the grace given us, let us use them. (ROMANS 12:6)

We are all gifted and graced differently to operate in the gifts God has given us. Today's verse says we are to use our gifts according to the grace that is upon us.

Two people can be gifted to teach, yet one may be a stronger teacher than the other because he or she has more grace from God for that particular calling. Why? Because the Holy Spirit distributes gifts to whomever He wills (see 1 Corinthians 12:11). He has His reasons for what He does, and we need to trust Him in that. We should be thankful for what He gives us and not become jealous of someone else's gift. We cannot walk in love with people and envy their gifts at the same time.

My husband could be jealous because God has given me a preaching gift that He did not give him. Dave realized a long time ago that he would not be happy if he tried to operate outside of the grace that has been given to him. If he tried to be who I am, he would lose his joy. Dave is anointed in administration and finances, and his part in our ministry is just as important as mine.

If you want to be really happy, give yourself to what you are called and graced to do. The Holy Spirit will speak to you about what you are to do and help you understand the grace you have been given. Don't be jealous of others, but walk in love toward them and in faithfulness to the calling and grace on your life.

GOD'S WORD FOR YOU TODAY: You are an awesome person with tremendous gifts and abilities, and you don't need to compare yourself to anyone else.

A More Excellent Way

Earnestly desire and zealously cultivate the greatest and best gifts and graces … And yet I will show you a still more excellent way [one that is better by far and the highest of them all—love].
(1 CORINTHIANS 12:31)

First Corinthians 13, which immediately follows our verse for today, tells us clearly that no matter how many of the gifts of the Holy Spirit we may operate in, they are of absolutely no good unless we are also operating in love. According to today's verse, love is a more excellent way and is better than everything else.

If we pray in tongues of men and angels, have prophetic abilities, can understand mysteries, and even have all knowledge and such faith that we can move mountains, but don't have love, we are "useless nobodies" (see 1 Corinthians 13:2).

In the early days of my Spirit-filled walk with God I heard a lot of talk about the gifts of the Spirit. Many people were focused on which gifts they had and being able to exercise them. Sadly, I heard much more about spiritual gifts than I heard about love or the other fruit of the Spirit.

There are nine gifts of the Spirit listed in 1 Corinthians 12 and several others in Romans 12. There are nine fruit of the Spirit listed in Galatians 5. The gifts of the Spirit are extremely important, and we should deeply desire them. We need to learn about them, know how to operate in them properly, and be sure to nurture the gifts that have been given to us. But, we should never emphasize the gifts or the ability to operate in the gifts more than we emphasize and operate in love.

***

GOD'S WORD FOR YOU TODAY: God loves you and He wants you to let His love flow through you to others.

The Foundation of Happiness

All has been heard; the end of the matter is: Fear God [revere and worship Him, knowing that He is] and keep His commandments, for this is the whole of man [the full, original purpose of His creation, … the foundation of all happiness …] and the whole [duty] for every man. (ECCLESIASTES 12:13)

The writer of Ecclesiastes was a man who literally tried everything to be happy. He had much wealth, great power, and many wives. He restrained himself from no earthly pleasure. Anything his eyes desired, he took. He ate, drank, and made merry. He had tremendous knowledge, wisdom, and respect, yet he hated life. Everything began to appear useless to him. He tried to figure out what life was all about and became more and more confused.

Finally, he realized what his problem had been all along. He had not been obeying God's commandments. He was unhappy because of it and made the statement that the foundation of all happiness is obedience.

There are many, many sad, grieved individuals walking around blaming their unhappy lives on people and circumstances, failing to realize that the reason for their dissatisfaction is their disobedience toward God.

I believe you want to be happy. The key to happiness is obeying God. Ecclesiastes 12:13 says that obedience is "the adjustment to all inharmonious circumstances." That means that anything out of order or harmony got that way through disobedience and only obedience can bring it back into harmony. Every time we obey God, something in our lives improves.

GOD'S WORD FOR YOU TODAY: Set your mind to obey God in all things and your joy will increase.

The Holy Spirit Cares About Relationships

Do not grieve the Holy Spirit of God [do not offend or vex or sadden Him], by Whom you were sealed (marked, branded as God's own, secured) for the day of redemption. (EPHESIANS 4:30)

Today's Scripture, in the context of the verses surrounding it, teaches us that the way we handle relationships is important to God. Handling them badly is one way we grieve the Holy Spirit.

Many times we develop a habit of mistreating those close to us, especially when we don't feel well; didn't get enough sleep; have had a rough day, received bad news, or suffered a disappointment. But God wants us to treat one another well all the time, not only when we feel like doing so.

I used to ask myself why I acted badly with my husband or children, but not with other people. The Holy Spirit quickly showed me that I controlled my negative emotions and attitudes when I was around people I wanted to impress. But when I was with my own family, with whom I already had relationships, I took liberties that clearly showed my character flaws and spiritual immaturity. I had myself convinced that I really could not help myself, that when I became grouchy or difficult, I simply could not discipline myself. I felt so frustrated it seemed I just had to explode.

When I became upset over financial struggles, something at work, or some insignificant matter at home, I took my frustration out on my family. Most of the time I was angry and treated them badly because of something unresolved within me, not because of what had happened. God helped me to face truth and thankfully I have been set free.

Relationships are some of our greatest assets, and God wants us to value them. The Holy Spirit will help us handle our frustrations properly if we go to Him with an open heart, ready to face whatever truth He shows us.

GOD'S WORD FOR YOU TODAY: Don't make other people pay for your internal frustrations.

Being Filled with God

May you be rooted deep in love and founded securely on love, . . . that
you may be filled [through all your being] unto all the fullness of God
[may have the richest measure of the divine Presence, and become a
body wholly filled and flooded with God Himself]!

(EPHESIANS 3:17, 19)

Being daily filled with the presence and power of God is wonderful and, according to the verse for today, it is God's will for us. Being filled with God is much better than being full of ourselves. Selfishness is a miserable way to live, but God has provided a way for us to live for Him and others, through Jesus Christ.

The Bible teaches us that Christ died for all, "so that all those who live might live no longer to and for themselves, but to and for Him" (2 Corinthians 5:15). Jesus has made a way for us to have a wonderful life, filled with peace and joy. He has made a way for us to love others rather than living only for our own pleasures and purposes.

Being filled with God's presence requires seeking Him, studying His Word, and developing behaviors that make room for Him in our lives. Starting your day with Scripture and fellowship with God is the way to get your day started right. This day is God's gift to you, so don't waste it. He is waiting to fill you with His presence, so ask and receive that your joy might be full.

GOD'S WORD FOR YOU TODAY: Be filled with God and let Him touch others through you.

The Everlasting Fruit

I have loved you, [just] as the Father has loved Me; abide in My love [continue in His love with Me]. (JOHN 15:9)

I will never forget when Dave decided the beautiful old tree outside our home needed pruning. It had some wild branches and was getting lopsided. I didn't think much about it when he said he was bringing in professionals to do the job of cutting it back and thinning it out. But I was appalled when I arrived home and found those saw-happy men had sabotaged my tree.

Dave said, "Just wait until next year. It will be beautiful again."

But I don't like waiting.

And I didn't like looking at the toothpick limbs that had once been lush and full. But Dave was right. The next year, the tree was more beautiful than before, strong enough to withstand powerful winds for many years to come, and more fruitful and productive than ever. This is a perfect example of the pruning work of the Holy Spirit in our lives— and His pruning results in beauty, strength, and fruitfulness in us.

Galatians 5 gives us a list of sins of the flesh and a list of the fruit of the Spirit, and it is important that the flesh be regularly pruned to make room for more and more good fruit. Like my tree, we sometimes get lopsided or out of balance and God must deal with us to straighten us out again. We should be grateful that God cares enough about us to watch over us and help us be the best we can be. Ask God to come through your life with His pruning shears regularly so you can bear richer and more excellent fruit.

GOD'S WORD FOR YOU TODAY: Discipline never feels good, but we enjoy the fruit of it later on.

Led by the Spirit

If we live by the [Holy] Spirit, let us also walk by the Spirit. [If by the Holy Spirit we have our life in God, let us go forward walking in line, our conduct controlled by the Spirit.] (GALATIANS 5:25)

Today's verse speaks of living and walking by the Spirit, which are the same as being led by the Spirit. There are many things available to lead us—people, the devil, the flesh (our own bodies, minds, wills, or emotions), or the Holy Spirit. There are many voices in the world that speak to us, and often several that do so at the same time. It is imperative that we learn how to be led by the Holy Spirit. Remember: He is the One Who knows the will of God and Who is sent to dwell in each of us to aid us in being all God has designed us to be and to have all He wants us to have.

The Holy Spirit lives in us to help us. His help may not always be welcome at first, but, thank God, He is persistent and will not give up on us. We should lift up our entire lives daily and say with all our might, "Holy Spirit, You are welcome in every area of my life!"

When you welcome the Holy Spirit in every area of your life, He will come. He will speak to you, guide you, correct you, help you, empower you, and lead you. Other forces may try to lead you, but the Holy Spirit gives you power to resist them and enables you to follow Him.

———————

GOD'S WORD FOR YOU TODAY: Ask yourself who is leading your life. Is it you, other people, emotions, the lies of Satan, or the Holy Spirit?

The Gift of Tongues

To one is given . . . various kinds of [unknown] tongues.
(1 CORINTHIANS 12:8, 10)

Believers in some segments of the body of Christ are known for operating in the gifts of the Spirit perhaps more than those from other spiritual backgrounds. Some church groups teach on the baptism and gifts of the Spirit regularly and see the operation of the gifts frequently, while some don't teach on them or even believe they are available for Christians today. These gifts are clearly part of Scripture and should be studied and sought by all believers in Jesus Christ.

Speaking in tongues is speaking in a spiritual language, one God understands but the speaker and others may not. It is useful for private prayer and communion with God and it is beneficial in corporate settings, but must be accompanied by the spiritual gift of interpretation (see 1 Corinthians 14:2, 27–28).

Ignoring the gifts of the Spirit may close the door to excesses and abuses of the gifts that do take place at times, but it also closes the door to countless blessings people desperately need in their daily lives.

I have to say as Paul did in 1 Corinthians 14:18 that I am glad I speak in tongues and I thank God for this gift. I speak in tongues a lot because it strengthens me spiritually; it increases my intimacy with God; and it enables me to hear His voice more clearly.

Clearly, Paul spoke in tongues. The 120 disciples who were filled with the Holy Spirit on the Day of Pentecost all spoke with other tongues. Other believers who received the baptism of the Holy Spirit as recorded in the book of Acts spoke in tongues. Why shouldn't you and I operate in this gift of the Spirit?

GOD'S WORD FOR YOU TODAY: Be open to the gifts of the Holy Spirit and never have a closed mind to learning new things.

Take Time to Get to Know People

Be honest in your judgment and do not decide at a glance (superficially and by appearances); but judge fairly and righteously. (JOHN 7:24)

Today's verse is a very clear, specific word from God to us. He tells us not to judge people superficially or by appearances.

For years I was the kind of person who made snap judgments. God seriously dealt with me about it several times, and I finally realized the danger of judging hastily and superficially.

Before we judge people, we must take time to get to know who they really are. Otherwise, (1) we can approve of someone because they appear to be something, when in fact they are not; or (2) we can disapprove of someone because of some outward appearance or action, when that individual is actually a wonderful person inside.

We all have our little quirks, our odd little actions, behaviors, and ways that are not easily understood by others. God Himself does not judge by appearances and we need to follow His example.

David would never have been chosen to be king if people had judged superficially. Even his own family disregarded him. But God saw David's heart, the heart of a shepherd. God saw a worshipper, someone who had a heart for Him, someone who was pliable and moldable in His hand. These are qualities God values, but they aren't always obvious at a glance.

I encourage you to seek God and let the Holy Spirit speak to you about people. He knows their hearts, and He will tell you whether to beware or pursue a relationship with them. Trust Him, not your own judgment, to lead you as you get to know people and develop relationships.

GOD'S WORD FOR YOU TODAY: Have the same attitude toward others that you would like them to have toward you.

Purified by Fire

The Lord went before them by day in a pillar of cloud to lead them along the way and by night in a pillar of fire to give them light, that they might travel by day and by night. (EXODUS 13:21)

The Bible mentions the fire of God and how it is used in our lives in several different portions of Scripture. If we want God's best, we must be willing to endure the fires of purification. We have gold in us (good things), but we also have impurities that must be removed.

Everyone wants to enjoy God's best, but few are eager to be pursued by His fire. Always remember that when the fire of God comes into your life He is in charge of the flame. He will never let the fire go completely out, but neither will He let it destroy you. He never allows more to come on us than what we can bear.

Throughout all of our lives we experience times that seem difficult and other times that are easier. Paul referred to these times and said that he had learned to be content in either one. He trusted that God's wisdom was perfect and that all things would eventually work out for his good. We can choose to do the same thing. Resisting the fire of God will not keep it from burning in our lives—it only makes it harder to endure.

The fire of God comes to burn up all the useless things in our lives and leave what is left to burn brightly for Him. Sometimes we sense this fire burning in us when we study God's Word and are convicted by it in an area that needs to change. At other times the fire of God comes through an unpleasant circumstance in which God is requiring us to remain stable and display behavior that is godly. Anytime we endure something difficult for the glory of God we can be assured that our reward will come in due time.

GOD'S WORD FOR YOU TODAY: If you go through things, then you won't have to run from them or ever be afraid of them.

Does Your Faith Work?

[If we are] in Christ Jesus, neither circumcision nor uncircumcision counts for anything, but only faith activated and energized and expressed and working through love. (GALATIANS 5:6)

Many people think great faith is the number one sign of spiritual maturity, but I believe the truest test of spiritual maturity is walking in love. Our love walk energizes our faith. We cannot have a good relationship with God without having faith in God, but love demonstrates, empowers, and expresses our faith. If we truly love God and have faith in Him, we will also love people.

Today's verse teaches us that faith works through love, and love is not talk or theory; it's action. In fact, the Bible says that we cannot be walking in love if we see a brother in need, have what it takes to meet his need, and will not help him (see 1 John 3:17).

Jesus also said all the law and all the prophets are summed up in love when He declared: "'You shall love the LORD your God with all your heart, with all your soul, and with all of your mind.' This is the first and great commandment. And the second is like it: 'You shall love your neighbor as yourself.' On these two commandments hang all the Law and the Prophets" (Matthew 22:37–40 NKJV). Jesus gave these words to people asking which commandment was most important. They basically said to Him: "Just give us the bottom line, Jesus." He replied: "Okay. You want the bottom line? You want to fully obey all the law and all the prophets? Then love Me and love people." It's that simple. Jesus let people know that walking in love is the key to living a life that is pleasing to Him. Trying to walk in faith without love is like having a flashlight with no battery. We must be sure that we keep our love battery charged at all times. Otherwise our faith will not work!

GOD'S WORD FOR YOU TODAY: God is love and the more we know Him, the more we will love others.

The Gifts of the Holy Spirit

About the spiritual gifts (the special endowments of supernatural energy), brethren, I do not want you to be misinformed.

(1 CORINTHIANS 12:1)

Much has been written about the gifts of the Spirit throughout Christian history. The Bible itself teaches us the importance of the gifts of the Spirit and the importance of our not being ignorant of them. Yet, in spite of all the information available today on the subject, many people are totally ignorant of these gifts. I, for one, attended church for many years and never heard one sermon or lesson of any kind on the gifts of the Spirit. I didn't even know what they were, let alone that they were available to me.

There are many varieties of "gifts" or "endowments," as they are called in the Amplified Bible, which also refers to them as "extraordinary powers distinguishing certain Christians" (1 Corinthians 12:4). The gifts vary, but they are all from the same Holy Spirit. When we let God lead us in the use of these gifts, they add a wonderful dimension of power to our lives. First Corinthians 12:8–10 (KJV) lists the gifts as: the word of wisdom, the word of knowledge, faith, the gifts of healing, the working of miracles, prophecy, discerning of spirits, divers (different) kinds of tongues, and the interpretation of tongues.

These are all abilities, gifts, achievements, and endowments of supernatural power by which the believer is enabled to accomplish something beyond the ordinary, and they are available to all believers. We cannot force the operation of any spiritual gift. We are to earnestly desire all the gifts, but the Holy Spirit chooses when and through whom they operate. Ask for and expect God's leading concerning the gifts of the Spirit.

GOD'S WORD FOR YOU TODAY: You don't have to live in weakness because God's power is available to you today and every day.

The Word of Wisdom

To one is given in and through the [Holy] Spirit [the power to speak]
a message of wisdom. (1 CORINTHIANS 12:8)

First Corinthians 1:30 (KJV) says that Jesus "is made unto us wisdom"
from God. And the writer of the book of Proverbs repeatedly tells us to
seek wisdom and do all we can to gain it. Wisdom is made available to
all people, but the "word of wisdom" is a type of wisdom different from
that which everyone can possess.

All wisdom is from God, and there is a wisdom that can be learned
from experience and attained intellectually. That is not the word of
wisdom mentioned in today's verse. The word of wisdom is a form of
spiritual guidance. When it is operating, an individual is made to know
supernaturally by the Holy Spirit how to handle a certain issue in an
exceptionally wise way, one that is beyond their natural learning or
experience and that lines up with God's purpose.[1]

We frequently operate in this gift without even being aware of it. We
may say something to someone that seems ordinary to us, but to the
listener it is a tremendous word of wisdom for his or her situation.

I have received words of wisdom from children I knew for sure did
not have a clue what they were saying. The Holy Spirit was trying to get
my attention and He was using a source through which I would know
He was speaking. Ask for and expect the guidance of God through
words of wisdom.

GOD'S WORD FOR YOU TODAY: Seek wisdom because
one word of wisdom spoken at the right moment can be life-
changing.

1 Stanley M. Burgess and Gary B. McGee, eds., *Dictionary of Pentecostal and Charismatic Movements* (Grand Rapids, MI: Zondervan, 1988), 890–92.

The Word of Knowledge

To another [the power to express] a word of knowledge and understanding according to the same [Holy] Spirit.

(1 CORINTHIANS 12:8)

The word of knowledge operates much the same way as the word of wisdom. There are several different interpretations of the word of knowledge, but most agree that it is in operation when God reveals something to an individual about what He is doing in a situation when the individual who receives the knowledge would have no natural way of knowing.[1]

Sometimes when God speaks to us and gives us a word of knowledge concerning other people, we know something is wrong with them, or we know they need to do a certain thing in a specific situation. We should never try to force this kind of supernatural knowledge on anyone. Instead, we should present it humbly and let God do the convincing. Sometimes all that God wants us to do is pray for the individual.

While the word of knowledge is often given as a ministry tool to help others, it is also very valuable in our personal lives. For example, this gift functions frequently when I have lost or misplaced something. I cannot seem to find what I am looking for anywhere and suddenly the Holy Spirit gives me a mental image, an idea, or a word about where it is. This is a very practical example of His giving me knowledge I do not have naturally and a way the word of knowledge can work in your life, too.

GOD'S WORD FOR YOU TODAY: Education is good, but God's knowledge is even better, so be sure to depend on Him.

---

1 Stanley M. Burgess and Gary B. McGee, eds., *Dictionary of Pentecostal and Charismatic Movements* (Grand Rapids, MI: Zondervan, 1988), 527–28.

The Gift of Faith

To another [wonder-working] faith by the same [Holy] Spirit.
(1 CORINTHIANS 12:9)

I believe there are certain individuals to whom God gives the gift of faith for specific occasions such as a dangerous missionary trip or a challenging situation. When this gift is operating in people, they are able to comfortably believe in God for something others would see as impossible.[1] They have total faith for something others would be daunted by or even terrified of.

A person operating with a gift of faith must be careful not to think others who do not have this gift are faithless, for when the gift of faith is operating in an individual, God is giving that person an unusual portion of faith to ensure that His purpose is accomplished. He can be used by God to bring courage and comfort to others, but he must remain humble and thankful for what God has given him. Romans 12:3 says, "By the grace (unmerited favor of God) given to me I warn everyone among you not to estimate and think of himself more highly than he ought…but to rate his ability with sober judgment, each according to the degree of faith apportioned by God to him."

God will always give us the faith we need to face whatever we have to face. However, the gift of faith makes a person unusually bold. Anyone who operates in it must be sensitive to realize that this boldness is a gift from God and always give Him thanks for it.

GOD'S WORD FOR YOU TODAY: Be thankful for the faith that God gives you to do difficult things.

1 Arnold Bittlinger, *Gifts and Graces* (Grand Rapids, MI: Eerdmans, 1967), 23–42.

The Gift of Prophecy

To another prophetic insight (the gift of interpreting the divine will and purpose). (1 CORINTHIANS 12:10)

The true gift of prophecy is in operation when someone hears and speaks a clear message from God for someone else, a group, or a situation. Sometimes a prophecy is very general and sometimes it is quite specific. It may come through a prepared message or sermon, or it may come by divine revelation.

While the gift of prophecy is vitally important, it regrettably has been abused and caused much confusion. There are certainly genuine prophets today, but there are also false prophets. Then there are those who mean no harm when trying to speak a word from God, but they do so from their own minds, wills, or emotions instead of by God's Spirit.

The purposes and goals of true prophecy are the "upbuilding and constructive spiritual progress and encouragement and consolation" of people (1 Corinthians 14:3). All the gifts of the Holy Spirit are for the good and profit of all. In addition, a true word will be accompanied by peace and "settle" in your heart and spirit as being from God; it will also confirm something already in your heart, even if only vaguely. These criteria can help determine whether a prophecy is genuine or not. Of course, the real test of prophecy is whether or not it comes to pass. Remember this: True prophecy comes true. Those with the gift of prophecy are not the only ones who hear from God. You have the ability and the right to hear His voice for yourself, so always try the spirit behind the prophecies you receive and test them to make sure they bear witness in your heart (see 1 John 4:1).

GOD'S WORD FOR YOU TODAY: When people give you advice and tell you it is from God, be sure it agrees with God's Word and is confirmed in your own heart.

The Gifts of Healing

To another the extraordinary powers of healing by the one Spirit.
(1 CORINTHIANS 12:9)

The gifts of healing work with the gift of faith. Although all believers are encouraged to pray for the sick and see them recover (see Mark 16:17–18), the Holy Spirit does distribute extraordinary gifts of healing to some people, just as He gives other spiritual gifts to certain people.

In our conferences we often pray for people and see many wonderful healings. We have received stacks of testimonies and reports of confirmed physical healings over the years. I pray the prayer of faith during our conferences and on our broadcasts and I believe by faith that God is working.

When a person receives healing through a spiritual gift, that healing may not be evident immediately. Healing can be a process that works somewhat like medicine. It is necessary to receive it by faith and believe it is working. The results often become visible later. I often encourage people to say, "The healing power of God is working in me right now."

We should trust God in the area of our health. I thank God for doctors and medicine when I need it, but Jesus is our Healer (see Isaiah 53:5).

GOD'S WORD FOR YOU TODAY: God is your physician and His Word is your medicine. Ask Him to heal you in every way.

Mind, Will, and Emotions

We have the mind of Christ (the Messiah) and do hold the thoughts (feelings and purposes) of His heart. (1 CORINTHIANS 2:16)

When we invite Jesus to come into our hearts, the Holy Spirit makes His home in us. From that position in our hearts, which are the very centers of our beings, the Holy Spirit begins a purifying work in our souls (our minds, wills, and emotions).

Our minds tell us what *we* think, not what God thinks. The Holy Spirit is working in us to change that. We have to learn how to think in agreement with God, how to be vessels for God to think through. Old thoughts must be purified from us, and new thoughts—thoughts from God—must become part of our thinking.

Our emotions tell us how *we* feel, not how God feels about situations, people, and the decisions we make. According to Psalm 7:9, God tests and tries our emotions. He works with us until we are not moved by human emotion alone, but by His Spirit.

Our wills tell us what *we* want, not what God wants. The will overrides emotions and even thoughts. We can use it to do the right thing even when we don't feel like doing it. We have a free will, and God will not force us to do anything. He leads us by His Spirit into what He knows will be good for us, but the final decisions are ours to make. God wants us to regularly make decisions that are in agreement with His will, not our wills.

As these three areas of our lives—mind, will, and emotions—come under the Lordship of Jesus Christ and the leadership of the Holy Spirit, we will become increasingly mature as believers.

GOD'S WORD FOR YOU TODAY: You can manage your emotions instead of letting them manage you.

People Belong to God

Fear not, for I have redeemed you … I have called you by your name;
you are Mine. (ISAIAH 43:1)

Do you have a possession that is extremely valuable to you, one you cherish and admire? If you saw someone tossing it around carelessly or otherwise risking damage to it, wouldn't you be grieved?

God feels the same way about His possessions as we feel about ours. People belong to God. They are His creations and His Spirit is grieved when He sees them being mistreated.

Not everyone shares the same calling in life, but every born-again person is an heir of God and a joint heir with Christ. Every individual has a right to peace, righteousness, and joy; to have their needs met, to be used by God, and to see His anointing flow through them.

Everyone has an equal opportunity to see fruit in their ministry, but their willingness to love others has a lot to do with how much fruit they are going to see. The Holy Spirit spoke to me years ago: "One of the main reasons people don't walk in love is that it requires effort. Anytime they walk in love, it's going to cost them something."

Love requires us to withhold some things we would like to say. Love demands that we not do some things we would like to do and that we give away some things we would like to keep. Love requires us to be patient with people.

Relationships are not always easy, but they are always important to God because He values people. We need to make the effort and the sacrifices needed to love people as God wants us to love them so we do not grieve Him.

GOD'S WORD FOR YOU TODAY: God sees people as His
own treasures, so be careful how you treat them.

Interpretation of Tongues

To another the ability to interpret [such] tongues.
(1 CORINTHIANS 12:10)

When a person speaks in tongues in public worship, the message must be interpreted, according to 1 Corinthians 14:27. I have sometimes been given understanding or interpretations of messages given in tongues. They come to me as an impression or a knowing in my spirit of what God is trying to convey to those listening.

To many sectors of Christianity, these things are a mystery simply because they have had no teaching concerning them. I believe we are living in difficult times and that we need all the supernatural help from God we can get. It is important not to be deceived, but it is also important not to be so afraid of being deceived that we end up closed-minded to God's gifts.

Paul encouraged believers to pray in tongues and to pray that they might interpret, and I believe we should do likewise. Having the gift of interpretation enables us to better understand what we are praying when we use our private prayer language. Interpretation is different from translation. We don't receive a word-for-word understanding, but more of a general sensing of what God is speaking to His people.

God is a Spirit and we are spiritual beings who must learn to sense in our spirits what God is saying to us. I encourage you to study these things for yourself and ask God for understanding concerning all of His wonderful gifts. The important thing is that you keep an open mind and follow the leading of the Holy Spirit as you pray and seek God.

GOD'S WORD FOR YOU TODAY: Be bold and ask God to lead you into understanding His secrets and mysteries.

Discerning of Spirits

To another the ability to discern and distinguish between [the utterances of true] spirits [and false ones]. (1 CORINTHIANS 12:10)

I believe the discerning of spirits is an extremely valuable gift, and I encourage you to desire and develop it. Some people say that the discerning of spirits gives people supernatural insight into the spiritual realm when God allows it. Many also believe that discerning of spirits is a gift given so we can know the true nature of a person or a situation. Our world is full of deception and many people are not who they appear to be. The gift of discerning of spirits helps us see behind the masks people often wear so we can know what is really going on. The gift also helps us sense when something is a good thing or a person has a good heart.

Dave and I have seen this gift work many times when hiring people to work in our ministry. Many times, people have seemed qualified, capable, dedicated, and "perfect" for the jobs for which they applied. I remember one specific occasion when we met with someone and everyone involved thought we should hire him, but I had a nagging feeling in my heart that we should not. We hired him anyway and he did nothing but cause trouble. I allowed my reasoning—thinking he would work out because his résumé was exactly what we wanted—to overtake my discernment, and I wish I had not.

The Spirit of God lives in our hearts and speaks to our hearts, not our heads. His gifts are not intellectual or operative in our minds; they are spiritual and they operate in our spirits. We must follow what we sense in our spirits, not what we think in our minds should be right. This is why God gives us discernment.

GOD'S WORD FOR YOU TODAY: Learn to discern and don't make decisions based only on what you see and think.

Seek the Gifts of the Spirit

*There are distinctive varieties and distributions of endowments
(gifts, extraordinary powers distinguishing certain Christians, due to
the power of divine grace operating in their souls by the Holy Spirit)
and they vary, but the [Holy] Spirit remains the same.*

(1 CORINTHIANS 12:4)

The gifts of the Spirit can be difficult to explain because they operate in the spiritual realm. Over the past few days of devotions, I hope and pray I have done an adequate job of describing them and their basic operation. There is much more to be said on the subject of spiritual gifts and I encourage you to read good books that are dedicated to the topic of the gifts of the Holy Spirit.

When we function in the supernatural realm we do need to be careful, but not afraid. Satan offers many perversions of God's true gifts, but we can stay on the right track through prayer and seeking truth from God's Word.

I also urge you to begin praying about the gifts of the Spirit. Ask God to use you in them and to allow them to flow through you as He sees fit. Don't seek the gifts that seem most attractive or interesting to you, but seek the gifts God has for you.

Allowing the gifts of the Spirit to work through us helps us in our everyday lives and demonstrates to nonbelievers the power and goodness of Christ, Who dwells within us. When the gifts of the Holy Spirit are operating in our lives, we reflect the glory of God's grace that is bestowed on us to others who desperately need to put their trust in Jesus.

Seek to operate in the gifts of the Spirit for your own edification and for the good of others. As you seek the gifts, don't forget to seek especially to walk in love because love is the greatest gift of all.

GOD'S WORD FOR YOU TODAY: The gifts of the Holy
Spirit should be a normal part of your everyday life.

Alone with God

After He had dismissed the multitudes, He went up into the hills by Himself to pray. When it was evening, He was still there alone.

(MATTHEW 14:23)

Spending time alone with God in a quiet place is vital to me and I believe it is also vital for you. I have an office in my home where I go each morning to meet with God before I begin my day. In addition to that, about four times a year I like to get away for a few days and be alone. I enjoy and need the extended time of quiet and focusing on God.

Most people take vacations yearly and plan some type of entertainment each week. We want to have fun and relaxation, and there is nothing wrong with that. We need it in order to maintain balanced, healthy lives and emotions. But we actually need the spiritual vacations even more and they should be the first thing we put on the yearly calendar or our weekly schedules.

Just imagine how it would honor God if you booked your time with Him before booking anything else. I conduct conferences in the United States and abroad and I am always impressed by the number of people who travel and take vacation time to be at one of these conferences. I always compliment them and I know that God is proud of their choices. They will grow spiritually because they are sacrificing something in order to spend time with God.

Don't wait until some difficulty or tragedy demands that you spend time with God in order to find answers to your situation. Seek God first and regularly, and then you will already be strong spiritually and enabled to deal with anything that comes. If Jesus needed to be alone with God the Father, then we certainly need it.

GOD'S WORD FOR YOU TODAY: Get your calendar out right now and schedule some special time with God.

God Gets His Messages Across

You shall obey the voice of the Lord your God.
(DEUTERONOMY 27:10)

God sometimes speaks to us through other people, as you know. I remember a specific time when God spoke to me through Dave concerning something in my life. When he shared it with me, I was angry. Dave simply said, "You do what you want to with it; I am only telling you what I believe God showed me." He did not try to convince me that what he had said was true; he simply reported what he believed God had said to him. Over the next three days God convinced me that the word He had given Dave was correct. I shed many tears because I was ashamed to admit that Dave was right!

Through the word of knowledge God gave me through Dave I was able to understand why I was having trouble in a certain area of my life. I had been seeking God about this situation and not getting any answers. Dave had given me my answer, but I did not like it because it convicted me of the sins of judgment and gossip. The fact that I did not want to hear it is probably why God gave it to Dave—because He knew I could not hear it from Him myself.

I cannot overemphasize the impact this experience had on my life. Had God dealt with me directly, I am sure I would have learned a lesson, but it would have been nothing like the lesson I learned because He spoke to me through Dave.

I encourage you to be open to hear God speak to you through trustworthy people who hear His voice and love you enough to say what He wants you to hear.

———————————

GOD'S WORD FOR YOU TODAY: Ask God daily to speak to you however, whenever, and through whomever He pleases.

God Chooses Our Gifts

A man can receive nothing [he can claim nothing, he can take unto himself nothing] except as it has been granted to him from heaven. [A man must be content to receive the gift which is given him from heaven; there is no other source.] (JOHN 3:27)

I think something very sad happens when people compete against each other or compare themselves with others in the area of spiritual gifts, natural abilities, and the callings God has placed on their lives. Comparison and competition cause us to lose the joy of being and doing what God has designed us to be and do.

Today's verse instructs us to be satisfied with the gift or gifts we have. Our gifts come from God and we need to be happy with the gifts He gives us because we will not get any other gifts unless God decides to give them to us. We need to trust the Holy Spirit, believing that He has been sent to Earth to help make sure God's will comes to pass on the earth and in each of our lives.

I encourage you to meditate on the fact that God has sent the Holy Spirit to dwell in us. He actually lives inside every person who has truly accepted Jesus Christ as Savior and Lord. The Holy Spirit was sent to keep us until the final day of redemption when Jesus returns to claim His own. He is attempting to speak to us so He can lead us into the fullness of what Jesus died for us to have. When we fight against our calling or are dissatisfied with what we are and what we have, we fight against the work and wisdom of the Holy Spirit. We need to submit to Him, obey His voice, develop the gifts He has placed within us, and with His help, live our lives passionately and fully for the glory of God.

GOD'S WORD FOR YOU TODAY: Contentment is a compliment to God. It tells Him that we trust Him and appreciate all He does for us.

Present Yourself to God, Then Relax

The LORD your God in your midst, the Mighty One, will save; He will rejoice over you with gladness, He will quiet you with His love, He will rejoice over you with singing. (ZEPHANIAH 3:17 NKJV)

I believe one of the biggest problems facing people today is the busy, hurried, frantic, stressful lifestyles we live. Busyness makes hearing from God very challenging, but today's verse promises that God will quiet us with His love. One of the best favors you can do for yourself is to find a place where you can be still and quiet.

Hearing God requires times of quiet solitude. If you really want to hear His still, small voice, you will have to be still. You need to go somewhere and be alone with Him. Jesus said, "Go into your most private room and shut the door" (see Matthew 6:6).

A few minutes of peace and quiet won't always do the job; you also need extended periods of quiet to seek God. It is important to be able to spend time with God free from distractions and interruptions.

When you are alone with God, don't think about your problems. Ask for His wisdom and strength. Ask for a refreshing and renewal.

Tell Him you want to know what He has for your life.

Ask Him to tell you what He wants you to do.

Ask Him to tell you what He *doesn't* want you to do.

Present yourself to God and listen. You are honoring Him by going to Him. You will get an answer from Him. If you don't hear Him speak during your time alone with Him, don't worry about it. You have done your part by seeking Him and He will guide you as you go through life.

GOD'S WORD FOR YOU TODAY: If you are too busy for time with God, then you are definitely too busy!

Jealous Love

Do you suppose that the Scripture is speaking to no purpose that says, The Spirit Whom He has caused to dwell in us yearns over us and He yearns for the Spirit [to be welcome] with a jealous love?

(JAMES 4:5)

Today's verse sums up the fact that the Holy Spirit wants to be made welcome in our lives. In fact, He yearns for fellowship with us.

According to James 4:4, which precedes today's verse, when we pay more attention to the things of the world than we do to God, He looks upon us as an unfaithful wife having an illicit love affair with the world and breaking our marriage vow to Him. To keep us faithful to Him, sometimes He must remove things from our lives when He sees they are keeping us from Him.

If we allow a job to come between God and ourselves, we may lose it. If money separates us from Him, we may have to learn we are better off with less money and things than alienated from God. If success gets in the way of our relationship with our heavenly Father, we may get demoted instead of promoted. If our friends take first place over God in our lives, we may lose some of our friends.

Multitudes of people fail to realize that they never receive the things they want because they don't really put God first. God is jealous for you; He wants first place in your life. Nothing else will do.

GOD'S WORD FOR YOU TODAY: Ask God to remove anything in your life that is taking the place that belongs to Him.

Fellowship: The Secret Place

Even when we were dead (slain) by [our own] shortcomings and trespasses, He made us alive together in fellowship and in union with Christ. (EPHESIANS 2:5)

Fellowship with God ministers life to us. It renews us; it charges our batteries, so to speak. We are made strong through union and fellowship with God—strong enough to withstand the attacks of the enemy of our souls (see Ephesians 6:10–11).

When we are fellowshipping with God, we are in a secret place where we are protected from the enemy. Psalm 91:1 speaks of this place and tells us that those who dwell there will defeat every foe: "He who dwells in the secret place of the Most High shall remain stable and fixed under the shadow of the Almighty [Whose power no foe can withstand]."

I believe the secret place is God's presence. When we are in His presence, fellowshipping with Him, we experience His peace. Satan simply does not know what to do with a believer who remains stable no matter what the circumstances may be. This is hard to do at times, but we draw strength for stability as we have communion and fellowship with God through His Spirit.

Fellowshipping with God takes time, but it is time well spent. It keeps you strong so you are not devastated by unexpected challenges. Proverbs 18:14 says, "The strong spirit of a man sustains him in bodily pain or trouble." Don't wait until you have trouble to get strong; stay strong!

GOD'S WORD FOR YOU TODAY: No matter what you're facing in life right now, through Christ you have the victory!

Expect More

I have still many things to say to you, but you are not able to bear them or to take them upon you or to grasp them now. (JOHN 16:12)

Jesus spoke the words of today's verse to His disciples, basically telling them they were not ready to hear everything He had to say, but promising that the Holy Spirit would come and lead them into all truth (see John 16:13). He also promised the Holy Spirit would continue to teach us all things and bring to our remembrance all that God has said through His Word (see John 14:26).

When Jesus spoke these words, He was talking to men with whom He had spent the previous three years. They had been with Him day and night, yet He indicated that He had more to teach them. We would think that if Jesus was with us personally for three years, day and night, we would have learned all there is to know. I think that if I had one uninterrupted month with people, I could tell them everything I know. But Jesus said to expect more because He will always have something to say to us about new situations we face. Revelation of God and His Word is progressive. As we mature in Him, we are able to understand what we could not previously understand. We may read a verse of Scripture ten times and then the next time we read it, we see something we did not know previously. Each day you can expect God to teach you something if you pay attention to what He is saying and revealing.

GOD'S WORD FOR YOU TODAY: Expect the Holy Spirit to teach you something new each day. Consider keeping a journal of what you learn.

The Baptism of Fire

I indeed baptize you in (with) water because of repentance … But He Who is coming after me is mightier than I, Whose sandals I am not worthy or fit to take off or carry; He will baptize you with the Holy Spirit and with fire. (MATTHEW 3:11)

As believers, we are called to do more than go to church on Sunday mornings, do more than follow prescribed rituals, and certainly do more than have water sprinkled on our heads or be immersed in baptismal pools. These are all extremely important and not to be ignored, but they must be followed up with a willingness to experience the "baptism of fire."

In response to James and John's mother, who asked if her sons could sit one on Jesus' right hand and one on His left when He came into His Kingdom (see Matthew 20:20–21), Jesus replied that they did not know what they were asking. He said, "Are you able to drink the cup that I am about to drink and to be baptized with the baptism with which I am baptized?" (Matthew 20:22).

What baptism was Jesus speaking of? He had already been baptized by John in the Jordan River and received the baptism of the Holy Spirit at the same time (see Mark 1:9–11). What other baptism is available?

Jesus was speaking of the baptism of fire. Fire is a purifying agent, something that causes discomfort while it does its work. Jesus was sinless and, therefore, did not need to be purified; but we do. Jesus is the One Who baptizes us with the Holy Spirit and with fire.

Have the courage to ask Jesus to baptize you with His fire. Ask Him to do a cleansing and purifying work in you so you can be a vessel fit for His use. It may be difficult to go through, but it will bring a satisfying reward.

GOD'S WORD FOR YOU TODAY: When you go through the fire God will be with you. He will never leave you or forsake you.

Don't Forget God

My people have committed two evils: they have forsaken Me, the Fountain of living waters, and they have hewn for themselves cisterns, broken cisterns which cannot hold water. (JEREMIAH 2:13)

The first and biggest mistake anyone can make is to forsake or ignore God, or act as though He doesn't exist. This is what the people Jeremiah wrote about in today's verse had done. Later in the same chapter that contains this verse, God says, "My people have forgotten Me, days without number" (Jeremiah 2:32). What a tragedy; it sounds as though God is sad or perhaps even lonely.

I sure wouldn't like it if my children forgot about me. I never go many days without talking to each of them. I have one son who travels extensively with the ministry. Even when he is overseas, he calls me every few days.

I remember a time when Dave and I had dinner with one of our sons two evenings in a row. Yet the next day he called just to see what we were doing and to ask if we wanted to do something together the following evening. He also called to simply say that he and his wife really appreciate all the things we do to help them.

These are the kinds of things that help build and maintain good relationships. Sometimes the little things mean the most. My children's actions let me know that they love me. Even though I know with my mind that they love me, it sure is good to also feel their love.

That is the way God is with us, His beloved children. He may know we love Him, but He also likes to experience our love for Him through our actions, especially our remembering Him and our desire to spend time with Him.

GOD'S WORD FOR YOU TODAY: God cares about everything that concerns you, so feel free to talk to Him about anything.

Bear Good Fruit

When you bear (produce) much fruit, My Father is honored and glorified, and you show and prove yourselves to be true followers of Mine. (JOHN 15:8)

In today's verse, Jesus said that God is glorified when we bear fruit. He also spoke of fruit in Matthew 12:33 when He said that trees are known by the fruit they bear, and in Matthew 7:15–16 He applied this same principle to people. These verses show us that as believers we need to be concerned about the kind of fruit we are bearing. We want to bear the good fruit of the Holy Spirit (see Galatians 5:22–23), but how do we do that?

We know that God is a consuming fire, and that Jesus was sent to baptize us with the Holy Spirit and with fire. Unless we allow the fire of God to burn in our lives, we will never exhibit the fruit of the Holy Spirit.

Bearing good fruit seems exciting until we realize that fruit-bearing requires pruning. Jesus said: "Any branch in Me that does not bear fruit [that stops bearing] He cuts away (trims off, takes away); and He cleanses and repeatedly prunes every branch that continues to bear fruit, to make it bear more and richer and more excellent fruit" (John 15:2). Just as fire describes the work the Holy Spirit does in our lives, so does pruning. Fire is necessary for purification and death of the flesh; pruning is necessary for growth. Dead things and things that are going in the wrong direction must be cut off so we can grow as "trees of righteousness" and bear rich fruit for God (Isaiah 61:3 KJV).

GOD'S WORD FOR YOU TODAY: When God cuts something off of your life, He always does so to make room for a better thing.

God Loves Us Enough to Change Us

Who can endure the day of His coming? And who can stand when He appears? For He is like a refiner's fire and like fullers' soap.

(MALACHI 3:2)

God uses His refining fire to change us and make us into the people He wants us to be. I realize that it isn't easy to change. I have been studying God's Word for more than thirty years, and I still have to work at many things and allow God to change me in certain ways. I'm still not where I need to be, but I thank God I'm not where I used to be.

If we become stubborn or unwilling to repent when God's refining fire comes to reveal a behavior that needs to be changed in us, then love gets stubborn. Let me explain. We know that God is love, and He is a jealous God. He doesn't want anything in us to occupy the place that belongs to Him. And love, God Himself, will be jealous enough and stubborn enough to stick with us until He gets His way. Love (God) will show us things we don't want to see in order to help us be what we need to be.

Fire devours all impurities and leaves all that remains ablaze for God's glory. A lot of the old Joyce Meyer has been burned up in God's refining fire over the years. It definitely has not been easy, but it definitely has been worth it.

God's refining fire may come to you in different ways. You may have a nudge in your heart to stop doing something and start doing something else; you may feel convicted as He speaks to you through His Word; or you may hear from His Spirit directly in your spirit. However it comes, God will bring His refining fire to your life. When it comes, don't resist it, but trust God and let the fire work.

GOD'S WORD FOR YOU TODAY: God is changing you daily and today you are better than you were yesterday.

Guaranteed!

That [Spirit] is the guarantee of our inheritance [the firstfruits, the pledge and foretaste, the down payment on our heritage], in anticipation of its full redemption and our acquiring [complete] possession of it—to the praise of His glory. (EPHESIANS 1:14)

The Holy Spirit is our guarantee of the good things that are to come. I often say, especially when I feel really filled with the Holy Spirit, "This is so good, I cannot imagine the glory of what the complete fullness will be like." If we experience only 10 percent (a typical down payment) of what belongs to us because of our inheritance, just think of what it will be like to actually see God face-to-face, to have no more tears, no more sorrow, no more dying. These thoughts leave me totally awestruck.

In Ephesians 1:13–14, the Bible says that we are sealed with the Holy Spirit, and He guarantees that we will arrive safe, preserved from all destruction, on the final day of deliverance from sin and all its effects. Think of the wonder of it—the Holy Spirit in us, preserving us for our final resting place, which is in not a grave but in heaven, in the presence of God.

The Holy Spirit does wonderful things for us here and now. He speaks to us, leads us, helps us, teaches us, gives us counsel, empowers us to fulfill God's exciting plans for our lives, and so much more. But no matter how wonderful our experiences with Him are in our earthly lives, they are only a foretaste of what we can look forward to. We have the down payment, but there's more to come!

GOD'S WORD FOR YOU TODAY: You can feel secure in knowing that your inheritance comes with a guarantee.

Live the Life of the Spirit

You are not living the life of the flesh, you are living the life of the Spirit, if the [Holy] Spirit of God [really] dwells within you . . . But if anyone does not possess the [Holy] Spirit of Christ, he is none of His.

(ROMANS 8:9)

We are called to walk in the Spirit or, as today's verse says, to live "the life of the Spirit." Making a decision to do this is the starting point, but I can tell you from the Word of God and from experience that it takes more than a decision; it takes a deep work of the Holy Spirit in our lives. He "operates" on us with God's Word, which divides soul and spirit (see Hebrews 4:12). He also uses circumstances to train us in stability and walking in love at all times.

These things we are called to do are not things that are just given to us; they must be worked in us. Just as leaven or yeast must be worked into dough—so Christ must be worked in us.

In Philippians 2:12 (KJV), the apostle Paul teaches us to "work out" our salvation with fear and trembling. That means we are to cooperate with the Holy Spirit as He begins in us a work of crucifixion or "dying to self." Paul said, "I die daily" (1 Corinthians 15:31 KJV). In other words, he was saying that he was constantly exposed to a "putting to death of the flesh." He was not speaking of physical death, but a death to his own will and ways.

If we really want to live the life of the Spirit, we also have to put to death our will and ways and choose God's will. We can count on God to lead us, and we want Him to be able to count on us to obey.

GOD'S WORD FOR YOU TODAY: If you die to self, you will be able to minister life to others.

Be Diligent in Prayer

I give myself to prayer. (PSALM 109:4 NKJV)

Prayer can be short and still be effective, but that does not mean extended seasons of talking and listening to God are not also necessary and valuable. They certainly are. In fact, in addition to daily prayer, I recommend setting aside entire days or even several days in succession a few times a year dedicated specifically to seeking God in prayer and studying His Word. Times of fasting can also be very beneficial spiritually. Even though prayer is simple and should never be viewed as complicated, there are also times when prayer is work. Sometimes we must labor in prayer until a specific matter that God has placed on our hearts is lifted or we have to wait patiently or sacrifice something in order to hear God's voice. But, at the same time, we should not allow Satan to make us believe that prayer must be hard and complicated.

Satan is working overtime trying to rob us of the honor of communicating with God. He does not want us to share our hearts with God and He certainly doesn't want us to hear God's voice. I encourage you to be diligent and faithful to communicate with God and to rediscover the simple privilege of a rich, fulfilling, rewarding relationship with God in which you speak to Him and He speaks to you.

GOD'S WORD FOR YOU TODAY: Stay in touch!

God Speaks Comfort and Consolation

Blessed be the God and Father of our Lord Jesus Christ, the Father of sympathy (pity and mercy) and the God [Who is the Source] of every comfort (consolation and encouragement). (2 CORINTHIANS 1:3)

We all desire to be accepted, not rejected. I hate the lonely, isolated feeling and emotional pain that come from feeling rejected, yet I experienced it for many years, not knowing I could do anything about it. Thank God, all that has changed!

Several years ago, something happened that brought back those old pains of rejection. I reached out to someone who had hurt me greatly during my childhood. Instead of an apology, I was blamed for something that wasn't my fault and received a clear message that this person had no interest whatsoever in me.

I wanted to hide and feel sorry for myself, but instead I immediately asked God for the comfort of the Holy Spirit. I asked Him to heal my wounded emotions and enable me to handle the situation as Jesus would have. As I continued to lean on God, I felt a warmth come over me, almost as though soothing oil was being poured over my wounds.

I asked God to forgive the person who had hurt me, and He brought to my mind the saying, "Hurting people hurt people." His intimate, personal response brought healing to my wounded spirit.

God is the source of all comfort, consolation, and encouragement. Please, do everything you can to develop and maintain an intimate relationship with Him because that is the context within which you will be able to hear His voice, receive His comfort and healing, and be strengthened by His encouragement and care.

GOD'S WORD FOR YOU TODAY: God knows how important it is to be comforted; He sent you the Holy Spirit to do just that.

Through the Fire

Our God [is indeed] a consuming fire. (HEBREWS 12:29)

God desires to consume everything in our lives that does not bring Him glory. He sends the Holy Spirit to live inside us believers, to be in close fellowship with us, and to bring conviction of our every wrong thought, word, or action. We must all go through the "refiner's fire" (Malachi 3:2).

What does it mean to go through the refiner's fire? It means God will deal with us. He will work to change our attitudes, desires, ways, thoughts, and conversations. He will speak to us about things in our hearts that are not pleasing to Him, and He will ask us to change those things with His help. Those of us who go through the fire instead of running from it are the ones who will bring great glory to God eventually.

Going through fire sounds frightening. It reminds us of pain and even death. In Romans 8:17, Paul said that if we want to share Christ's inheritance, we must also share His suffering. How did Jesus suffer? Are we expected to go to the cross also? The answer is yes and no. We don't have to physically be nailed to a cross for our sins, but in Mark 8:34, Jesus did say we should take up our cross and follow Him. He went on to talk about laying aside a selfish, self-centered lifestyle. The Bible says we are to die to self. Believe me, getting rid of selfishness takes some fire—and usually a lot of it. But if we are willing to go through the fire, we will later know the joy of bringing God glory.

GOD'S WORD FOR YOU TODAY: God loves you very much and He will continue working in you until the day of His return.

He Wants to Be Involved in Everything

All who are led by the Spirit of God are sons of God.
(ROMANS 8:14)

Being led by the Holy Spirit means allowing Him to be involved in every decision we make, both major and minor. He leads us by peace and by wisdom, as well as by the Word of God. He speaks in a still, small voice in our hearts, or what we often call "the inward witness." Those of us who desire to be led by the Holy Spirit must learn to follow the inward witness and respond quickly.

For example, if we are engaged in a conversation, and we begin to feel uncomfortable inside, it may be the Holy Spirit signaling us that we need to turn the conversation in another direction or be quiet. If we feel uncomfortable inside as we are about to purchase something, we should wait and discern why we are uncomfortable. Perhaps we don't need the item, or we may find it on sale somewhere else, or it may be the wrong time to buy it. We don't always have to know why; we simply need to obey.

I remember being in a shoe store one time. I had chosen several pairs of shoes to try on when I suddenly felt very uncomfortable. This discomfort increased until I finally heard the Holy Spirit say, "Get out of this store." I told Dave we had to go, and out we went. I never knew why, and I do not need to know. Maybe God saved me from some harm that was coming my way, or perhaps the people in the store were involved in something unethical. Maybe it was just a test of obedience. As I have said, we don't always have to know why God leads us in certain ways. Our part is simply to obey His voice.

GOD'S WORD FOR YOU TODAY: The greatest way to honor God is to obey Him promptly.

God Will Satisfy Your Longing

As the hart pants and longs for the water brooks, so I pant and long for You, O God. My inner self thirsts for God, for the living God.

(PSALM 42:1–2)

I went to church for many years without knowing that God wanted to speak to me, even though I sincerely loved Him. I observed all the religious rules and holidays and attended church every Sunday. I did everything I knew to do at that time, but it wasn't enough to satisfy my longing for God.

I could have spent every moment in church or in Bible study, but that wouldn't have quenched my thirst for a deeper relationship with the Lord. I needed to talk to Him about my past and hear Him talk to me about my future. But nobody taught me that God wanted to talk directly to me. No one offered a solution for my spiritual yearning.

Through reading the Bible, I learned that God does want to speak to us and to satisfy our longings for His presence and interaction in our lives. He has plans for our lives—plans that will lead us into peace and contentment, and He wants us to gain knowledge and understanding of Him and His will through divine guidance.

God is concerned about everything that concerns you and His plan is to be intimately involved in every aspect of your life. Knowing and believing this truth has made my walk with Him an adventure rather than a religious obligation.

GOD'S WORD FOR YOU TODAY: Spend part of your quiet time today being quiet! Be still and listen for what God wants to impart to you.

Honor God's Voice Above All

[Most] blessed is the man who believes in, trusts in, and relies on the Lord, and whose hope and confidence the Lord is. (JEREMIAH 17:7)

One attitude that welcomes the presence of God into our lives is the attitude that honors Him above everyone and everything else. Our attitudes need to say, "God, no matter what anyone else tells me, no matter what I think myself, no matter what my own plan is, if I clearly hear You say something and I know it's You, I will honor You—and honor what You say—above everything else."

Sometimes we give more consideration to what people tell us than to what God says. If we pray diligently and hear from God, and then start asking people around us what they think, we honor their human opinions above God's. Such an attitude will prevent our being able to consistently hear God's voice. If we are ever going to develop an ability to hear from God and be led by His Spirit as a way of life, we have to stop listening to so many opinions from so many people and begin trusting the wisdom God deposits in our hearts. There is a time to receive good counsel, but needing the approval of people will keep us out of the will of God.

The devil wants us to think we are not capable of hearing from God, but God's Word says that is not true. The Holy Spirit dwells inside of us because God wants us to be led by the Spirit in a personal way and to hear His voice for ourselves as He leads and guides us.

In the verse for today, God says we will be blessed when we look to Him. According to Jeremiah 17:5–6, severe consequences come to those who trust in the frailty of mere men and women, but blessed are those who trust in and honor the Lord. Good things happen if we listen to God. He wants to be our strength and we must honor His Word above all else.

GOD'S WORD FOR YOU TODAY: Hear what others have to say, but listen to God.

Red Light, Green Light

Now we are discharged from the Law and have terminated all inter-course with it, having died to what once restrained and held us captive. So now we serve not under [obedience to] the old code of written regulations, but [under obedience to the promptings] of the Spirit in newness [of life]. (ROMANS 7:6)

There have been times in my life when I was not happy, even though I was a Christian and did everything I thought a Christian was supposed to do. I look back now and realize that one of the main reasons I wasn't happy was that I didn't know much about the inner life. I didn't know how to listen to God's voice guiding me on the inside by the power of the Holy Spirit or how to obey Him when He prompted me to do or not do certain things.

Now, the Holy Spirit acts somewhat like a traffic cop inside me. When I do the right things, I get a green light from Him, and when I do the wrong things, I get a red light. If I am about to get myself in trouble, but have not fully committed to proceed in a certain direction, I get a caution signal.

The more we stop and ask God for directions, the more sensitive we become to the internal signals the Holy Spirit gives us. He speaks to us in a still, small voice or what I call a "knowing." Pay attention to the gentle signals of the Holy Spirit in your inner being just as you would pay attention to the red and green lights when driving in traffic. If you get a green light, then go ahead; and if the light is red, stop!

GOD'S WORD FOR YOU TODAY: When you're in new territory, use your GPS (God's prayer signals).

Fellowship with God

Truly our fellowship is with the Father and with His Son Jesus Christ.
(1 JOHN 1:3 NKJV)

God wants fellowship with us. In today's verse, John writes of fellowship with the Father and the Son, and in 2 Corinthians 13:14, Paul writes of fellowship or communion with the Holy Spirit. The communion of the Holy Spirit refers to our fellowship with other believers and with the Spirit Himself. Since the Holy Spirit lives inside us, we don't have to go very far to have fellowship and communion with Him.

Perhaps a good parallel to use to describe fellowship is that of two people who live together, such as a husband and a wife. I live in a house with my husband, Dave, and we are very close. We work together and do most other things together. There are times when he goes to play golf, but we stay in close contact by phone. He may watch sports on television, and even though I am not particularly interested in them, I am still in the house. Dave and I eat meals together, sleep together, and share the bathroom in the mornings as we get ready to go about the day. We spend a lot of time in each other's presence. We don't always talk, but we are always aware of each other. While we have quiet moments, we also communicate a great deal. I talk to Dave about things that are important to me and things that are unimportant. He does the same to me. When one of us speaks, the other listens.

In its simplest form, fellowship is about being together, talking and listening. The Holy Spirit is with us all the time. He lives in us and is never apart from us. We can talk to Him and He will listen. And He will speak to us, so we need to listen.

GOD'S WORD FOR YOU TODAY: Learn to be comfortable with God. Treat Him as an honored guest in your home.

The Holy Spirit Speaks to Our Spirit

*When He comes, He will convict and convince the world and bring
demonstration to it about sin and about righteousness (uprightness
of heart and right standing with God) and about judgment.*

(JOHN 16:8)

The Holy Spirit speaks to our spirit to convict us of sin and convince us
of righteousness. His conviction is intended to convince us to repent,
which means to turn and go in the right direction rather than in the
wrong direction in which we are currently going.

Conviction is entirely different from condemnation. It took me a
long time to learn that, and as a result, I erringly became condemned
every time the Holy Spirit convicted me of something in my life that did
not align with God's will. Conviction is meant to lift us out of something, to help us move up higher in God's will and plan for our lives.
Condemnation, on the other hand, presses us down and puts us under
burdens of guilt.

Feeling a healthy shame or guilt when we are initially convicted of sin
is normal. But, to continue to feel guilty after we have repented of the sin
is not healthy, nor is it God's will. In the story of the woman caught in
adultery (see John 8:3–11), Jesus proves that condemnation leads only
to death, but conviction delivers us to a new life free from sin.

Since God does not condemn us, we can fearlessly pray: "Lord,
show me my sin. Convict me of anything I am doing that breaks Your
law of loving others or that keeps me from doing Your will. Keep my
conscience tender to Your voice. Give me power to be free from sin.
Amen." Living in this way will increase our sensitivity to the voice of
God in our lives.

GOD'S WORD FOR YOU TODAY: Satan condemns; the
Holy Spirit convicts.

Are You Listening?

The Lord came and stood and called as at other times, Samuel!
Samuel! Then Samuel answered, Speak, Lord, for Your servant is
listening. (1 SAMUEL 3:10)

The verse for today comes from a story in which God wanted to tell Samuel what He planned to do in a certain situation. He had to speak several times before Samuel knew the voice he heard belonged to God. Once Samuel realized God was speaking to him, he responded by saying, "I'm listening."

Hearing God's voice is vital to enjoying His plans for your life, but whether or not you will listen to Him is a personal decision. No one else can make it for you; you must make it for yourself. God wants you to listen to Him. He will not force you to choose His will, but He will do everything He can to encourage you to say yes to Him.

God wants you to know what He wants you to do, how He feels about you, and what His plans are for your life. Proverbs 3:7 says "Be not wise in your own eyes." In other words, don't even think you can run your life and do a good job without God's help and direction. The more confidence you have that you can hear His voice, the better you can receive His guidance and instruction.

Decide today that God wants to speak to you, that you are going to listen when He speaks, and that you will give your full attention to His voice.

GOD'S WORD FOR YOU TODAY: God has good plans for your life and will tell you everything you need to know. Remember to listen!

Let Your Conscience Be Your Guide

Keep praying for us, for we are convinced that we have a good (clear) conscience, that we want to walk uprightly and live a noble life, acting honorably and in complete honesty in all things. (HEBREWS 13:18)

God gives us a conscience so we can stay out of trouble. If we ignore our conscience long enough, we will no longer sense God's conviction when we are guilty of sin. People become hardened when they ignore their natural sense of right and wrong. This happens even to people who are born again. The more hard-hearted people are, the more difficult it is for them to hear God's voice. Their conscience does not work as God designed it to work.

The conscience is a function of the spirit and it works like an internal monitor of our behavior. It lets us know when something is right or wrong; consequently, our knowledge of the standards and guidelines God has established for us greatly affects our conscience.

His Word awakens our conscience from its coma-like state. People who are not Christians may know when they are doing wrong, but they don't feel conviction like those of us who are born again, filled with the Spirit, and fellowshipping with God on a daily basis.

The more time we spend in the presence of God, the more sensitive we become to the things that don't reflect God's heart. When we behave in ungodly ways, we quickly sense that we have stepped out of line with the way Jesus would want us to handle a situation.

We can have wonderful lives if we fill our minds with God's Word and then simply obey our conscience.

GOD'S WORD FOR YOU TODAY: Let your conscience be your guide.

Abide in God

If you live in Me [abide vitally united to Me] and My words remain in you and continue to live in your hearts, ask whatever you will, and it shall be done for you. (JOHN 15:7)

The verse for today tells us we can ask whatever we "will" and it will be done for us if we abide in Christ. The only way this is possible is for a merging of our desires with God's desires to take place as we mature in Him.

The goal of every true believer is to be one with God. This happens spiritually when we are born again, and it occurs in mind, will, and emotions as we continue to grow and mature in Him. As we do so, our desires become His desires and we are safe in following them.

The call that Dave and I have to our ministry is a good example of this. God's desire was for us to be in ministry and help people in the ways He has gifted us to help them. That has also been the desire of our hearts. We could not have spent many years traveling every weekend, staying in hotels, and being away from our family if our desire for ministry was not God-given. He has put such a strong desire to minister in us that we are willing to make any sacrifice necessary or overcome any opposition that may come against us in order to accomplish His will for us.

To abide with God is to "hang out" with Him, to spend time with Him, live in His presence, and nurture the desires He puts in our hearts, because that is His will for us. He speaks to us and puts desires in our hearts so we will pray and ask for those things He wants to give us. He will be faithful to give us our desires as long as they are also His desires and as long as we abide in Him.

GOD'S WORD FOR YOU TODAY: "Hang out" with God today; He's a great companion.

Make It Personal

You are My friends if you keep on doing the things which I command you to do. (JOHN 15:14)

In today's verse, Jesus tells us we are His friends if we obey Him. In the following verse, He says He no longer calls us His servants, but His friends. Clearly, He wants a personal relationship with us and He wants us to get personal with Him. He proves this by the fact that He lives in us. How much more personal can anyone get than to live inside another person?

If God had wanted a distant, businesslike, professional relationship with us, He would have lived far away. He might have visited occasionally, but He certainly would not have come to take up permanent residence in the same house with us.

When Jesus died on the cross, He opened up a way for us to get personal with almighty God. What an awesome thought! Just think about it: God is our personal friend!

If we know someone important, we love to have an opportunity to say, "Oh, yes, that person is a friend of mine. I go to his house all the time. We visit with one another often." We can say the same about God if we do our part to fellowship with Him, listen to His voice and obey what He says, and stay in His presence every day.

GOD'S WORD FOR YOU TODAY: You can have a personal relationship with God; He's your friend.

Our Refiner

He will sit as a refiner and purifier of silver, and He will purify the
priests, the sons of Levi, and refine them like gold and silver.

(MALACHI 3:3)

Looking back over the years, I can see that I have been on a fascinating journey with God. He has definitely changed me and is still changing me daily. I had many problems in my soul (my mind, will, and emotions) and in my circumstances at the time I received the fullness of the Holy Spirit. Little did I realize what was about to take place in my life. I was asking God for change, but I was totally unaware that what needed to be changed in my life was *me*!

God began a process in me—slowly, steadily, and always at a pace I could endure. As a Refiner, He sits over the fires that burn in our lives to make sure they never get too hot and that they never die out. Only when He can look at us and see His own reflection is it safe to turn the fire off, and even then we continue to need a few alterations at times.

When God was dealing with me about patience, I faced many circumstances in which I could either be patient or behave badly. Quite often, I behaved badly, but the Holy Spirit kept convicting me, teaching me, and giving me a desire to live for God's glory. Gradually, little by little, I changed in one area, then in another. I usually got to rest a bit in between battles and often thought that perhaps I had finally graduated, only to discover something else I needed to learn.

This is the way it works as the Holy Spirit changes us. Keep your heart open to His leadership; keep your ears open to His voice; obey what He speaks to you—and soon, you'll find yourself changing more and more into the person He created you to be.

––––––––

GOD'S WORD FOR YOU TODAY: Don't get discouraged when God shows you areas in you that need to change.

"Martha, Martha"

The Lord replied to her by saying, Martha, Martha, you are anxious and troubled about many things; there is need of only one or but a few things. Mary has chosen the good portion [that which is to her advantage], which shall not be taken away from her. (LUKE 10:41–42)

In the story leading up to today's verse, Jesus went to visit two sisters, Mary and Martha. Martha was busy getting everything ready for Him—cleaning house, cooking, and trying to make an impression by having everything just right. Mary, on the other hand, took the opportunity to fellowship with Jesus. Martha became angry with her sister, wanting her to get up and help with the work. She even complained to Jesus and asked Him to tell Mary to get busy!

Jesus' response began with "Martha, Martha," and these two words imply more than we may first realize. They tell us Martha was too busy for relationships, she was choosing work over intimacy, and she was misusing her time and missing what was vital.

Mary, though, was operating in wisdom; she was taking advantage of the moment. She could spend the rest of her life cleaning, but on that day, Jesus had come to her house, and she wanted Him to feel welcome and loved. He had come to see her and Martha, not to inspect their clean house. While I think a clean home is important, this was not the time to focus on it. It was time to focus on Jesus because He was there.

I remind myself and encourage you to use wisdom and not miss God's presence when it is available. There are times when we sense the Holy Spirit prompting us to pray or spend time in His presence, but we prefer to work or play. When He calls, we should respond immediately. The blessings of His presence far, far outweigh the benefits of anything else we could do.

GOD'S WORD FOR YOU TODAY: Don't miss an opportunity to enjoy God's presence.

Let God Lead You to Life

I have set before you life and death, the blessings and the curses; therefore choose life. (DEUTERONOMY 30:19)

In John 16:8, Jesus said the Holy Spirit would "convict and convince" the world about sin and righteousness. He didn't say anything about the Holy Spirit bringing condemnation. He said He brings "demonstration … about sin and about righteousness."

The Holy Spirit reveals the results of sin and the results of righteousness so people may understand which path to follow. He makes clear distinction between right and wrong, between blessings and curses, and between life and death so people can ask God to help them choose life.

People who live in sin have wretched, miserable lives. I occasionally run into people I knew years ago and haven't seen in quite some time. Some of these people have not been living for God and the rough, rugged lifestyles they have chosen have taken a toll on them. The sour, sad, miserable choices they have made are visible because sin has left them looking sad and often older than they are. They are unhappy, negative, and discontented individuals often filled with bitterness because their life has not been a good one. They fail to realize that their life is the direct result of bad choices they made.

The result of sin may be observed everywhere. The line between those who love and serve God and those who don't is becoming quite clear. God pleads with us to make right choices, ones that will lead us into the life He desires for us to enjoy. There are two paths before each of us: a broad path that leads to sin and destruction and a narrow path that leads to life (see Matthew 7:13–14). I encourage you to choose life today and every day.

GOD'S WORD FOR YOU TODAY: Good choices become a good life.

His Dwelling Place

Do you not discern and understand that you ... are God's temple
(His sanctuary), and that God's Spirit has His permanent dwelling
in you? (1 CORINTHIANS 3:16)

I am amazed and in awe as I think of the great blessing of the indwelling Holy Spirit. He inspires us to do great things. He endues us with power for all our tasks. He stays in close communion with us, never leaving us or forsaking us.

Just think about it—if you and I are believers in Jesus Christ, we are the home of the Holy Spirit of God! We should meditate on this truth over and over until it becomes a personal revelation in our lives. If we do, we will never be helpless, hopeless, or powerless, for He promises to be with us to speak to us, strengthen us, and empower us. We will never be without a friend or without direction, for He promises to lead us and go with us in everything we do.

Paul wrote to his young disciple Timothy, "Guard and keep [with the greatest care] the precious and excellently adapted [Truth] which has been entrusted [to you], by the [help of the] Holy Spirit Who makes His home in us" (2 Timothy 1:14).

The truths you know about the Holy Spirit are so precious; I encourage you to guard them and keep them in your heart. Don't allow them to slip away from you. Since you are a believer in Jesus Christ, the Holy Spirit is in you to help you not only maintain what you have learned about Him, but to help it grow and enable you to share it with others. Appreciate Him, honor Him, love and adore Him. He is so good, so kind, so awesome. He is wonderful—and you are His dwelling place!

GOD'S WORD FOR YOU TODAY: Say out loud several times a day: "I am the dwelling place of God. He makes His home in me."

Three in One

There are three witnesses in heaven: the Father, the Word and the Holy Spirit, and these three are One. (1 JOHN 5:7)

Today's verse speaks of the Father, the Son, and the Holy Spirit—which we know as the Holy Trinity. Though the verse doesn't use the term *Son,* it refers to Jesus as "the Word," but we know from John 1 that Jesus and the Word are one and the same.

When we think of the Trinity, we must remember that they are three, and yet they are One. This does not compute for us mathematically, but it is true according to Scripture. By having the Holy Spirit living in us, we also have the Father and the Son living in us.

This is a wonderful reality. It is too awesome to explain. We must simply believe it with our hearts. Don't try to understand it. Be like a little child and just believe it because the Bible says it: The entire Godhead—Father, Son, and Holy Spirit—lives inside you and me and every born-again believer who has accepted Jesus Christ as Savior and Lord (see Colossians 2:9–10).

This truth should make us bold, fearless, and aggressive in a balanced way. We should believe we can do whatever we need to do in God's plan for our lives because the Holy Trinity equips us. He gives us everything we need and more. God loves you, is with you all the time, and has a good plan for your life. Through His presence, you are equipped to do whatever you need to do in life.

GOD'S WORD FOR YOU TODAY: Face this day boldly because God has already been where you are going and He has prepared the way.

Nothing Else Satisfies

My soul yearns for You [O Lord] in the night, yes, my spirit within me seeks You earnestly. (ISAIAH 26:9)

The world makes it easy for us to fill our ears with all kinds of things that drown out the voice of God and push Him far, far into the background of our lives. However, the day comes for every person when only God remains. Everything else in life eventually passes away; when it does, God will still be there.

The Bible teaches that what is known about God is evident to all because He has made Himself known in the inner consciousness of humankind (see Romans 1:19–21). Each person will someday stand before Him and give an account of his or her life (see Romans 14:12). When people don't want to serve God with their lives, when they want to go their own way, they find ways to hide from and ignore this instinctive knowledge of their Creator, Who wants to talk to them and guide them in the way they should go.

The truth is, whether people try to hide from God or not, nothing can satisfy our longing for Him except communion and fellowship with Him. Even when people try to ignore Him, deep down they would love to hear His voice.

I encourage you to satisfy your longing for God by spending time with Him, sitting in His presence, and listening to His voice.

GOD'S WORD FOR YOU TODAY: Live your life in such a way that you have no fear or dread of standing before God when your life on Earth is over.

Talking and Listening

Hear the sound of my cry, my King and my God, for to You do I pray.
(PSALM 5:2)

Prayer is so simple; it is nothing more than talking to God and listening to what He has to say. God wants to teach each one of us to pray and hear His voice in personal ways. He wants to take us just the way we are and help us discover our own unique rhythm of prayer and develop a style of prayer that maximizes our personal relationship with Him. He wants prayer to be an easy, natural, life-giving way of communicating with Him as we share our hearts with Him and allow Him to share His heart with us.

God is far too creative to teach every person on Earth to interact with Him through prayer in exactly the same way. He is the One Who designed us all differently and delights in our distinctiveness. All of us are at different places in our walk with Him, we are at different levels of spiritual maturity, and we have different types of experiences with God. As we grow in our ability to talk to God and listen to His voice, we need to continually say to God, "Teach me to pray; teach me to talk to You and listen to You in the ways that are best for me. Teach me to hear Your voice on a personal level. God, I'm depending on You to make me effective in prayer and to make my relationship with You through prayer the richest, most rewarding aspect of my life."

GOD'S WORD FOR YOU TODAY: You are God's unique creation. Celebrate that in your life and in your prayer.

It's Better This Way

I am telling you nothing but the truth when I say it is profitable
(good, expedient, advantageous) for you that I go away. Because if I
do not go away, the Comforter … will not come to you … but if I go
away, I will send Him to you. (JOHN 16:7)

The presence of the Holy Spirit in our lives is wonderful beyond what we can imagine. He is our Comforter and that means He will help and comfort us anytime we are hurt as we journey through life. I like to think of the Holy Spirit being as near to me as my next breath.

The Holy Spirit leads and guides us into the plan of God for our lives. Learning to follow His leadership is definitely a journey. We are accustomed to living by our own thoughts, feelings, and desires, but as Christians we need to learn to be led by the Holy Spirit. Jesus came in the body of a man and understands all that we go through in life. It gives me great comfort to remember that *Jesus understands me*! He is patient and will continue working with us as long as we are willing to continue learning.

Why would Jesus say that it would be better if He went away and sent the Holy Spirit? What could possibly be better than having Jesus in person on the earth? Jesus could be only one place at a time, but the Holy Spirit can be everywhere, working in everyone all at the same time. It is amazing! He *never* leaves us, not even for one moment. He knows everything about us and is working to heal all that is broken or wounded in us, and to put everything in its proper working order. Every day we get better and better in every way through the awesome power and wisdom of the Holy Spirit.

GOD'S WORD FOR YOU TODAY: Ask the Holy Spirit to
take you as you are and make you what He wants you to be.

We Need a Guide

This God is our God forever and ever; He will be our guide [even] until death (PSALM 48:14)

It thrills me to know that God is our guide through every day of our lives. How wonderful to know that we have Someone to guide us and ensure that we get from one destination in life to the next.

Sometimes when Dave and I travel, we hire a guide to show us the best and most important sites to see. One time, we decided we would explore a certain place by ourselves; that way, we reasoned, we could do what we wanted to do when we wanted to do it. However, we quickly found that our independent trip was nearly wasted. We spent large portions of each day getting lost and then trying to find our way again. We have learned from our mistakes and we now know the best use of our time is to follow a guide rather than wandering aimlessly to find places ourselves.

I believe this example from our travels relates to how most people are in life. We want to chart our own courses, be our own guides, and do what we want to do at our convenience. But we typically lose our way and end up wasting our time. God has promised in today's verse to guide us through our lives. He does this through the Holy Spirit, Who will speak to us and tell us where to go and what to do if we will simply ask Him to lead us.

———————————

GOD'S WORD FOR YOU TODAY: Every moment of your life, even unto death, wherever you are, God is there!

God's Greatest Desire

Behold, the virgin shall become pregnant and give birth to a Son,
and they shall call His name Emmanuel—which, when translated,
means, God with us. (MATTHEW 1:23)

Jesus came into the world so we could be redeemed from our sins, know God, and experience His very best in our lives. He wants to have close fellowship with us and to be invited into everything about us. This is why one of the names of God, Emmanuel, means, "God with us." He wants to be *with* us, intimately involved in our lives. He wants us to know His voice and follow Him.

God's will is that we hear clearly from Him. He does not want us living in confusion and fear. We are to be decisive, secure, and free. He wants each of us to fulfill our destiny and to walk in the fullness of His plan for us.

Yes, we can hear from God in a personal, intimate way. The depth of our personal relationship with God is based on intimate communication with Him. He speaks to us so that we are guided, refreshed, restored, and renewed regularly.

The first step toward hearing anyone, including God, is to listen. Turn your ear toward Him and be still. He will speak to you to tell you He loves you. God wants to meet your needs and do more than you could ever think or imagine (see Ephesians 3:20). He will never leave you or forsake you (see Hebrews 13:5). Listen to Him and follow Him all the days of your life.

You belong to God; you are one of His sheep, and the sheep know the Shepherd's voice—the voice of a stranger they will not follow (see John 10:4–5). You can hear from God; it is part of your inheritance as a Christian. Don't ever believe otherwise!

GOD'S WORD FOR YOU TODAY: God's gift to you is a new life filled with righteousness, peace, joy, and intimacy with Him.

Enjoy God's Presence

You will show me the path of life; in Your presence is fullness of joy, at Your right hand there are pleasures forevermore. (PSALM 16:11)

I love to lie facedown on the floor and pray—talking to God and listening to His voice. This posture helps me shut everything else out and feel as if I am alone with God. I prayed that way until it started hurting my back and I had to quit! I am glad I did not have to feel unspiritual because I had to change my posture in prayer. All I can tell you is that there is no certain posture you have to struggle to maintain in order to pray, experience God's presence, or hear His voice. If your knees hurt, lie on the floor. If your back hurts or you fall asleep on the floor, get up and walk around. If you are like Dave and you can pray while sitting and looking out the window, then pull up a chair. Just find a place and a way in which to talk and listen to God that makes you comfortable and allows you to focus on Him.

Be free from everything you have heard about the formulas of prayer or the positions of prayer—and just pray! I challenge you to simplify your communication with God. Talk to Him and listen to Him in ways that are comfortable and easy for you—and above all, enjoy His presence!

GOD'S WORD FOR YOU TODAY: Just pray!

Saved to Serve

Be mindful to be a blessing, especially to those of the household of faith. (GALATIANS 6:10)

As you begin your day, ask God to speak to you about what you can do to help others today and every day. We are saved by God so we can serve Him and others. God told Adam and Eve in the beginning of time to use all of their resources in the service of God and man. A truly great man or woman is one who serves. Even a leader should be a servant-leader.

When Jesus' disciples asked Him which of them was the greatest, He replied that whoever wished to be great had to be a servant (see Matthew 20:26). Are you interested in hearing from God? If so, then ask Him to speak to you about whom you can help and bless. If we only want to hear from God about what will help *us,* then He may not have much to say because He is not interested in helping us be selfish. If we truly care for others we often find that in the midst of our effort to serve them, our own problems are divinely solved by God without much effort on our part.

In God's Kingdom, the position of "servant" is the highest. Christ came to serve and not to be served (see Mark 10:45). Anyone can serve if they are willing to do so. Just listen to what people say they want and need and get busy serving. As you serve others your intimacy with Christ will increase because He is a Servant.

GOD'S WORD FOR YOU TODAY: Pray right now and ask God what you can do to help someone else today. Listen for the still, small voice and get busy being obedient.

Prove Your Love

When He had finished washing their feet and had put on His gar-
ments and had sat down again, He said to them, Do you understand
what I have done to you? (JOHN 13:12)

I believe that only secure people can be true servants. Jesus was able to put on a servant's towel and wash the feet of His disciples because He knew Who He was, where He came from, and where He was going. He had no fear and nothing to prove, so He was free to serve.

Many people in our society need a high position to make them feel that they have worth and value. Being a servant is often looked on as a low job, but in God's mind it is the highest position that exists. Being a true servant begins with a humble heart, and that is a heart and spirit that is acceptable to God. No matter what our natural employment may be, our call from God is to serve Him and others.

In washing the disciples' feet, Jesus gave them an example of how they should live, and told them that if they would serve others, they would be blessed and happy to such a degree that they would be envied (see John 13:17). When we serve one another, we become part of one another. We experience the true meaning of love. Jesus was the highest of all, yet He humbled Himself and became a servant. Are you willing to follow His example?

———————

GOD'S WORD FOR YOU TODAY: Help as many people as you can, as often as you can.

No Dividing Walls

Christ is all and in all [everything and everywhere, to all men, without distinction of person]. (COLOSSIANS 3:11)

In Christ, God created one new creation where all distinctions vanish and we all become one in Him. In practical terms, that means we must trust God to take care of whatever we are not able to do and receive as a gift from Him whatever good is in us or whatever we can do well. Everything is in Him! We are made right with God in Him, our life is in Him, our joy and peace are in Him. All things are to Him, for Him, in Him, and through Him (see Romans 11:36).

We no longer need to compare ourselves with anyone else. It doesn't matter what they can do that we cannot do because our only worth and value is found in Him. We are free from comparisons and competition, and that enables us to be fully ourselves. Just be the best you that you can be. When you are able to do something well, then thank God; and when you are unable, thank Him that He loves you anyway and will take care of what needs to be done.

This truth allows you to enter God's rest and to avoid the agony of self-rejection or spending your life trying to be something you will never be. If you are listening to God's voice, then hear Him tell you right now that you are special; you have no need to compare yourself with anyone. All of the dividing walls have been broken down in Christ and we are all one in Him.

GOD'S WORD FOR YOU TODAY: God will never help you be somebody else, but He will help you be all you can be.

God Knows What You Need

Return to the stronghold [of security and prosperity], you prisoners of hope; even today do I declare that I will restore double your former prosperity to you. (ZECHARIAH 9:12)

One day I was emotionally hurt over something that had happened. Dave and I had been treated unfairly and unjustly in a situation, and I was feeling down about it. I was on an airplane, so I decided to read the Bible. When I opened it to Zechariah 9:12, the verse for today, the words seemed to jump off the page at me.

When I saw this verse, my faith went to a new level. I knew without a doubt that God was speaking to me about my situation. I knew that if I would not give up hope, if I would have the right attitude, that I would see the day when God would give me back double what had been taken from me in that situation.

Almost one year later, to the day, God did an outstanding work and proved Himself true to His promise by restoring double what had been unjustly taken from us, and He restored it through the same people who had mistreated us!

The Holy Spirit knows exactly what you need. I opened my Bible that day expecting Him to speak to me and help me in my situation, but He surpassed my greatest hope by not only comforting me, but promising to restore my loss. This Scripture—and all the others—are your promises, too, and God is speaking them to you.

Anytime you need comfort or direction in life I encourage you to go to God's Word. It truly contains all the answers we need for every situation in life.

GOD'S WORD FOR YOU TODAY: God will give you double for your trouble! (He will give you double blessing for your former trouble.)

We Do the Walking

The steps of a [good] man are directed and established by the Lord when He delights in his way [and He busies Himself with his every step]. Though he falls, he shall not be utterly cast down, for the Lord grasps his hand in support and upholds him. (PSALM 37:23–24)

God is busy with our every step! That means we are never alone. When we fall down He helps us back up and encourages us to go forward again. No person will learn to be led by God without making some mistakes, but remember that God knew about them before they took place. God is not surprised by our slips and failures. As a matter of fact, God has every day of our lives written in His book before even one of them takes place (see Psalm 139:16). Remember that God delights in you and is busy with your every step. If you fall, He will lift you up.

All of the great men and women we read about and admire in the Bible and throughout history made mistakes. God does not choose us because we are perfect, but so He can show Himself strong through us. He actually chooses on purpose the weak and foolish things of the world to amaze everyone and show His greatness (see 1 Corinthians 1:28–29). Don't accept pressure from the enemy to be perfect and never make mistakes. Every day, do your best and trust God to do the rest! Don't ever be afraid of your mistakes, but instead have an attitude of learning from them. Let all of your mistakes be a college course in what not to ever do again!

GOD'S WORD FOR YOU TODAY: Do not fear; God is with you.

About the Author

JOYCE MEYER is one of the world's leading practical Bible teachers. A #1 *New York Times* bestselling author, she has written more than eighty inspirational books, including *100 Ways to Simplify Your Life, Never Give Up!,* the entire Battlefield of the Mind family of books, and two novels, *The Penny* and *Any Minute,* as well as many others. She has also released thousands of audio teachings, as well as a complete video library. Joyce's *Enjoying Everyday Life®* radio and television programs are broadcast around the world, and she travels extensively conducting conferences. Joyce and her husband, Dave, are the parents of four grown children and make their home in St. Louis, Missouri.

Joyce Meyer Ministries
U.S. & Foreign Office Addresses

Joyce Meyer Ministries
P.O. Box 655
Fenton, MO 63026
USA
(636) 349-0303
www.joycemeyer.org

Joyce Meyer Ministries—Canada
P.O. Box 7700
Stn. Terminal
Vancouver, BC V6B 4E2
Canada
1-800-868-1002

Joyce Meyer Ministries—Australia
Locked Bag 77
Mansfield Delivery Centre
Queensland 4122
Australia
(07) 3349 1200

Joyce Meyer Ministries—England
P.O. Box 1549
Windsor SL4 1GT
United Kingdom
01753 831102

Joyce Meyer Ministries—South Africa
P.O. Box 5
Cape Town 8000
South Africa
(27) 21-701-1056

Other Books by Joyce Meyer

* Study Guide available for this title.

Any Minute

Never Give Up!

The Secret to True Happiness

New Day, New You Devotional

I Dare You

The Penny

The Power of Simple Prayer

The Everyday Life Bible

The Confident Woman

Look Great, Feel Great

*Battlefield of the Mind**

Battlefield of the Mind Devotional

Battlefield of the Mind for Teens

Battlefield of the Mind for Kids

Approval Addiction

Ending Your Day Right

21 Ways to Finding Peace and Happiness

The Secret Power of Speaking God's Word

Seven Things That Steal Your Joy

Starting Your Day Right

Beauty for Ashes (revised edition)

*How to Hear from God**

Knowing God Intimately

The Power of Forgiveness

The Power of Determination

Do It Afraid!

Expect a Move of God in Your Life…Suddenly!

Enjoying Where You Are on the Way to Where You Are Going

A New Way of Living

When, God, When?

Why, God, Why?

The Word, the Name, the Blood

Tell Them I Love Them

Peace

If Not for the Grace of God*

Joyce Meyer Spanish Titles

Las Siete Cosas Que Te Roban el Gozo
(Seven Things That Steal Your Joy)
Empezando Tu Dia Bien (Starting Your Day Right)

* Study Guide available for this title.

Books by Dave Meyer

Life Lines